Masters of the Ninth Art

Bandes dessinées and Franco-Belgian Identity

Contemporary French and Francophone Cultures 3

MATTHEW SCREECH

Masters of the Ninth Art

Bandes dessinées and Franco-Belgian Identity

LIVERPOOL UNIVERSITY PRESS

First published 2005 by
Liverpool University Press
4 Cambridge Street
Liverpool L69 7ZU

British Library Cataloguing-in-Publication data
A British Library CIP record is available

ISBN 0–85323–938–X cased

Typeset in Sabon by Koinonia, Manchester
Printed and bound in the European Union by
Bell and Bain Ltd, Glasgow

Contents

List of Illustrations

Acknowledgements

My thanks are due to the following who have helped with this book: the editors of *The Journal of Popular Culture*, *Francophone Bandes dessinées* and *Belphegor* for letting me re-use some material on Franquin, Moebius and Gotlib, which had been already published, or has been accepted for publication, by them in a different form; the British Academy for providing a research grant which enabled me to spend time in libraries at Paris and Angoulême, and which helped cover the cost of illustrations; the BA grant also met the cost of interviewing artists; Dave Huxley who, drawing on his encyclopaedic knowledge of American comics, has prompted me with comments and suggestions; and my friends Katia Brozek, Greg Williams and Liliane Zekri, for my frequent and prolonged stays at their flats in Paris.

Introduction

Comic strips are a powerful means of expression. They are portable, cheap to buy and easy to read; they can be produced rapidly, in large numbers and at relatively low cost. Comic strips enjoy widespread appeal and they offer amusing topics of conversation, which are accessible to almost everyone. In Europe, just as in the USA, heroes from comics have entered popular mythology.

Comic strips are particularly highly esteemed in France and Belgium, where they are known as *bandes dessinées* or BDs. Unlike most English-speakers, the French and the Belgians believe their comics to be a genuine art form: they even go so far as to call *bandes dessinées* 'the ninth art', a phrase rarely uttered in the USA or the UK. This places *bandes dessinées* on a level with the seven liberal arts, the traditional branches of learning: grammar, logic, rhetoric, arithmetic, geometry, astronomy and music.[1] In France and Belgium, three new arts were added to the list: cinema (somewhat confusingly known as 'the seventh art'), photography, and *bandes dessinées* as the ninth.

In the USA and the UK, comic strips are far less highly regarded. As Richard Reynolds remarked in his study of superhero mythology, the comic strip

> continues to be (at least in American and British culture) a margin-alized channel of communication held by many to be an irredeem-ably corrupt and corrupting form of discourse, or else suitable only for children and the semi-literate.[2]

Masters of the Ninth Art explains why Francophone comic strips command such extraordinary respect in their countries of origin; it will also enable a wider audience to appreciate *bandes dessinées* better. The following chapters consider a variety of French and Belgian BD artists, whom I have interviewed where possible. It builds upon three articles of mine: a study of the Belgian humorist André Franquin; an article about the Frenchman Jean Giraud (aka Moebius), who is best known for his science fiction; and a discussion of the French humorist Marcel Gotlib.[3] *Masters of the Ninth Art* extends my analysis to other genres, among them Westerns, war comics, historical dramas, animal stories and social satire.

The masters of the ninth art work in diverse genres but, as we shall see, a common thread links them. They are united by their collective achievement: each artist has successfully turned the ninth art into a unique, distinguishing feature of French and Belgian cultural life, and in so doing, has strengthened Franco-Belgian cultural identity. The ninth art's achievement inspires genuine respect in France and Belgium, not least at a time when Anglophone mass culture is dominant.

Before considering the artists themselves, we must examine the nature of Franco-Belgian identity. Questions about what qualities make each country different have long been debated.[4] Anne-Marie Thiesse lists the following attributes that, by common consent, now define the identity of any 'nation digne de ce nom':

> Une histoire établissant la continuité avec les grands ancêtres, une série de héros parangons des vertus nationales, une langue, des monuments culturels, un folklore, des hauts lieux et un paysage typique, une mentalité particulière, des représentations officielles – hymne et drapeau – et des identifications pittoresques – costume, spécialités culinaires ou animal emblématique.[5]

France and Belgium have different 'représentations officielles' and different 'identifications pittoresques'; unquestionably the two countries are individual, sovereign states. Nevertheless France and Belgium, to varying degrees, share the other elements on Thiesse's list. They enjoy a uniquely close relationship, which marks them off from the other French-speaking parts of the globe such as Switzerland, Quebec or Francophone Africa. That special relationship is due to geography, history and language, as well as to cultural factors.

No natural border has ever separated France from Belgium, as the plains of Flanders stretch on uninterruptedly into northern France. The Franco-Belgian frontier has been contested for centuries, and numerous Belgians speak French. France annexed what is now Belgium from 1794 to 1815, and Belgium only gained full independence in 1830. Henri Pirenne states that already by the early/mid-twentieth century, the two countries were almost indistinguishable to many outsiders:

L'action de la France demeurait prépondérante. Favorisée par une tradition plusieurs fois séculaire, par l'analogie des mœurs, par la communauté de la langue, par le voisinage de Paris que les trains rapides mettaient à quatre heures de Bruxelles, elle dominait incontestablement dans la vie sociale ... La Belgique était baignée d'une atmosphère française et, à première vue, l'étranger pressé de conclure, la considérait souvent comme une contrefaçon de la France.[6]

Since Pirenne wrote, events have driven Belgium and France still closer together: they were fiercely fought over in World War II, which accelerated their retreats from empire; after that, both formed a solid alliance within the European Union.

Post-war writers have underlined the similarities between Belgium and France, just as Pirenne did over a generation earlier. Frank Huggett commented:

With very few exceptions, most Belgian writers, artists, actors and musicians are ... thought to be French. This confusion is understandable, for throughout Belgium's history, Paris has exercised so pervasive a cultural attraction that for many writers the fact of being Belgian has become almost a mere accident of birth.[7]

David Gordon observed: 'Those who speak French easily are in part Frenchmen and partake in France's destiny as a culture'; in addition Belgium's 'identity, on a cultural level, had been originally French'.[8]

Of themselves, geographical, historical and linguistic affinities would not have been sufficient to build bridges between France and Belgium: a sense of shared cultural identity is also indispensable to their special relationship, as Huggett and Gordon pointed out. In order to exist, that cultural identity needs the following elements, which were first named by Ernest Renan in 1882:

L'une est dans le passé, l'autre dans le présent. L'une est la possession en commun d'un riche legs de souvenirs; l'autre est le consentement actuel, le désir de vivre ensemble, la volonté de continuer à faire valoir l'héritage qu'on a reçu indivis.[9]

The cultural dimension should never be underestimated. As Renan commented, no truly common identity is ever complete without those specific, key ingredients.

By its nature the ninth art works primarily at the cultural level, and its function is twofold. As Renan put it: 'L'une est dans le passé, l'autre dans le présent'. First, *bandes dessinées* stimulate what Renan called 'le consentement actuel, le désir de vivre ensemble': every day,

BDs offer millions of French and Belgian people shared pleasures. Secondly, and equally importantly, the ninth art engages simultaneously with a common past: *bandes dessinées* actively promote 'la volonté de continuer à faire valoir l'héritage qu'on a reçu indivis'; they do so by finding inspiration in 'la possession en commun d'un riche legs de souvenirs'. The ninth art draws heavily, though not exclusively, upon the rich cultural and historical legacy of France and Belgium: folktales, novels, paintings, plays, poems, songs, historical events and so forth. Consequently *bandes dessinées* rework the past into the present, giving Franco-Belgian culture a powerful new voice in the age of mass communication.

Bandes dessinées perpetuate and renew a specifically Franco-Belgian culture in exactly the same way as more traditional folkloric forms. They operate this dual process of conservation and renewal, which was first spoken of by Vladimir Propp:

> The process of reworking the old into the new is the basic creative process in folklore, observable right up to the present. To say this is not to belittle the creative aspect of folklore. The concept of creative art does not mean the production of something absolutely new. Folklore is creative by its very nature, but creation is not an arbitrary process.[10]

The ninth art's creative process is indeed anything but arbitrary: BD artists are profoundly influenced by their native culture; for that reason, they produce a uniquely Franco-Belgian folklore. BD folklore evolves within the context of a distinctively European Francophone tradition. The crucial importance of folklore in constructing identity has already been mentioned by Thiesse.

The decisive influence of a Franco-Belgian culture is all the more apparent when we compare the ninth art to American comics. One simple example: the *bande dessinée* humorists share a common fount of knowledge with their readers; often, to get the jokes, readers must know the culture being described. Quite unintentionally, much BD humour locks English-speakers outside this frame of reference. The predominantly Franco-Belgian influence explains the ninth art's generally lacklustre sales in America and the UK.

Masters of the Ninth Art begins with the first artist to give *bandes dessinées* an identity distinct from that of American comics: Georges Remi, better known as Hergé, who emerged in pre-war Belgium. To put Hergé's emergence in context, I shall now briefly survey the history of *bandes dessinées* up to the 1940s.

In France, the art of telling stories by combining words with pictures goes back to the eleventh-century Bayeux tapestry and beyond. Medieval art forms frequently combined words with pictures: woodcuts and stained glass windows in churches integrated words into pictures by employing a device which foreshadowed the speech-balloon: it looked like a scroll containing words, and it protruded from the mouths of characters when they spoke. With the Renaissance, however, words and pictures became increasingly divorced from one another, and combinations of the two were often consciously avoided in art. Scott McCloud notes that for several centuries the two 'stayed separate, refusing to mix like oil and water'.[11]

Words and pictures came back together to make a new art form in French-speaking Switzerland, when the Genevan Rodolphe Töpffer drew *L'Histoire de M. Vieux Bois* (1827), a humorous story about a love-struck man; as the historians of the comic strip Thierry Groensteen and Benoît Peeters make clear, Töpffer's contribution to the ninth art was paramount.[12] Töpffer is crucial because, whether later artists read him or not, his innovative technique came to be adopted on both sides of the Atlantic. Töpffer enabled fixed images to develop through time by dividing events up into sequences of panels, which he arranged in chronological order; each panel grew out of the previous panel and prepared for the following one. Töpffer's panels were accompanied by handwritten text, not by speech-balloons, but his definition of the form he invented holds true for most comic strips to this day:

> Les dessins, sans le texte, n'auraient qu'une signification obscure; le texte, sans les dessins, ne signifierait rien. Le tout ensemble forme une sorte de roman d'autant plus original qu'il ne ressemble pas mieux à un roman qu'à autre chose. (M. *Jabot et M. Vieux Bois*, p. 10).

As Peeters and Groensteen point out, Töpffer was the ninth art's first practitioner and its first theoretician: he was the first of many to realise the full potential of text/image interaction. Töpffer saw that, in order to communicate clearly, he had to strike a harmonious balance between pictures and words. Both are equally important to telling his stories, and the one cannot be understood fully without the other. Töpffer's words and pictures form a unified, interdependent whole, thereby opening up new dramatic and humorous possibilities.

With the growth of literacy, illustrated stories became popular, especially in late nineteenth/early twentieth-century France. Examples include George Colomb's *Famille Fenouillard*, Maurice Languereau's and Joseph-Porphyre Pinchon's *Bécassine*, and Louis Forton's *Bande des Pieds Nickelés*. These stories still had explanatory texts printed beneath pictures.[13] However, when the Frenchman Alain Saint Ogan integrated words into his drawings by using speech-balloons in *Zig et Puce*, all of the requirements for a modern *bande dessinée* came together for the first time.[14] Speech-balloons, which were descended from the medieval scroll device, had already been used by the American comic-strip artist Rudolph Dirks in *The Katzenjammer Kids* (1897);[15] but speech-balloons predated comic strips, having previously been used by European caricaturists, notably the Englishman James Gillray (1757–1815).

Many early French illustrators looked to America for inspiration, not to their native history and culture or even to Töpffer: *La Famille Fenouillard* tells of a French family's travels in the USA; *La Bande des Pieds Nickelés* is about a band of swindlers who visit (among other places) America during the Prohibition; *Zig et Puce* is about two youngsters obsessed by the New World, with America portrayed as a mythological country that is always just beyond their reach.

Bécassine, more than the other stories, played upon characteristics specific to France. Bécassine is a likeable if slow-witted country girl, who leaves her native Britanny to work for an aristocratic family in Paris. Her rustic manners clash amusingly with Parisian sophistication.

1929 saw the first Belgian artist: Hergé. Hergé's Tintin dominated *bandes dessinées* from the 1940s to the 1970s, as we shall see. While Tintin was growing in popularity, America was in the ascendant. In 1934, *Le Journal de Mickey* introduced Walt Disney's Mickey Mouse to French-speakers in comic-strip form; in 1936 *Robinson* magazine carried *Popeye* and *Bringing up Father* (called *La Famille Illico*), followed by *Flash Gordon* (sometimes called *Guy L'Eclair*) in 1938; the same year, in Charleroi, Editions Dupuis launched the first Belgian *bande dessinée* magazine, *Le Journal de Spirou*, which featured *Tarzan* and *Superman*.[16] World War II, paper shortages and the Nazi occupation abruptly halted most BD production, although some magazines were still published. Most notably, in occupied France a magazine called *Le Téméraire* (1943) tried to indoctrinate its young readers with pro-Nazi propaganda, sometimes using comic strips.[17]

Immediately after the war *bandes dessinées* continued to be over-shadowed by America, and the newly liberated governments were acutely aware of the impact made by US comics. In 1947, the Belgian government used characters from *Popeye, The Katzenjammer Kids* and others in anti-inflation publicity;[18] but in France, comics were mistrusted. On 16 June 1949, the French government passed a law aimed at censoring comics which forbade any 'apologie du banditisme, du mensonge, du vol, de la paresse, de la lâcheté, de la haine, de la débauche ou de tout acte qualifié de délit ou de crime et de nature à démoraliser l'enfance et la jeunesse'.[19] Belgian artists who wanted to tap the larger French market had to comply with French law.[20] The more relaxed attitude taken by the Belgian authorities partly explains why Belgium, rather than France, spearheaded the *bande dessinée*'s post-war renaissance.

There are other reasons why Belgium dominated *bandes dessinées* immediately after World War II. Hergé's enormous success no doubt encouraged Belgians such as Franquin to follow his lead. *Le Journal de Tintin* and *Le Journal de Spirou* put Belgium on an equal cultural footing with France; *bandes dessinées* raised Belgium's profile in the eyes of her bigger, richer, more powerful neighbour. René Henoumont speaks for other Belgians when he calls *Spirou*'s artists, the song-writer Jacques Brel and the detective novelist Georges Simenon 'les Belges qui ont fait la France'.[21]

One could even explain Belgium's early pre-eminence by risking a comparison between the ninth art and the Belgian nation itself. Belgium turned French-speaking Catholics and Flemish-speaking Protestants into a single, coherent country. The ninth art turns words and pictures into a single, coherent art form. *Bandes dessinées* are composite, as is Belgium: they both unite disparate elements, which were once deemed incompatible. That curious coincidence made *bandes dessinées* a uniquely suitable mode of expression, when Belgian artists emerged as the first major talents.

Masters of the Ninth Art is divided into two parts, each of which spans roughly thirty years. Part I, 'The *Bande dessinée* Classics', concentrates on the period from 1945 to 1975. Part II, 'Innovation and Renewal', chiefly focuses on the years from 1975 to 2000. In the first part I look at Hergé and Franquin, as well as René Goscinny and Albert Uderzo, whose collaborations were published in France. These artists are best known for *Les Aventures de Tintin, Gaston Lagaffe* and *Les Aventures d'Astérix* respectively. Goscinny and

Uderzo also set up the first notable French BD magazine, *Pilote* (1959), which launched the careers of many of the artists studied in Part II. Critics have already referred to Hergé, Franquin, Goscinny and Uderzo as 'classical'.[22] The term 'classical' is appropriate because the French and the Belgians almost universally treat *Tintin*, *Gaston Lagaffe* and *Astérix* as cultural achievements of outstanding importance. Hergé, Franquin, Goscinny and Uderzo are the ninth art's Old Masters. They arouse enduring interest and are widely acknowledged to have perfected their chosen genres: adventure stories and funny gags.

Part I ends by enlarging upon the link between comic strips and popular mythology, which was first pointed out by Umberto Eco.[23] Tintin, Gaston and Astérix are mythological heroes. To borrow Thiesse's phrase, they are 'héros parangons des vertus nationales': together, they assert a strong sense of joint, Franco-Belgian identity. As we shall see, these three *bande dessinée* heroes behave very differently from the almighty superheroes who are so beloved of American readers.

During the period covered in Part II the *bande dessinée* scene became increasingly heterogeneous. Many of the artists studied here came of age during and after the Paris uprising of May 1968, and rebelled against the traditions formulated by the BD 'classics'. There was a growing tendency to experiment; alternative strategies for depicting everyday reality were developed; censorship laws drafted in the 1940s became untenable; and explicit sex and violence grew more acceptable. The next generation of *bande dessinée* magazines appeared, including *L'Echo des savanes* (1972) and *Métal hurlant* (1975), which catered more specifically for adults. Some artists broke radically with the past, while others drew inspiration from more traditional sources, such as European Francophone history, culture and current affairs.

Chapter 4 studies Jean Giraud/Moebius, who was the most influential BD artist after Hergé. Giraud experimented with genres that are generally associated with the USA (Westerns and science fiction), and he produced effects very different from those of American comics. This chapter also evaluates Giraud's contribution to *bande dessinée nouveau réalisme*. *Nouveaux réalistes* no longer used historical events and genuinely existing places to produce effects of reality, as the 'classical', Hergéen realists had done; instead, like their forerunners in the European avant-garde, *nouveaux réalistes* questioned where reality ends and where the imaginary begins; in so doing, they asked what is known as 'la question du réel'. *Nouveau réalisme* has no direct equivalent in American comics.

Chapter 5 looks at Jacques Tardi, whose war comics and historical dramas ask 'la question du réel'. Tardi's best-known strip, *Les Aventures extraordinaires d'Adèle Blanc-Sec*, set in early twentieth-century Paris, ironically parodies *romans feuilletons*, the French popular novels of the day.

Chapter 6 explores the link between shared laughter and shared identity by considering three humorists: Marcel Gotlib, Claire Bretécher and Régis Franc. These artists all make jokes about Franco-Belgian history, culture and topical events; some of Franc's strips humorously raise 'la question du réel'; and with each of them, readers require some knowledge of Franco-Belgian culture in order to appreciate the jokes.

Chapter 7 reviews some of the developments that have taken place in the last two decades of the twentieth century: a return to more traditional narrative forms in the 1980s; a revival in humour and experimentalism during the 1990s.

The thriving Franco-Belgian *bande dessinée* culture has spawned such a vast number of artists that they cannot possibly all be discussed here; some artists who are worthy of study, such as Christian Binet, Régis Loisel and Cabu (Jean Cabut), have had to be omitted. The choice of artists discussed in the following pages is, inevitably, a somewhat personal one. However, the artists selected have all given *bandes dessinées* a distinctly Franco-Belgian voice: they are inspired by European Francophone writers and artists; they are influenced by Franco-Belgian history, as well as by current affairs in French-speaking countries; they break the rules by which American comics function; they change (and often substantially weaken) the position of the hero; and they produce Franco-Belgian mythology and folklore.

In France and Belgium, the ninth art is just as worthy of critical attention as the other eight arts, and numerous BD studies have already appeared. Although the ninth art's contribution to Franco-Belgian cultural identity has not yet been fully established, some critics do touch briefly upon related issues. Let us now consider the state of *bande dessinée* scholarship.

Bandes dessinées began attracting serious critical attention in Paris in 1962, when a group of enthusiasts based around Francis

Lacassin, Alain Resnais and Evelyne Sullerot formed CELEG (Centre d'Etudes des Littératures d'Expression Graphique). CELEG coined the term 'the ninth art'. Their fanzine *Giff Wiff* (1963) mostly published articles about famous artists from the 1930s. Evelyne Sullerot was among the first to suggest that *bandes dessinées* illustrate the workings of the French mind:

> La fresque des types produits par notre société et celle des rêves fantastiques de cette société, on la trouve dans les bandes dessinées, lumineux réservoir d'imaginaire, immense caricature. Elles ne pourront pas être ignorées des historiens des mentalités et de la sensibilité de notre époque.[24]

As Sullerot suggested, *bandes dessinées* are both the stuff of fantasy and valuable historical documents: the ninth art faithfully depicts, and sometimes even anticipates, succeeding prejudices, ideals, dreams and fears in France and Belgium. The *bande dessinée*'s mythology and folklore tell us much about what it was like to be French or Belgian during the period under discussion; the 'classical' heroes give particularly revealing insights into how the two countries viewed the world, and their place in it, during the mid/late twentieth century.

In 1965 Claude Moliterni, Pierre Couperie and others formed SOCERLID (Société Civile d'Etudes et de Recherches des Littératures Dessinées). SOCERLID's magazine, *Phénix* (1966), ran articles about *bandes dessinées* and about American comics. Some research by SOCERLID's members makes essential reading. Pierre Couperie and his collaborators wrote an *Histoire de la bande dessinée*, which traces the history of comics in France, Belgium and the USA up to the 1960s; more recently, Claude Moliterni and Patrick Gaumer compiled an encyclopaedic *Dictionnaire mondial de la bande dessinée*, with 1,800 entries on Belgian, French and American artists.[25]

In Grenoble in 1969 Jacques Glénat founded *Les Cahiers de la bande dessinée*, which lasted until 1990. Each issue of *Les Cahiers de la bande dessinée* profiled one Belgian or French artist in an interview with a bibliography, together with articles about influences, graphic styles and narrative techniques. These three publications are a mine of information for anyone researching BDs; so too is Henri Filippini's *Dictionnaire de la bande dessinée*, which has 1,700 entries mostly on French and Belgian artists.

BD sales soared in the 1970s; meanwhile, more French and Belgian scholars became interested in them. Pierre Fresnault-Deruelle's above-mentioned study, *La Bande dessinée*, was influenced by the prevailing academic theories: putting aside historical and biographical approaches, he looked at strips by Hergé's generation in the light of structuralism and semiology. Fresnault-Deruelle took the comic strip's characteristic combination of text and image to be a coherent system of signs, and he set out to determine the laws by which those signs worked together to produce meaning. Later, Thierry Groensteen applied semiology to a wider range of Belgian, French and American comics which he scrutinised in minute detail, placing strong emphasis upon the visual aesthetics of panels.[26]

Others critics used different apparatus. Jean–Bruno Renard's *Clefs pour la bande dessinée* probed into the relationship between *bandes dessinées* and folklore:

> Comme le folklore, la bande dessinée est à la fois vivante, actuelle, liée aux problèmes du temps présent, et permanente, de toutes époques, du fait des archétypes auxquels elle empreinte ses thèmes … Comme pour le folklore, c'est la création collective qui répond à ses propres besoins d'imaginaire, par une sorte de dynamique compensatrice naturelle.[27]

This book, like *Clefs pour la bande dessinée*, demonstrates how *bandes dessinées* operate precisely that folkloric process of conservation and renewal that was mentioned by Propp and alluded to by Renan. However, my focus of attention differs from Renard's. Renard assesses BDs' re-use of archetypes, which are recognisable the world over. I concentrate on BDs' ability to perpetuate and renew French-speaking culture, thus producing an unmistakeably Franco-Belgian folklore.

Bruno Lecigne's and Jean-Pierre Tamine's *Fac-Similé* is another study whose importance cannot be exaggerated.[28] *Fac-Similé* is a philosophical treatise on BD realism, influenced by Jean Baudrillard. Lecigne and Tamine coined the phrase 'la question du réel', and their book was the first to apply the term *nouveau réalisme* to *bandes dessinées*. I shall refer to *Fac-Similé* again in the chapters on Giraud and Tardi.

Serge Tisseron saw *bandes dessinées* through the prism of Freudian psychoanalysis. He interpreted BD narratives as manifestations of the fears, desires, dreams and fantasies that lurk in the subconscious. Tisseron's studies, like mine, link comic strips to 'la question de l'identité'; however, unlike this book, Tisseron explores the theme of identity itself. In *Psychanalyse de la bande dessinée* Tisseron thinks about masks, 'les changements d'apparence sans changement d'identité' (disguises), and 'les changements d'identité sans changements d'apparence' (characters possessed by aliens).[29] My conclusions do not coincide with Tisseron's, although our arguments do run parallel very occasionally, as we shall see with reference to Hergé in Chapter 1.

On continental Europe, research into *bandes dessinées* is now entering the multi-media age. For example, François Schuiten and Benoît Peeters have compared *bandes dessinées* to other forms of mass communication which combine text and images (e.g. photonovels), as well as to the audio-visual media such as TV and cinema.[30] Today, the ninth art has a flourishing critical industry. *Bande dessinée* museums, complete with archives, are open to researchers in Brussels and Angoulême, France.

In France and Belgium *bandes dessinées* are avidly consumed, both by the wider public and by the 'intellos'. West of the English Channel, the picture could scarcely be more different. Comic strips are not generally believed to be a serious art form, and market-penetration by *bandes dessinées* remains strictly limited. No monograph about *bandes dessinées* has ever been published in English, although Roger Sabin's books contain useful sections on European comic strips.[31] The English-speaking critics Scott McCloud, Jerry Robinson, Maurice Horn, Denis Gifford, Steve Duin and Mike Richardson make only passing references to *bandes dessinées*.[32]

There are tentative signs of growing interest. *The International Journal of Comic Art*, founded in Philadelphia (1999), which publishes scholarly articles about the historical, practical and theoretical aspects of comics, has carried two articles about *bandes dessinées*: one is on the upheavals at Goscinny's and Uderzo's magazine *Pilote* in the late 1960s/early 1970s; the other is about Tardi's heroine Adèle Blanc-Sec.[33] The link between comic strips and notions of identity is becoming increasingly recognised: a conference by the Popular Culture Association in Toronto in 2002 had a series of papers exploring the relationships between comics and 'the question of identity'. However, the papers dealt with lesbian, Chinese and American comics, not with *bandes dessinées* and Franco-Belgian identity.

Despite valiant attempts by artists, critics, publishers, enthusiasts and academics, the ninth art remains a cultural phenomenon chiefly restricted to France and Belgium. Most *bandes dessinées* are still unknown in the USA and the UK. The ninth art deserves greater recognition than it currently receives. This book will open an important, largely undiscovered area of Franco-Belgian culture up to scrutiny. I hope that it provokes debate among scholars, students and aficionados alike.

PART I

The *Bande dessinée* Classics

CHAPTER ONE

Constructing the Franco-Belgian Hero: Hergé's *Aventures de Tintin*

Tales of Adventure

Hergé (Georges Remi) is the ninth art's pioneer. He achieved massive popularity with his series *Les Aventures de Tintin,* which appealed strongly to the empathy between France and Belgium: Hergé called directly upon the two countries' shared language, history, culture, current affairs and even geography; some of Hergé's carefully documented, visually realistic landscapes and urban settings look remarkably like both Belgium and France.

Tintin himself can be seen as the ninth art's first mythological hero, and he differed sharply from his American counterparts. America's emergence as the Western superpower coincided with the rise of US superheroes. These superheroes embodied an American force of good in the world, which had to prevail; superheroes were morally superior, they always triumphed and they exerted their power with absolute authority. Tintin, on the other hand, developed within a Franco-Belgian context: loss of empire, wartime occupation, reduced global influence and dominance by Anglophone popular culture. Tintin's reality is not that of a superhero: it gradually turns him into a human being.

Hergé (1907–1983) was born in Etterbeek, a French-speaking area of Brussels. Young Hergé was a keen member of the boy scouts, and in July 1935 he drew a series for *Le Boy Scout belge* called *Totor.*[1] After a very brief stint studying at the Collège Saint Luc in Brussels, Hergé joined the Roman Catholic newspaper, *Le Vingtième Siècle*; this newspaper was run by a strict, right-wing disciplinarian called Abbé Norbert Wallez. Hergé soon moved to the children's supplement, *Le Petit Vingtième*, for which he invented a new character, Tintin, who first appeared on 10 January 1929.[2] Tintin had a tuft of ginger hair, he wore plus-fours, and he was always accompanied by a fox-terrier called Milou. Hergé improvised Tintin's story, drawing two pages per week.

Early *Tintin* clearly shows Hergé's influences. Hergé had already read French and American comic strips including *Zig et Puce*, *Bringing up Father* and *Krazy Kat*, which taught him how to make characters speak with balloons; this technique was unusual in Europe at the time.[3] Hergé also drew inspiration from sources specific to his native, French-speaking culture. Hector Malot's *Sans Famille*, a novel which Hergé had loved as a boy, told of a young man called Rémi who, like Tintin, travelled far and wide with his white dog.[4] Benjamin Rabier and Fred Isly had already drawn *Tintin Lutin*, an illustrated story about a mischievous child who, like Tintin, had a tuft of hair and wore plus-fours.[5] Hergé said that although he liked Rabier, he had not consciously modelled Tintin on Tintin Lutin. Physically, Tintin also resembled popular novelist Gaston Leroux's journalist-hero Rouletabille whose head, like Tintin's, was 'ronde comme un boulet'.[6]

At the outset *Les Aventures de Tintin* were funny but, following Abbé Wallez's strict editorial policy, they also sent out a clear moral message. Tintin was a positive role-model whom young Christian boys were supposed to emulate; he was an angelic example of youthful virtue, the perfect boy scout. Tintin was brave, strong and magnanimous. He did good turns, putting others before himself. Hergé later said: 'Tintin, c'est moi quand j'aimerais être héroique, parfait'.[7]

Hergé was not the first to have associated humour with moral improvement. As Dominique Labesse suggests, *Les Aventures de Tintin* renew a European Francophone tradition that dates back to the seventeenth-century French comic playwright François Molière:

> Hergé, tout comme Molière, n'a qu'un but: plaire à ses lecteurs, à son public. Mais il ne peut empêcher que la vertu comique de ses albums viennent contribuer à l'idéfication [sic] de ses jeunes lecteurs; lui aussi à sa façon 'corrige les mœurs en riant'.[8]

Le Petit Vingtième's young readers took to Tintin instantly. A major factor in his immediate success was Hergé's ability to create the illusion that Tintin actually existed: Hergé authenticated Tintin by making him a reporter for *Le Petit Vingtième*, the magazine in which the strip itself appeared. Tintin was thus far more accessible than Moliére's aristocratic, pre-revolutionary heroes and heroines: he supposedly lived in exactly the same world as his youthful public. The opening panel of Tintin's very first adventure, *Tintin au Pays des Soviets,* called Tintin 'un de ses meilleurs reporters', adding: 'la direction du *Petit XXe* certifie toutes ces photos rigoureusement authentiques, celles-ci, ayant été prises par Tintin lui-même' (p. 1). Hergé's ploy integrated Tintin, a make-believe hero, firmly into real life; readers could imagine Tintin working for *Le Petit Vingtième* in between his weekly appearances.

Hergé fostered the notion that Tintin really existed by turning *Le Petit Vingtième* into a place where the real and the imaginary intersect. Hergé's idea worked particularly well because it was complemented by the very nature of comic strips. Comic strips intersect with the real because readers witness events directly, rather than reading continuous lines of prose and forming mental pictures as they would do when reading a novel. What is more, readers see the 'real' hero, and not an actor who impersonates him, as in a play or a film; consequently comic strips have an unusual degree of visual immediacy. Comic strips simultaneously intersect with the imaginary because readers animate the drawn hero by visualising what happens during the white spaces between each panel; readers also breathe life into the hero by imagining the sound of his voice, as it is printed in the balloons.[9]

The comic strip's combination of text and image requires active reader-participation: readers engage their imagination in order to bring the drawn hero to life when they read. Moreover, it follows logically that the readers must want the hero to be alive; if they did not, they would simply stop reading. Comic strips, in their own inimitable way, invite readers to suspend disbelief.

Like any successful artist, Hergé gave his public precisely what it asked for: *Le Petit Vingtième*'s young readers wanted to believe that Tintin existed, and Hergé connived with them. From the very first panel of his very first adventure Tintin was entering popular mythology.

Tintin's first assignment as *Le Petit Vingtième*'s roaming reporter took him to Russia, just 12 years after the Russian revolution. Hergé recalled that in *Le Petit Vingtième*'s right-wing Catholic circles, 'le bolchevik c'était ... pratiquement le diable',[10] and *Tintin au Pays des Soviets* follows this line. In a nightmarishly Bolshevist Russia, Tintin comes across the Secret Police, rigged elections, and cardboard factories producing nothing. However, despite the story's moral and political undertones, *Tintin au Pays des Soviets* amounts to little more than sequences of chases. Towards the end, Tintin is thrown out of a car and onto a westbound train, which miraculously takes him home to Belgium. Tintin then makes his triumphal entry into

Brussels, where he is greeted by an ecstatic crowd at La Gare du Nord. When *Tintin au Pays des Soviets* ended, *Le Petit Vingtième* staged a homecoming reception, which replicated the hero's return: a boy resembling Tintin, dressed in Russian clothes, alighted at the Brussels Gare du Nord to a rapturous welcome from *Le Petit Vingtième's* readers.[11]

Tintin's second adventure, *Tintin au Congo* (1930), took him on safari to the Belgian Congo. Again the story is fairly simple, chiefly consisting of visual humour as Tintin tussles with alligators, leopards and elephants. From this point onwards, Tintin's job was played down. Instead of being *Le Petit Vingtième's* star journalist, he became a righter of international wrongs. Rather than authenticating Tintin with references to his publisher, Hergé tried a different tactic: he brought a real person, Al Capone, into Tintin's fictional world. In *Tintin au Congo*, Tintin defeats villains working for Al Capone, who are seeking to control the diamond trade.

Tintin au Congo depicts the Africans as lazy, backward and immature, and it has been accused of being racist: the Congolese need to be organised by white, European Tintin.[12] Such paternalistic notions of superiority were widely taken for granted in colonialist Europe, not least in the right-wing Roman Catholic circles around Abbé Wallez; after all, Belgium did not lose the Congo until 1960. Hergé himself came to regret the assumptions underlying the story, calling *Tintin au Congo* and *Tintin au Pays des Soviets* his 'péchés de jeunesse'.[13] As Frédéric Soumois notes, Hergé deliberately toned down suggestions that Tintin was a colonising Belgian in later editions of *Tintin au Congo*: in the original version, Tintin gives Congolese schoolchildren a geography lesson which begins: 'je vais vous parler aujourd'hui de votre patrie: la Belgique'; that scene became a maths lesson on republication (*Tintin au Congo*, p. 36).[14]

Al Capone reappeared in Tintin's next adventure, *Tintin en Amérique* (1932), where Tintin takes on the Chicago mafia under Prohibition. The story again strains credibility: on page 2 a kidnapped Tintin escapes from the mafia by producing a saw out of nowhere, and by cutting his way out of their car.

Although *Tintin en Amérique* lacked sophistication, Hergé paced his narrative more effectively than in Tintin's first two adventures: as befits a serialised strip, he often ended a page at a particularly exciting moment, creating suspense and encouraging readers to buy the next instalment. One example of Hergé's dramatic use of page-breaks is the episode that ends with Tintin about to be hanged by rednecks (p. 35).

Despite Hergé's anti-Communism in *Tintin au Pays des Soviets*, *Tintin en Amérique* is anything but pro-American: it depicts the USA as wasteful, racist and corrupt. As Thompson notes, the story reflects Abbé Wallez's 'own fear of America and its dissolute ways'.[15] However, Hergé was no longer simply taking orders from Abbé Wallez: he had his own reservations about America, which resurfaced throughout his career. Years later, when Numa Sadoul asked him 'Tintin, lui, est-il aussi contre la société de consommation?', Hergé replied: 'tout à fait contre, bien sûr! ... Tintin a toujours pris parti pour les opprimés'.[16] In particular, *Tintin en Amérique* displayed an unexpected sensitivity towards the suffering that white America was inflicting upon its ethnic minorities: when oil is discovered on a Red Indian reservation, the US army forces the Indians off the land at gunpoint (p. 29); later, a radio news-bulletin announces that 44 Afro-Americans have just been lynched (p. 36).

Sympathy for the Red Indians did not appear in American comics until the 1950s, and still then only rarely. In the Western strip 'War of 1812' from Harvey Kurtzman's *Frontline Combat*, for example, the Indians are driven from their ancestral homes and massacred.[17] Sympathy for the Afro-Americans is rarer still. Even the scathing, socially critical Underground artists of the late 1960s and early 1970s were, with remarkably few exceptions, coy about white American racism. Mark Estren criticises the 'real absence of social awareness in the cartoonists' general lack of sensitivity to the problems of blacks and other minority groups in the United States'.[18]

Hergé's sympathy for the Native Americans makes him heir to a specifically French-speaking tradition. As Jon Tuska wrote in his history of Westerns:

> The French, almost since the advent of military forays into the New World, have been possessed of an *idée fixe* glamourizing the American Indian as a godlike pagan, a fierce but untutored ally in whom barbarism, while deplorable, is wholly forgiven due to a childish simplicity.[19]

René Gonnard suggests that the relatively benign French attitudes towards indigenous peoples may have their roots in colonial history:

> Les Français, dès le lendemain des grandes découvertes géo-graphiques de la fin du XVᵉ siècle ... se sont intéressés aux sauvages,

d'une manière plus humaine, et avec moins de préjugés que la plupart des autres Européens, surtout ceux de religion protestante. C'est parce que, dès les débuts de la colonisation française d'Amérique, cette colonisation s'est inspirée de sentiments de sympathie pour les indigènes.[20]

In Tintin's next adventure, *Les Cigares du Pharaon* (1934), Tintin goes to Egypt where he foils heroin smugglers. Although the anti-drugs message would obviously have met with Abbé Wallez's approval, Hergé was nonetheless gradually freeing himself from his editor's diktats. As Thompson says, there is evidence to suggest that 'Hergé was now polarising power away from him [Wallez] successfully'.[21] From *Les Cigares du Pharaon* onwards, Hergé displayed an ever-growing interest in the art of telling a good story, and he no longer simply subordinated plot and character to Wallez's requirements. A new emphasis on characterisation and narrative pacing is detectable in Tintin's adventures from this point onwards.

Regarding characterisation, *Les Cigares du Pharaon* features the comic policemen, Dupond and Dupont, who often reappear in later adventures. Although funny policemen are frequently recurring fictional characters, Dupond and Dupont are highly original. Despite their slightly different surnames, they are identical twins; they mirror each other's gestures symmetrically and they dress exactly the same, with matching bowler hats and walking-sticks. Dupond and Dupont deform each other's words, they follow rules and regulations to the letter, and they never fully grasp what is going on.

Pierre Sterckx suggests that Hergé's mutually reflecting Dupondts were inspired by the French novelist Gustave Flaubert's comic duo in *Bouvard et Pécuchet* (1881):

> Bouvard et Pécuchet fonctionnent en miroir, exactement comme les Dupondt. Ce miroir ne leur permet nullement de s'identifier ... Dédoubler le savoir en la parole ne renforce pas le sens, mais la mine et la détruit. Plus la bêtise se repète, moins elle signifie ... A chaque instant, la symétrie des personnages de Flaubert et la bêtise qu'elle dégage, renvoient aux Dupondt.[22]

Sterckx also points out that Dupond and Dupont, like Bouvard and Pécuchet, have surnames ending with the letters 'd' and 't'. Although Sterckx does not specify whether Hergé had ever read *Bouvard et Pécuchet,* Hergé certainly knew about Flaubert. He said: 'Tintin (et tous les autres) c'est moi, exactement comme Flaubert disait "Madame Bovary, c'est moi"'.[23]

By *Les Cigares du Pharaon* Hergé was also paying greater attention to narrative rhythm. This adventure is the first not to read like a series of improvised, weekly instalments that have been cobbled together. Rather than relying heavily upon slapstick, Hergé now linked visual gags into the plot, suspending the action momentarily to provide comic relief. *Les Cigares du Pharaon* shows Hergé starting to perfect an adventure-narrative structure, which he used almost exclusively for the next forty years. As such, this narrative structure needs to be examined in detail.

The structure, which predates comic strips by several centuries, is a simplified descendant of the traditional folktale as defined by Vladimir Propp in his study *Morphology of the Folktale*. Of course, Hergé did not consciously base Tintin's adventures on Propp's academic study of folklore; nonetheless, he would have absorbed the Proppian narrative structure from childhood fairytales, from Hector Malot, from Alexandre Dumas' *Trois Mousquetaires* (1844) and from Jules Verne's *Michel Strogoff* (1816), all of which he is known to have read.[24]

Tales of adventure are, to quote Propp, a 'development proceeding from villainy or a lack, through intermediate functions to marriage ... a reward, a gain or in general the liquidation of misfortune'.[25] Tintin, like d'Artagnan, Strogoff and Rémi, is the hero defined thus: 'That character who either directly suffers from the action of the villain ... or who agrees to liquidate the misfortune or lack of another person'.[26]

As in folktales, the hero (whether Tintin, d'Artagnan, Strogoff or Rémi) leaves home to venture into dangerous places and/or foreign countries. During his adventure the hero is tested, and he may have to contend with the forces of nature, as well as confronting wrongdoers. Chance or good fortune help the hero at critical moments, and he does not commit serious blunders. The hero has exceptional talents and he triumphs by using his intelligence, not simply by brute force. Suspense is maintained because the hero never wins too easily; victory is only assured after his final showdown with the villains.

According to the conventions of the genre, good triumphs over evil, so the hero ultimately defeats villainy and 'liquidates' misfortune. In traditional folktales (just as in *Sans Famille* and in *Michel Strogoff*), the hero could be rewarded with marriage after his triumph. Angelic Tintin cannot marry because he must stay forever young, independent and ready for his next adventure.

Hergé was the first to popularise the Proppian narrative structure in *bandes dessinées*, although in American comics it was being used by Walt Disney, whose Mickey Mouse first appeared just one year before Tintin; the Proppian structure also reappears in *Superman,* and in countless other comic strip 'classics'.[27] One reason for the traditional structure's enduring and international popularity is its flexibility: artists can adapt tales of adventure to suit their fancy. A brief comparison between Hergé, Disney and *Superman* shows how artists can use the same structure in different ways.

In Disney's comics, as in *Superman,* heroes are often prompted into action by a well-intentioned North America's national interest. Morally and politically, Mickey and Superman are patriots: they defend 'the set of values ... summed up by the Superman tag of "Truth, Justice and the American Way"'.[28] The villains are frequently agents of foreign powers: wrongdoers, dictators and despots tend to be anti-American. Money is an important consideration for America's heroes: villains try to steal Uncle Scrooge's cash; Donald Duck goes far afield to accumulate wealth for Uncle Scrooge and for himself. Superman is not interested in personal gain, but his steady job at the *Daily Planet* proves that he chooses to earn an honest wage, despite his superhuman strength. Finally, America's heroes have a love-life: Mickey has Minnie; Superman desires Lois Lane.

Tintin cannot be defined in such simple terms as America's heroes, even at this early stage. Like Mickey and Superman, Tintin is a force for good in the world; but, being an angel, he needs no love-life and he is far above financial constraints; he knows no deadlines and he has unlimited expenses. Tintin is roused to action by his moral convictions about truth and justice, although he is unaligned on the international stage: he is anti-Communist but he is not fully convinced by America. Soon, as we shall see, the outbreak of World War II was to push Tintin still further away from the American heroes.

Hergéen Realism

Tintin's first four adventures were amusing, but they were only partially successful: the countries to which he travelled were described in clichés and, despite Hergé's efforts to authenticate the stories, they were not convincing. That situation changed radically with *Le Lotus bleu* (1936): from now on, Hergé took pains to research the history, the culture and the customs of every country Tintin visited. In *Le Lotus bleu* Tintin goes to China, which is evoked by visually realistic street scenes, accurately drawn military uniforms, and signs written in genuine Chinese characters. An abundance of authentic-looking local colour counteracts the unrealistic speech-balloons.

Throughout his career Hergé perfected his distinctive brand of mimetic, carefully documented realism, causing the French anthropologist Claude Lévi-Strauss to remark later: 'Tintin était la bande dessinée la plus respectueuse des coutumes du monde.'[29] Hergé was helped with the research by his Chinese friend Chang Chong Chen, who appears in the role of Tintin's friend in *Le Lotus bleu*.

Hergé's new-found interest in documentary realism did not merely involve copying visually correct details: he further authenticated *Le Lotus bleu* with events that had recently been in the news. For example, the story includes an attack on a Japanese train, which actually happened (p. 21). The attack was committed by Japanese bandits, yet officials blamed it on the Chinese, in order to justify Japan invading China.[30] Most Western governments were pro-Japanese at the time but Hergé, perhaps because of his friendship with Chang, supported China, and so Tintin resists Japanese imperialism. *Le Lotus bleu* also criticised the British empire: Dawson, Shanghai's corrupt British police-chief, is a particularly unscrupulous villain.

Despite *Le Lotus bleu*'s political intrigue, Hergé was still drawing mostly for children. He therefore combined realism with visual humour, which is mostly generated by the Dupondts. In an attempt to travel through China incognito, the Dupondts dress up in traditional Chinese costumes: gowns embroidered with dragons, pigtails and fans. Their attempt at disguise has the opposite effect of the one intended, and they attract a huge crowd. Dupond and Dupont repeat exactly the same mistake when they visit other foreign countries in later adventures.

Mindful of his young readers' sensitivities, and of Abbé Wallez, Hergé toned down the violence inherent in war-comics by presenting it elliptically, and by making it funny. For instance, when three burly soldiers pick a fight with Tintin, the action takes place behind a closed door (*Le Lotus bleu*, p. 11). We can see the onomatopoeic words 'boum', 'bang' and 'dzing', coming from behind the door, but we can only guess at what is happening. A comic reversal of roles follows: Tintin has beaten his assailants off single-handedly.

L'Oreille cassée (1937) took Tintin to the fictitious South American republic of San Theodorus, in an adventure which was again partly authenticated by current affairs. Tintin is pitted against Anglo-American oil barons, who are destabilising an imaginary region called Gran Chapo; Gran Chapo recalls Gran Chaco, a particularly bloody war between Bolivia and Paraguay (1932–35) which, some said, was being waged by international oil companies, who were competing for drilling rights.[31] *L'Oreille cassé* also features the arms-dealer Basil Bazarov, who sells arms to both sides in Gran Chapo. His name recalls Basil Zaharoff, a Greek who was knighted by the English king, and who made a fortune arming both sides in World War I.[32]

L'Ile noire (1938) is a non-politicised adventure in which Tintin visits Britain, where he outwits forgers on a remote Scottish island. The story is full of unexpected twists and turns, and the Dupondts' antics provide much humour. *L'Ile noire* was redrawn for English-language publication (1966), in order to make the décor more visually realistic. The landscapes, buildings, vehicles and police uniforms do indeed look distinctively British in the later edition.

By *Le Sceptre d'Ottokar* (1939), Hergé's authenticating strategy was becoming even more effective. This story is a fast-moving political thriller with a very mundane opening: Tintin goes for a walk in a city park, finds a briefcase which has been left on a park bench and returns it to its owner. The opening sequence eases readers into the story, by reducing the gap between fiction and the real world: Tintin's good turn could be done by almost anybody, in any park, anywhere. Hergé is encouraging the impression that Tintin shares every reader's reality.

This impression is enhanced by the fact that the park and its urban surroundings are not necessarily located in the Belgian capital. Soumois suggests that the modern buildings in Tintin's home town resemble those on the avenue Louise in Brussels;[33] even so the Art Nouveau style, which characterises Brussels architecture for most outsiders, is absent from Tintin's city. There is no obvious Brussels landmark such as the Gare du Nord, as there had previously been in *Tintin au Pays des Soviets*. For those who do not know the Belgian capital well, *Le Sceptre d'Ottokar* could easily be set in France. Tintin's clean, visually realistic and distinctively Franco-Belgian town is a far cry from the superhero's sprawling, futuristic urban jungle.

Reynolds mentions 'the New York (or Gotham City, or Metropolis) that dominates the superhero story and has become its almost inevitable milieu'.[34]

Thanks to Hergé's authenticating strategy, his youthful French readers believed without question that Tintin was living in France. The French *bande dessinée* artist Jacques Tardi recalled:

> On ne peut plus identifier une rue de Bruxelles d'une rue de Paris. Quand je lisais *Tintin* quand j'étais môme je pensais qu'il était français, je ne savais pas qu'il était belge. Il n'y avait pas d'indica- tions.[35]

The owner of the briefcase found by Tintin, Professor Alembique, is impressed by his honesty. He immediately offers Tintin a place on a research trip to Syldavia, an imaginary Balkan kingdom. Hergé successfully depicts Syldavia as a genuinely existing country with its own history and traditions; yet the parallel between *Le Sceptre d'Ottokar* and the situation in Europe is perfectly clear. Just before Hergé began *Le Sceptre d'Ottokar,* Hitler's Nazi Germany had invaded neighbouring Austria; in *Le Sceptre d'Ottokar*, Tintin saves Syldavia from invasion by Borduria, its fascist neighbour; the villain's name, Müsstler, combines Mussolini's name with Hitler's.

Le Sceptre d'Ottokar's comparatively complex plot shows Hergé paying still greater attention to narrative rhythm. In particular, Hergé alternated sequences rich in text with amusing pictures. For example, after a wordy explanation that ties down all the loose ends, there is visual humour when the Dupondts fall into the sea (pp. 60–62). *Le Sceptre d'Ottokar* is also noteworthy because it introduced Hergé's only significant female character: the Italian opera-singer Bianca Castafiore, who is best known for her version of Margarita's 'Jewel Song' from Gounod's opera *Faust* (1859).

As well as working on characterisation and on narrative rhythm, Hergé was honing a distinctive graphic style, which came to be called 'ligne claire' or 'clear line'. Hergé spent the rest of his career perfect- ing 'clear line'. 'Clear line' enabled Hergé to organise perceptible reality, and to recreate it his own way: carefully selected, thoroughly researched and scrupulously copied details had precise, well-defined lines, that lack of shadow emphasised; everything was arranged according to the rules of perspective and proportion. 'Clear line' demanded technical precision and tight graphic control; nothing was arbitrary or left to chance.

Colour was an important component of 'clear line'. When *Les Aventures de Tintin* came out in colour from 1946, Hergé selected fresh, pastel shades, sky blues, pale pinks and light greens, all of which conjured up an attractive, non-threatening and clean-looking world, where goodness triumphed. Hergé's neat letters, held within rectangular speech-balloons and captions, matched his pictures perfectly; they were elegant, free from confusion and agreeable to look at. 'Clear line' turned some of Hergé's panels into beautifully finished, mini-masterpieces.

Hergé's well-researched décor and his polished, orderly, even restrained artwork distanced *Les Aventures de Tintin* from most contemporary American adventure comics, which had no direct equivalent of Hergéen realism. Disney's bulbous, elastic graphic style was far more exuberant, and it set little store by effects of visual reality. Superheroes inhabited fantastic mega-cities, which were loosely based on New York.

Tintin's closest early equivalent is Tarzan, who first appeared in comic strips in the same year as he did (1929). Tarzan, like Tintin, was a peripatetic righter of wrongs, whose adventures were drawn with concern for realism: Tarzan's muscular body was anatomically correct; but Tarzan's artists, unlike Hergé, made no attempt to authenticate foreign settings with carefully researched mimetism. Tarzan's Africa has gothic castles, Roman soldiers, troglodyte cities, medieval knights, Vikings and vampires.[36]

A further parallel exists between *Les Aventures de Tintin* and the American artist Milton Caniff's strip *Terry and the Pirates*. Caniff told of a youthful hero, who went to China on a treasure-hunt; like Hergé, Caniff took pains to research the Chinese setting, drawing with carefully documented, visual realism. However, Caniff's graphic style is totally different from 'clear line': Caniff's artwork is black and white, with a strong emphasis on the black; moreover, unlike Hergé, Caniff produced dramatic effects of contrast between light and shadow.[37]

Tintin/Haddock/Tournesol/Moulinsart

On 9 May 1940 the Nazis invaded Belgium, putting a stop to *Le Petit Vingtième* and interrupting *Tintin au Pays de l'or noir* (1939), which Hergé did not complete until 1950. Having lost his beloved *Petit*

Vingtième Abbé Wallez, 'a sad and disillusioned man', retired to a monastery.[38] Hergé then began a new Tintin adventure, *Le Crabe aux pinces d'or* (1940), which was serialised in *Le Soir jeunesse*, a paper under Nazi control.

Le Crabe aux pinces d'or introduced Captain Haddock who was to become a vitally important character in Tintin's adventures, later almost upstaging Tintin. When Tintin meets Haddock, the captain is a miserable incompetent and a dangerous drunk: his ship is smuggling opium without his knowledge. Bringing a violent alcoholic into a children's comic was a very surprising development, and Haddock is remarkably lifelike: he drinks himself into psychosis, and he even tries to kill Tintin; maudlin repentance then follows his appalling behaviour. Over the years Haddock gradually became less menacing and more likeable. His litanies of comical insults became his most endearing characteristic. Haddock's amusing tirades allowed Hergé to dodge the censor, who would not have tolerated swearing in a children's comic.

Le Crabe aux pinces d'or avoided Nazi censorship, but it later ran into trouble in America. A picture of Haddock, his white first mate Allan and an African sailor was altered at the request of Hergé's American publisher, who felt uneasy about seeing a mixture of races in the same panel.[39] The offending picture was on page 53, panel 6.

Tintin's next adventure, *L'Etoile mystérieuse* (1942), was drawn at the height of World War II. The story is about a race to claim a meteorite containing a rare metal, which crashes into the sea near the North Pole. Tintin and a group of scientists set out to find it on Haddock's ship. They are opposed by a gang of unscrupulous rivals whose ship, *The Peary*, flew the US flag in the original drawings.[40] *The Peary* was named after the American explorer Robert Peary (1856–1920), who made eight journeys to the Arctic. The ship's flag was redrawn in post-war editions, although the American name remained unchanged. Another enemy ship, *The Kentucky Star,* which tries to ram Haddock's ship, has an even more obviously American name (p. 26).

Wisely, Hergé avoided sensitive topics for the rest of the war and Tintin's next two adventures, *Le Secret de la Licorne* (1943) and *Le Trésor de Rackham le Rouge* (1944), are a treasure-hunt. Tintin's treasure-hunt shows him evolving in precisely the opposite direction to Caniff's Terry: Terry joined the American war effort by enrolling with the US air-force, but Hergé disengaged Tintin from World War

Figure 1. Tintin, Captain Haddock and François Hadoque, *Le Secret de la Licorne* © 2005 Hergé/Moulinsart

II, which does not figure at all in *Le Secret de la Licorne* and *Le Trésor de Rackham le Rouge*. Moreover, as we shall see, Tintin's treasure-hunt, unlike Terry's, appeals strongly to notions of Franco-Belgian identity. The treasure-hunt begins when Tintin and Haddock discover a complex series of riddling clues left by Haddock's ancestor, François Hadoque (Figure 1). François Hadoque was a ship's captain under Louis XIV, and his galleon, *La Licorne*, sank off a tropical island, loaded with treasure.

Captain Haddock resembles his ancestor. The two captains look similar, and they use the same comically abusive epithets. When Haddock recounts the sinking of *La Licorne* he imitates Hadoque's movements, while the panels jump abruptly between past and present. A comical climax is reached when Hadoque's portrait falls off the wall, landing on top of Haddock; Haddock's face then pokes through the canvas in place of Hadoque's (p. 25).

After much research, Tintin and Haddock locate *La Licorne*'s wreck, but they find no treasure in it. However, Tintin discovers ancient documents in the wreck that prove that the French King Louis XIV gave Hadoque a luxurious stately home: the Chateau de Moulinsart. Tintin and Haddock are helped in their treasure-hunt by Professor Tournesol, an eccentric inventor, whose submarine enables Tintin to explore the wreck. Tournesol also deciphers the ancient documents (Figure 2). Tournesol's deafness makes him deform what people say, which gives rise to verbal humour. Hergé said that

Figure 2. The Dupondts, Tintin, Tournesol, Haddock and Milou, *Le Trésor de Rackham le Rouge* © 2005 Hergé/ Moulinsart

Tournesol was inspired by Professor Auguste Piccard (1844–1962), a Frenchman who invented the bathyscaphe.[41]

Tintin, Haddock and Tournesol leave *La Licorne*'s wreck empty-handed; but they buy back Moulinsart with money earned from the patent on Tournesol's submarine. Tintin and Haddock then discover Hadoque's treasure at last, hidden in Moulinsart's cellars.

With his usual painstaking realism, Hergé modelled Moulinsart on the sumptuous French Loire chateau at Cheverny.[42] Yet *Le Trésor de Rackham le Rouge* did not suggest that Tintin had left Belgium to go and live in France: the countryside around Haddock's French-style chateau looks as much like Belgium as northern France. As Diane Hennebert points out, Moulinsart recalls Brabant, which has villages named Sart-Moulin, Maransart and Rixensart.[43] Moulinsart, where Tintin, Haddock and Tournesol relax between their adventures, is a haven of tranquillity. The chateau and its environs are a mythological Utopia, where France and Belgium mingle to the point of becoming indistinguishable; as such, Moulinsart is the image of Franco-Belgian identity.

By now, Hergé was quite deliberately encouraging readers to believe that Tintin was living in both Belgium and France. He even rewrote the dialogues, in order to remove typically Belgian turns of phrase. Jean-Marie Apostolides notes that the Belgian-sounding expression, 'ça veut juste réussir, Monsieur', became the neutral 'je regrette, Monsieur', in later editions of *Le Secret de la Licorne*.[44]

Tintin's next adventure was another two-album series, *Les Sept Boules de cristal* (1948) and *Le Temple du Soleil* (1949). Again, the story appeals strongly to notions of Franco-Belgian identity. It begins as a tale of the supernatural. In *Les Sept Boules de cristal*, scientists returning from an expedition to South America go down with a strange illness; they are apparently cursed by Rascar Capac, an Inca mummy that they brought back to Europe. Tournesol, having tried on Rascar Capac's bracelet, is mysteriously spirited off to Peru; he leaves the country through the French port of La Rochelle. Hergé was partly inspired by Frenchman Gaston Leroux's novel *L'Epouse du Soleil* (1913).[45] Leroux's adventure, like Hergé's, is about a Peruvian Inca curse, and it features an Indian called 'Huascar'; both Leroux and Hergé tell of South American Indians who make human sacrifices to the sun, and whose victims wear sacrificial bracelets; Hergé's Inca name Rascar Capac recalls Leroux's name Manco Capac.

Les Sept Boules de cristal is given a true sense of mystery by Hergé's narrative techniques. For instance, when Rascar Capac comes through the bedroom window as Tintin sleeps, readers are left wondering: does the mummy really enter the room, or does Tintin dream it? It is impossible to tell where Tintin's dream ends and where reality begins (p. 32).

In the sequel, *Le Temple du Soleil*, Tintin and Haddock follow Tournesol's trail to Peru, which is depicted with Hergé's characteristically close attention to local colour. Any lingering notions that Tintin may be a racist are definitively scotched when Tintin rescues Zorrino, an Indian boy, from being bullied by mestizos (pp. 18–19). Zorrino becomes Tintin's guide. After a long, hard trek through South America's mountains and jungles Tintin, Haddock and Zorrino reach the Inca temple, where Tournesol is held prisoner. They persuade the Great Inca to lift his curse, and to release Tournesol. As a good-will gesture, the Great Inca offers Tintin, Haddock and Tournesol gifts of treasure.

Tintin and Haddock go to truly heroic lengths to rescue Tournesol, with the captain now firmly on the path to redemption. Haddock never gives up, even though he invariably comes off worse than Tintin from brushes with the forces of nature: Haddock is caught in an avalanche, knocked down by a tapir, spat at by llamas, overrun by ants, and so on.

Tintin Psychoanalysed

Serge Tisseron has psychoanalysed Hergé's life and work in minute detail. Tisseron suggests that Tintin's, Haddock's and Tournesol's behaviour can be explained by Hergé's subconscious desire to establish an identity; as such, Tisseron's research is particularly relevant to this book.[46] Tisseron is well argued and persuasive. He highlights Hergé's original use of the Proppian adventure-narrative structure, while emphasising the thematic richness of Hergé's oeuvre and the unique-ness of Hergé's characterisation. Tisseron's ingenious theories can even explain why angelic Tintin spends his time with such unlikely friends: an alcoholic sea-captain and a deaf, eccentric old professor. In this section, I shall briefly summarise Tisseron's reading of *Les Aventures de Tintin*.

As Tisseron found out, Hergé's family history is mysterious: Hergé never knew the identity of his paternal grandfather. His paternal grandmother, one Marie Dewigne (1860–1901), was a servant for the Countess Errembault de Dudzeele, who owned a chateau in Brabant. In 1882, while she was still unmarried, Marie Dewigne gave birth to Hergé's father Alexis and to a twin brother called Léon; in 1893 she married Philippe Remi, a workman employed by the countess. Philippe Remi gave Marie's children, Alexis and Léon, his surname; but, as Marie and Philippe never lived together, their relationship appears to have been a marriage of convenience, possibly designed to save appearances. The countess bought fine clothes for Alexis and Léon and supervised their schooling. The identity of the twins' father (Hergé's paternal grandfather) was never revealed.

The question arises: who was Hergé's unknown grandfather?

Tisseron writes: 'Quant au grand-père secret, son identité n'a, semble-t-il, jamais été révélée, mais il fut dans la famille Remi l'objet d'une considération extrême'.[47] The older family members apparently wanted to keep the grandfather's name secret, but nobody seems to have been quite sure why. When the children asked who their grandfather was they were told, 'sur un ton de légende: "On ne vous dira pas qui était votre grand-père, cela vous tournerait la tête"'.[48]

Such an enigmatic reply raises more questions than it answers, encouraging unlimited speculation. Given the lack of concrete information, almost anything is possible. Perhaps Hergé's mysterious grandfather was a man of very high social rank, with a reputation to protect. Tisseron continues: 'Ainsi le père de Hergé était-il un enfant illégitime que la légende familiale désignait pour être d'ascendance illustre, voire noble, et même royale!'[49] Hergé's grandfather may even have been the Belgian king, Léopold II, who is known to have fathered numerous illegitimate children. Perhaps the countess was the go-between for the king and his two unacknowledged sons: that would explain why she educated Alexis and Léon and bought clothes for them. Tisseron adds: 'L'identité probablement prestigieuse du géniteur secret ... était en quelque sorte officialisée par la générosité de la comtesse de Dudzeele'.[50]

According to Tisseron, characters in *Les Aventures de Tintin* correspond to actors in Hergé's family drama: 'Il a su donner à chacun de ses héros une identité en rapport avec les personnages qui avaient marqué son enfance'.[51] Hadoque personifies the family mystery; his actions in *Le Secret de la Licorne* and *Le Trésor de Rackham le Rouge* are indeed shrouded in mystery, and they are not easily accounted for.

Under the laws of Hadoque's time, any booty captured at sea belonged to the crown. A loyal captain should have handed his treasure straight over to his king, Louis XIV; but instead Hadoque kept the king's treasure, and carefully hid it in his own cellar. Hadoque also went to astonishing lengths to make the treasure difficult to discover, even by his own descendants. Hadoque was more interested in hushing the treasure up than he was in enriching himself. Why? Did Hadoque harbour a secret grudge against the king for not openly acknowledging his son? Did the king give Hadoque Moulinsart in order to buy his silence? The treasure, hidden away like a guilty secret, may represent a paternal and filial love that cannot speak its name: 'mon trésor' is a term of endearment, which is used especially for children.

Castafiore, says Tisseron, resembles Hergé's grandmother Marie

Dewigne, as she creates confusion about who is who: Castafiore is unable to acknowledge Haddock's family background, as she cannot say his real surname. Moreover, Castafiore is closely associated with Margarita's 'Jewel Song' from Gounod's opera *Faust*. That is significant, because Margarita (like Marie Dewigne?) becomes pregnant outside marriage, by a man whose social station is far above hers.

According to Tisseron, the Dupondts are the second generation, that of Alexis and Léon, because they physically resemble Hergé's father and uncle: like Alexis and Léon, the Dupondts are identical twins with matching moustaches, bowler hats and walking-sticks. Hergé himself commented on the striking resemblance: 'Ce qui est curieux, c'est que je n'ai pas songé une seconde à eux en créant les Dupondt. Mais la rencontre est tout de même assez étrange.'[52]

Like Alexis and Léon, the Dupondts have two surnames, and nobody knows what the real one is; furthermore the Dupondts cannot comprehend what is going on around them. In their efforts to understand, they take whatever they are told literally. Finally, the Dupondts resemble young Alexis and Léon because attempts to disguise their identity are undermined by their clothes: the Dupondts' habit of dressing up in the national costume of the countries that they visit persistently arouses curiosity.

Hergé's three main characters, Tintin, Haddock and Tournesol, are the third generation, that of Hergé himself. They represent three possible ways for Hergé to approach the mystery of his grandfather's identity: 'Chacun de ces trois personnages incarne, à sa façon, une facette de Hergé aux prises avec le secret familial'.[53]

Tintin, like the others, is of unknown genealogy; his family background is obscure, and there is uncertainty about what he is really called: is Tintin a Christian name or a surname? All we know is that Tintin is a paragon of good behaviour: he is sober, brave, generous and clever. Tintin practises virtue and he uses his ingenuity. Tintin embodies the best way to solve the mystery.

Captain Haddock is the opposite of virtuous Tintin; the family secret torments him, driving him to drink. Haddock bursts into tears at the mere mention of his mother (*Le Crabe aux pinces d'or*, p. 16). In addition, a clue suggests that Haddock may be of royal lineage. A coat-of-arms above the door at Moulinsart implies royal ancestry, as it shows a crowned dolphin *(Les Sept Boules de cristal,* p. 2). The heraldic symbol puns on the dual meaning of the French word 'dauphin': 'dolphin' and 'heir-apparent to the French throne'.

Professor Tournesol is neither a bold righter-of-wrongs like Tintin, nor a distressed Haddock. The professor would rather turn a deaf ear than listen to disturbing speculation; hence, he refuses to wear a hearing aid. Tournesol wrestles with the mystery by shutting himself away and by channeling his curiosity into his work.

In *Le Secret de la Licorne* and *Le Trésor de Rackham le Rouge* Tintin, Haddock and Tournesol collaborate to solve Hadoque's mystery (i.e. to solve the mystery of Hergé's grandfather's identity). During their expedition, each of them turns out to be indispensable to the other. Although they are three separate characters they complement each other perfectly, as if they were one person: Hergé. Haddock captains the ship, Tournesol builds the submarine, Tintin locates *La Licorne's* wreck. Hadoque's treasure is eventually discovered and Tintin, Haddock and Tournesol gain access to Moulinsart, their rightful, ancestral home. From now on, nothing can ever part the threesome. In *Les Sept Boules de cristal* and *Le Temple du Soleil,* Tintin and Haddock spare no effort to bring Tournesol back home.

A king and his treasure reappear at the end of *Le Temple du Soleil,* but this time the treasure is not stolen and hidden. Quite the reverse: treasure is now given freely and legitimately, by its royal owner. Thus, mutual reconciliation is achieved between Tintin/Haddock/Tournesol (Hergé) and a regal figure (his unknown grandfather); that reconciliation is symbolised by a gift of treasure (love). *Le Temple du Soleil's* ending resolves the conflict that prevailed in the previous adventures:

> Hergé n'a pas seulement constitué avec *Tintin* un équivalent romanesque et heureux de ce drame familial. Il a aussi utilisé son œuvre pour exorciser les figures historiques du secret telles qu'il avait pu, enfant, les imaginer.[54]

Having been reconciled, Tintin, Haddock and Tournesol can come out from under the shadow of their 'secret d'une filiation royale mais inavouable'.[55] Their new, happy state accounts for the way their characters develop in the adventures that follow *Le Temple du Soleil*: Tintin becomes more human and less angelic; Haddock leaves his worst drunken excesses behind; Tournesol joins the international scientific community.

Hergé was not on a conscious mission to establish his familial identity by solving the mystery of his grandfather. Tintin's adventures are not some kind of encrypted autobiography. However, as Hergé himself made clear:

> Je cherchais 'avant tout' à raconter une histoire ... Mais une histoire, quoi qu'on fasse, est toujours porteuse d'un 'message'. Que j'en aie été conscient ou non, je me suis exprimé dans ce que j'ai écrit et dessiné ; sans le vouloir et sans le savoir, j'y ai mis ce que je pensais, ce que je sentais, ce que j'étais.[56]

Tisseron saw *Les Aventures de Tintin* as expressing Hergé's subsconscious desire to establish an identity at the personal level. However, it should be borne in mind that Tisseron offers only one interpretation of Tintin's adventures. Some readers may find Tisseron's psychoanalysis thoroughly implausible. A very different case can be put. Perhaps Tintin embodies goodness because he is a conventional hero, and Haddock is simply his foil. Maybe Tournesol and the Dupondts are no more than reworkings of stock comic figures: absent-minded professors and bumbling policemen. The Dupondts' habit of dressing up in national costumes may simply be included to make readers laugh; so too may Castafiore's inability to pronounce Haddock's name. Numerous other examples can be cited to cast doubt upon Tisseron's thesis.

Yet, whether or not one accepts Tisseron's reading, he indisputably highlights ways in which Hergé established an identity at the Franco-Belgian level: Hergé is Belgian but Tisseron is French. What is more, Tisseron's argument delves deeply into the long-standing linguistic, historical, geographical and cultural links between Belgium and France; finally Tisseron sees Moulinsart, where Léopold II meets Louis XIV, as a place where France and Belgium can overlap. One is tempted to suggest that the treasure, unearthed at Moulinsart, is nothing less than Franco-Belgian identity itself.

Tisseron's work is just one example of the scholarly interest that Tintin attracts in France and Belgium. Others abound: Jean-Marie Apostolides' Freudian study interprets *Les Aventures de Tintin* as 'un itinéraire psychologique' based upon the search for a father-figure, not for a grandfather, with Tournesol as the 'figure paternel';[57] Pierre-Louis Augereau analyses Tintin's treasure-hunt in the light of occult, mystical and masonic symbolism; Jean-Paul Tomasi and Michel Deligne examine the French novelist Jules Verne's influence over Hergé.[58] Books by Tisseron, Apostolides, Augereau and others are a measure of the fascination that Hergé's life and work hold for Tintinographers.

Perfecting Clear Line

When World War II ended, Hergé briefly found himself in trouble for publishing work in a newspaper run by the Nazis. He was arrested four times, but he was never formally charged.[59] On 26 September 1946, Hergé founded his own magazine, *Le Journal de Tintin*. The magazine gave Hergé full editorial control and, for the first time, an outlet worthy of his talent. *Le Journal de Tintin* used good-quality paper and colouring; it also enjoyed wider distribution than *Le Petit Vingtième* and *Le Soir*. Freed at last from both Abbé Wallez and the iron fist of Nazi censorship, Hergé could now perfect the art of storytelling.

One of Hergé's first tasks was to complete *Tintin au Pays de l'or noir* (1950), a Middle Eastern adventure, which World War II had interrupted. Appropriately enough, the story begins in an atmosphere of foreboding, depicting the world on the brink of war. Hergé had started *Tintin au Pays de l'or noir* before Tintin met Haddock. He explained Haddock's long absence by having the captain mobilised. Without Haddock, humour is chiefly generated by the Dupondts, who get misled by mirages in the desert.

By 1950, the political context of the Middle East had changed and the original version of *Tintin au Pays de l'or noir*, begun in 1939, suddenly looked dated. For example, it showed the Jewish underground organisations Hagannah and Irgun struggling against British occupation, before the state of Israel was established.[60] In the postwar editions Hergé, with his usual concern for keeping up with events, dropped the Jewish sub-plot; he also replaced the British soldiers with Arabs. In addition, Hergé redrew the décor, making it look more up to date.

Next, Hergé drew another two-album series: *Objectif Lune* (1953) and *On a marché sur la Lune* (1954). Tournesol (who now uses a hearing aid) designs a rocket that takes him to the moon along with Tintin, Haddock and the Dupondts. *Objectif Lune* and *On a marché sur la Lune* are relatively untouched by the nascent Cold War. Tintin and friends blast off from imaginary, unaligned Syldavia, not from France, Belgium, the USA or Russia. Unlike in contemporary American strips about space-travel, such as New York publisher's EC titles *Weird Science* and *Weird Fantasy* (which both started in 1950), there were no zap guns, no space monsters and no alien civilisations. Instead, Hergé took extreme care to make the adventure seem plausible. Hergé stuck closer to the tradition of the French novelist Jules Verne's *De La Terre à la Lune* (1865). He acknowledged his debt to Verne, saying: 'En fait de précurseur, il y a eu un certain Jules Verne. Moi je n'ai fait que "romancer" des bouquins qui existaient déjà.'[61] As with a Verne novel, much of the story's interest arises from interaction between the characters: the complex, scientific explanations offered by Tournesol and by Wolff, the other scientist, alternate with Haddock's and the Dupondts' amusing misbehaviour.

Hergé further perfected his technique as a storyteller, exploiting the possibilities offered by *bandes dessinées* to generate suspense. Panels jump from the main plot to the scheming villains; but the significance of the villains' actions is not revealed until Colonel Boris unexpectedly overpowers Tintin on the moon (*On a marché sur la Lune*, p. 39). Tintin then learns that Wolff, whose gambling problem made him vulnerable to blackmail, is a spy and a traitor.

With Wolff, Hergé's characterisation became more complex, as clear-cut distinctions between good and evil started to break down. Wolff is treacherous but he is nonetheless likeable, and on the way back to Earth he sacrifices his own life to save the others. There is not enough oxygen left to go round, so Wolff leaves the rocket and disappears into space (*On a marché sur la Lune*, p. 55). Hergé recalled that the censor was unhappy about showing suicide in a children's comic, so Wolff's farewell note had to read 'peut-être un miracle me permettra-t-il d'en réchapper aussi'.[62]

By going to the moon Tintin made one of humankind's oldest dreams come true, and the adventure sold exceptionally well. By now, almost everybody in France and Belgium knew about Tintin. When the Americans landed on the moon over ten years later, many comparisons were made with Tintin's feat. *Paris Match* invited Hergé to draw pictures of the US rocket; the French journalist Jean Cau wrote that one of the American astronauts had 'des cheveux qui forment un cran sur le front. Comme Tintin'; on hearing about the expedition, a little boy sadly told a journalist from *France soir* 'c'était déjà dans Tintin'.[63]

In the next adventure, *L'Affaire Tournesol* (1956), Tournesol is kidnapped by the Bordurians, who want his ultrasonic weapon. Tintin and Haddock follow Tournesol to Switzerland, and then on to Syldavia and to Borduria, where they rescue him. *L'Affaire Tournesol* is a Cold War spy-thriller, with Syldavia cast as the liberal, Western democracy and Borduria as the repressive, Stalinist state. The two

imaginary countries parallel Europe divided by the Iron Curtain. Yet the distinction between 'good' Syldavia and 'bad' Borduria is not as clear-cut as might be expected: Syldavia is not Tintin's unconditional ally; the Syldavians, like the Bordurians, attack Tintin and kidnap Tournesol.

Hergé's implication that a degree of moral equivalence existed between the capitalist West and the Communist East was utterly unknown in contemporary American comics. Unlike his American counterparts, Tintin remained politically unaligned: even during the Cold War he championed neither American-style consumerism, nor Stalinist Communism. Hergé's choice of neutral Switzerland as a setting for much of *L'Affaire Tournesol* is not insignificant.

L'Affaire Tournesol is generally acknowledged to be one of Hergé's finest works. The adventure is a masterful piece of narrative pacing, with moments of dramatic tension balanced by well-timed humour. There is frequent use of cinematic techniques (long shots, close-ups, aerial views etc.), which dramatise the action. Hergé also used panels of different sizes to great dramatic effect. He alternated small panels that accelerate the action (as the reader's eye travels over them rapidly) with larger panels that are bursting with detail. One particularly successful example is a sequence in which Tintin and Haddock, hot on Tournesol's trail, hitch a ride with an Italian boy-racer. A small panel shows the driver's foot jammed on the accelerator (p. 38). A panoramic view then reveals what is happening outside, as their car careers through a Swiss village market, scattering people everywhere (Figure 3).

Hergé continued working on his distinctive brand of realism, which reached new heights in *L'Affaire Tournesol*, with the Swiss decor looking particularly authentic. At one point, the Bordurians force Tintin's car off the road and into Lake Geneva (p. 20). Hergé visited Lake Geneva himself, in order to make sure that such a scene would be possible; he even copied down in his sketch-book the exact point at which Tintin's car leaves the road.[64] Hergé's mimetic, 'clear line' realism was also becoming ever more detailed: in earlier albums (such as *Le Trésor de Rackham le Rouge*), the newspapers characters read were blank sheets of paper; in *L'Affaire Tournesol*, their newspapers are covered with lines of print.

Tintin's next adventure, *Coke en stock* (1958), has a very strong opening. Tintin and Haddock are at the cinema, watching the end of a film; they then go out onto a city street. The prologue at the cinema shows a slice of fiction ending; the street scene shows reality beginning. When they are put together, the sequence which they form suggests that *Coke en stock* is set in the real world. Hergé's effect of reality is strengthened because Tintin's city, with its recognisable road signs and makes of car, looks even less like Brussels than the city in *Le Sceptre d'Ottokar*. As noted, some of the buildings in *Le Sceptre d'Ottokar* resembled those on the avenue Louise to readers familiar with the Belgian capital; but in *Coke en stock*, there is nothing to prevent Tintin's city from being French. Once again Hergé is creating common ground, where France and Belgium overlap; thus he strengthens a sense of Franco-Belgian identity, with mimetic realism driving the point home.

Coke en stock, in which Tintin and Haddock take on slave-traders, shows how far Hergé had come since *Tintin au Congo*. The African slaves still need Tintin to free them, but there is no more colonialism: the Africans are now responsible adults, who make their own choices. Nonetheless, Hergé was rather unfairly accused of racism, because of a dialogue between Haddock and the Africans in pidgin French. Hergé was sensitive to that accusation and so he rewrote the dialogue, but amusingly he left Haddock's words unchanged: in the redrawn edition the Africans speak passable French, but Haddock still speaks pidgin (p. 47). Hergé continued experimenting with devices specific to comics to produce unusual effects. In particular, he integrated balloons into pictures by new, ingenious means. When an enemy frogman mines Haddock's ship, his thoughts are represented by air-bubbles coming out of his diver's helmet (p. 57).

By the late 1950s Tintin was a household name in Europe, but he had not made any serious headway in the vast American market. Perhaps that is why *Coke en stock* uncharacteristically brought in the Americans as a *deus ex machina*. The USS *Los Angeles* rescues Tintin and Haddock when they are torpedoed by a submarine (pp. 56–59).

Tintin's Final Adventures

Tintin au Tibet (1960) was different from all of Tintin's previous adventures: there were no dastardly intrigues and no scheming villains. This time, Tintin has a dream in which his friend, Chang, survives an air crash in the Himalayas. Tintin and Haddock go to Tibet to find Chang, who has been rescued by the yeti. Typically,

Tibet's landscapes, street life and people are depicted with 'clear line' realism. *Tintin au Tibet* has less emphasis on action than previous adventures, and more on sentiment. Tintin weeps when he thinks Chang is dead (p. 35); the yeti turns out to be a lonely, sensitive creature, and not the savage monster of local legend. Haddock reveals the full extent of his nobility: he tries to lay down his own life to save Tintin, when they are stranded on a mountainside (p. 40).

By the early 1960s, Hergé had perfected his 'clear line' realism and his storytelling techniques. However, the structure of Tintin's adventures had never deviated once from the Proppian folktale narrative, structured by the hero's 'absentation', testing and return, which we discussed above. That situation changed with *Les Bijoux de la Castafiore* (1963), which dismantled the traditional adventure story. Hergé enjoyed breaking the rules he had spent almost thirty years putting into place. He said that he wanted to write 'une histoire où il ne se passerait *rien*. Sans aucun recours à l'exotisme ... Simplement pour voir si j'étais capable de tenir le lecteur en haleine jusqu'au bout.'[65]

Les Bijoux de la Castafiore is the only Tintin adventure with no travel abroad. The entire story takes place at the Chateau de Moulinsart, and nothing happens as it should. Tintin is frightened by an owl; Haddock is confined to a wheelchair; Tournesol's invention (a colour TV) does not work properly. Castafiore invites herself to stay at Moulinsart and her emerald is stolen; but the culprit is only a magpie, and not a band of gypsies as the Dupondts believe. The plot is a series of false trails and clues leading nowhere. For example Igor Wagner, Castafiore's pianist, overhears her telling her maid Irma where she is putting the key to her jewel box (p. 14, Figure 4); that is just one of the misleading clues, planted by Hergé, to suggest Wagner may be the thief.

Les Bijoux de la Castafiore provides ample evidence to support Tisseron's psychoanalysis of *Les Aventures de Tintin*. The story brings Tintin, Haddock, Tournesol, the Dupondts and Castafiore together at Moulinsart, an aristocrat's chateau, which may be in Brabant. There, Castafiore's treasure (ie. her love) is stolen. Tisseron suggests that the theft of Castafiore's love raises a distressing question, which cannot fail to have troubled Hergé: did his grandmother Marie Dewigne consent to his mysterious grandfather, or was she raped? Among other things, Tisseron points out the similarity between the words 'vol' (theft) and 'viol' (rape).[66] Tisseron also notes that when

...et la clef de ce tiroir, je la cache dans le vase qui se trouve sur ce meuble. Faites un effort pour vous en souvenir, ma fille!

Oui, madame.

Figure 4. Castafiore, Wagner and Irma at Moulinsart, *Les Bijoux de la Castafiore* © 2005 Hergé/Moulinsart

the Dupondts interview Tintin about the theft, they draw attention to the one letter that distinguishes 'vol' from 'viol', saying: 'vous tenez absolument à mettre les points sur les i' (*Les Bijoux de la Castafiore*, p. 37).[67] Marie Dewigne carried her secret with her to the grave; Castafiore hid her jewels in a writing-desk, called in French a 'secrétaire', or 'secret taire'. As Tisseron explains: 'Les bijoux sont cachés dans le "secrétaire", c'est-à-dire, littéralement, dans le "*secret*" qu'il faut "*taire*"'.[68]

Vol 714 pour Sydney (1968), in which Tintin, Haddock and Tournesol take a plane that is hijacked and diverted to a tropical island, is a more conventional adventure, even though Tintin lacks worthy opponents: Rastapopulous, the villain, is a ridiculous, fancy-dress cowboy. In an extremely amusing scene Rastapopulous and Carreidas, a mean-minded millionaire, bicker about who has been the naughtiest (p. 31). Haddock is now a reformed character: not a drop of alcohol ever passes his lips, and at one point he holds a glass of what looks like iced water (p. 60). Hergé further exploited the possibilities offered by the form, making speech-balloons and pictures support each other in new, dramatic ways. When Tintin guides Haddock, who has been blindfolded, through the tropical vegetation, Tintin's speech-balloons zigzag across the panel; the balloons make the reader's eye participate in Haddock's abrupt turns left and right (p. 22).

Tintin et les Picaros (1976), the last Tintin album that Hergé completed, overturned expectations entirely: Tintin drives a motor-bike, wears jeans and sports a ban-the-bomb sticker. He participates unenthusiastically in the adventure, and he seems to be uncertain about what to do. When Tintin hears that Castafiore has been arrested in San Theodorus, the fictitious Latin American banana republic, he first decides to stay at home, leaving Haddock to go and rescue her. Alain Chante notes that Haddock is stealing the limelight from Tintin: the captain appears in 47.9% of the panels, Tintin only in 41.7%.[69]

As Hergé said, *Tintin et les Picaros* is about ' la dictature', 'la misère des Indiens', 'la guérilla', and 'l'emprise de certaines sociétés commerciales'.[70] Despite Hergé's characteristically well-timed humour, this story paints social injustice in South America with a bleakness that is absent from the other Tintin adventures. *Tintin et les Picaros* is also unusually pessimistic because, unlike all of the previous stories, it suggests that goodness does not triumph. Despite Tintin's intervention, the San Theodorans remain poverty-stricken and unfree. General Tapioca, the ousted dictator, is replaced by Tintin's man General Alcazar; but nothing changes except for uniforms on the soldiers patrolling the shanty towns. Alcazar, who is supported by the International Banana Company, seems scarcely better than his corrupt and brutal predecessor.

Hergé's International Banana Company has sinister connotations: it calls to mind the United Fruit Company, a North American con-glomerate, which abetted the fascist coup d'état against the democratically elected Guatemalan government in 1954; the name also recalls the American Banana Company in *Cien Anos de Soledad* (1967), which brutalised a little Colombian town.[71] Hergé is implying that US business interests sponsor oppressive, terror-states south of the border; his condemnation of US foreign policy had no equal among mainstream English-language comics until *Brought to Light*, a 'graphic docudrama' about covert CIA operations in Latin America.[72]

Tintin's last adventures end the process that began after *Le Temple du Soleil*: almost imperceptibly, Tintin evolves from an angel in plus-fours into a flawed human being. In *Tintin au Tibet*, Tintin displayed a new capacity for emotion through his attachment to Chang. In *Les Bijoux de la Castafiore*, Tintin was unusually fallible. In *Tintin et les Picaros*, Tintin finally came off the moral high ground: he sided with a dubious dictator, who is bankrolled by US big business.

The gradual weakening of Tintin's status, apparent from the early 1960s, finds a very distant echo in some superhero strips, particularly those involving Stan Lee. Lee's and Steve Ditko's *Spiderman* told of an unusually insecure superhero, who had his share of human failings; Lee's and Jack Kirby's *X Men* introduced a human element, by depicting a quarrelsome band of mutant superheroes; Lee's and Kirby's *Incredible Hulk* brought in a note of ambivalence by telling of a misunderstood hero, who was mistaken for evil when he was simply frightened.[73] Parallels between Hergé and Lee should not be exaggerated, however: Spiderman, the X Men and the Hulk, unlike Tintin, never lost their exceptional strength and/or their agility, and they always defeated the wrongdoers.

Why did Tintin and the superheroes develop along such different lines? As White and Abel suggest, America's heroes are the product of a superpower, which is utterly convinced of its own invincibility and of its own goodness:

> Always the struggles were depicted according to the rules of the American game ... The hero's eventual victory was ensured because he represented the might of right. In America it could not be otherwise, and the public remained secure in this belief.[74]

In *Les Aventures de Tintin,* on the other hand, struggles are by no means always 'depicted according to the rules of the American game'. Many Americans may indeed believe, without question, in myths about their country's invincibility and goodness; but the French and the Belgians, for their part, can ill afford such a national mythology. Having been the theatre for two world wars, France and Belgium have a very different view of the world and of their place in it. They have learnt severe lessons from their shared, historical experiences of being invaded and occupied. Their common history makes it perfectly plain: victory is not always assured, and 'might' does not necessarily make 'right'. As Jacques Tardi pointed out:

> On ne peut pas se permettre d'avoir des superhéros. Notre histoire nous empêche d'avoir des superhéros. Notre histoire de petits pays

européens qui n'ont cessé de se faire la guerre. Notre histoire nous empêche d'avoir cette idée d'une suprématie, d'une force extrême.

According to the French BD artist Régis Franc, cultural influences can also explain the ninth art's lack of appetite for superheroes. When I interviewed Franc, he detected a deep-seated reluctance in French culture to accept the simple, even naive aspects of the super-power's comic strip mythology. Franc also humorously alluded to a French national tendency to rebel against convention, and to delight in breaking rules on purpose:

> Si vous prenez Batman, Superman, Tarzan etc, ils sont tous un peu de la même famille. Aux Etats-Unis les choses sont simples. Un et un égalent deux. En France, un et un ne peuvent pas égaler deux; et si un et un égalaient deux il faudrait absolument le détruire. Et, dans la BD française, dans cet esprit-là, il y a des gens qui ont saboté ça.[75]

As we shall see, the historical and cultural influences cited by Tardi and Franc had a strong impact on *bandes dessinées* from Hergé onwards: an absence of superheroes, combined with a persistent tendency to challenge other US comic strip conventions, are promin-ent features of the ninth art.

Hergé died on 3 March 1983, while working on *Tintin et Alpha Art*, an adventure about art-forgers.

The Tintin Phenomenon

By the time Hergé died, Tintin's adventures had sold over 70 million copies in French alone, and they had been translated into 33 different languages.[76] Interest in Tintin continues unabated, in France as much as in Belgium: on 29 September 1976, a statue of Tintin was erected at Parc de Wolvendaal, Uccle, Brussels; in 1977, Hergé was awarded the prestigious Grand Prix at the French *bande dessinée* festival in Angoulême;[77] in 1979, Tintin appeared on a Belgian postage stamp; and in 1982 the *Société Belge pour l'Astronomie* named a planet after Hergé. On 3 February 1999 MPs at the French *Assemblée nationale* used parliamentary time to stage a serious debate about whether Tintin is left-wing or right-wing.[78] In 2000 Tintin appeared on a French postage stamp to commemorate *La Fête du Timbre*. In 2004 Tintin appeared on a Belgian euro coin. Tintin's adventures have spawned an entire industry, of which Tisseron, Apostolides, Soumois and Augereau are just a few examples. Numerous studies in 'Tintinography' are published by the Bibliothèque de Moulinsart (Brussels).

There are many reasons why people still love Tintin today, even though he first appeared in 1929. Almost to the end Tintin was a valiant force for goodness, crusading against villains whom we still know only too well: warlike dictators, drug smugglers, gun runners, people traffickers, corrupt politicians, criminal businessmen. Hergé's secondary characters (Haddock, Tournesol, the Dupondts, Castafiore) are funny and original; readers enjoy rediscovering them and watching them develop as story follows story. Hergé's immaculate 'clear line' realism and scrupulously researched settings satisfy the most demanding adult; meanwhile, his knockabout humour pleases younger readers. Hergé's experiments with panels and balloons give rise to exciting effects.

Tintin was Belgian in origin but he crossed over into France perfectly naturally, and the French rapidly adopted him. Tintin's distinctive face has advertised French products such as Citroën cars, *La Vache qui rit* cheese and Olivet Brioches. Tintin's political non-alignment serves him well. The French press has regularly compared politicians from across the political divide to characters from his adventures. Henri Amouroux likened members of François Mitterrand's Socialist government to Tintin and Haddock, with 'M. Jacques Delors dans le rôle de Tintin, M. Pierre Mauroy dans celui du furibard capitaine Haddock ... Milou fait cruellement défaut à l'équipe gouvernementale'; Jean-Michel Helvig made a similar comparison about the right wing, likening Jacques Chirac to Tintin and Giscard D'Estaing to Castafiore.[79]

Tintin's iconic importance is best summed up by ex-French president General Charles de Gaulle, himself a Tintin fan, who said: 'Au fond, vous savez, mon seul rival international, c'est Tintin! Nous sommes les petits qui ne se laissent pas avoir par les grands.'[80] De Gaulle's comparison is perfectly justified. Like de Gaulle, Tintin towered above post-war France and Belgium; like de Gaulle, Tintin sought to steer a European middle course somewhere between Washington and Moscow.

De Gaulle is by no means the only person to have behaved as though Tintin really existed, albeit in a spoofing manner. Among many others, President Mobutu of Zaire 'wrote to Richard Nixon to remind him that it was actually Tintin … who had got to the moon first'.[81] The French journalist Jacqueline Dana asserted 'Tintin existe … en chair et en os', and then she went on to claim that she had actually interviewed him; Jean-Pierre Allaux declared that Tintin's dog Milou existed, alleging that Milou had told him about daily life with his master; Ariane Valadié later based an entire book around the same idea; when Hergé died, the French newspaper *Libération* ran the headline 'Tintin est mort'.[82]

Hergé's influence has been profound. By putting the traditional, Proppian folktale structure into a comic strip, Hergé popularised an entirely new genre and inspired countless imitators, in France as in Belgium. Quite forgetting that Hergé was Belgian, the distinguished French philosopher Michel Serres not only called Hergé 'l'auteur qui a le plus marqué la culture contemporaine', but also added: 'aucun auteur français ne peut lui être comparé au point de vue importance et grandeur'.[83] *Bande dessinée* artists influenced by Hergé are far too numerous to be listed in full. A selection of examples follows.

From the 1940s Hergé started the *Ecole de Bruxelles*, which combined adventures and humour with a mimetic realism, strongly influenced by 'clear line'. One early example, *Bob et Bobette*, depicts two adventurous children; another, *Félix*, is about a youthful detective; yet another is *Guy Lefranc*, about a freelance reporter; lastly, in *Les Quatre As,* a group of young friends and a dog resembling Milou solve mysteries.[84]

As Tintin's fame spread, French and Belgian artists grafted 'clear line' onto a variety of different settings: *Blake and Mortimer* applied 'clear line' to science fiction thrillers; *Alix*, drawn with well-researched 'clear line' realism, took place in pre-Christian Rome; *Hassan et Kaddour* adapted 'clear line' to an Arabian Nights setting; *Cori le Moussaillon* is a seventeenth-century, seafaring adventure influenced by 'clear line'; *Le Rendez-vous de Sevenoaks* is an English whodunnit, drawn in 'clear line'; *Gaspard de la Nuit* used 'clear line' in the context of a magical fantasy; *Ray Banana* grafted 'clear line' onto an American cop-drama.[85] Tintin even influences the way some latterday *bande dessinée* heroes look: Maurice le Cowboy has a distinctly Tintinesque quiff, as does the Parisian troubleshooter Freddy Lombard.[86]

Hergé's influence is not restricted to comics. The French novelist Françoise Sagan's *Femme fardée* recalls *Les Aventures de Tintin*: it features a bearded seadog called Capitaine Ellédocq, whose name echoes Haddock's. *La Femme fardée* also has an Italian opera singer who, like Castafiore, consistently mispronounces the captain's name; at one point, she even calls him 'Haddock'.[87]

Although Tintin has been less influential in the USA, he is not unknown in English-speaking countries: film-maker Steven Spielberg approached Hergé about movie rights. Chris Donald, founder of the British comic *Viz,* cites Tintin as an influence; there has been talk of a Tintin film starring Leonardo di Caprio.[88]

As well as influencing artwork and narrative techniques, Hergé has established *bande dessinée* artists' commercial practices which, to this day, differ from those in America. Allowing for some exceptions, most American comic-strip artists still published their work in paperback or in newspapers, with no guarantee of royalties; in the USA, artists are usually paid per page by a syndicate, which retains control of the strip and can change the artists around or drop them at will. Geoff Klock notes that the concept of 'creator owned' work did not catch on in the USA until Image Comics was founded in Fullerton California during the early 1990s.[89]

Hergé, on the other hand, remained firmly in control of *Les Aventures de Tintin* from the mid-1940s onwards. Like many later *bande dessinée* artists, Hergé was considerably better paid than most of his American counterparts, as he got two sets of royalties: the first from newsstand sales of *Le Journal de Tintin*; the second from republication of Tintin's adventures in hardback album form.[90]

Hardback albums, an essential characteristic of *bande dessinée* packaging pioneered by Hergé, used good-quality paper and colouring. Hergé's albums set very high production standards, which were unusual in America; they facilitated the ninth art's transformation from an infantile, throwaway product into an aesthetic object that adults keep and treasure. Tintin is giving generations of French and Belgian people lifelong enjoyment.

Thanks to Hergé, the ninth art carved out a new, Franco-Belgian identity: the French and the Belgians, divided and humiliated under occupation, needed to fashion a strong, new identity in the post-war, post-imperial world; new mythological 'heros parangons' were called for, and Tintin rose to the challenge. Throughout the historical and political upheavals of the mid-20th century, Tintin resolutely stood his ground as a steadfast Franco-Belgian hero: Tintin was a bold righter of wrongs, who lived both in France and Belgium; like General de Gaulle, Tintin remained politically unaligned on the international stage; Tintin evinced a certain scepticism about American society and US foreign policy; setting the trend for later *bandes dessinée* heroes Tintin evolved away from the American superhero tradition, and he came to exist on a human scale.

Les Aventures de Tintin aim unashamedly at the mass market, and they require no education in taste; for many English-speakers, those would be sufficient grounds to banish Hergé from the respectable-sounding realm of 'art'. Nonetheless Hergé's impeccable craftsmanship and his superb storytelling techniques, always beautifully presented, raised comic strips to the level of an art form. After *Les Aventures de Tintin,* the Franco-Belgian cultural landscape would never look the same again.

CHAPTER TWO

Creating Ambiguity: André Franquin's Humorous Strips

Early Spirou

The Belgian humorist André Franquin is our second master of the ninth art. Following the path beaten by Hergé, Franquin became enormously popular in France with his strips *Spirou et Fantasio* and *Gaston Lagaffe*. Franquin even influenced the great Hergé, who is known to have admired his work. Hergé laid down the ground rules governing *bandes dessinées,* and Franquin was the first to break them, particularly with regard to the hero. Long before *Tintin et les Picaros*, Franquin changed the hero's position and made it morally ambiguous, in contrast to Tintin, Mickey, Superman and Charlie Brown.

André Franquin (1924–1997) was born in the Etterbeek area of Brussels, like Hergé who was seventeen years his senior. As a child Franquin devoured comics, later saying, 'Je lisais beaucoup de bandes américaines dans *Mickey* et *Robinson* ... et aussi le *Tintin* d'Hergé'.[1] Like Hergé, Franquin went to the Ecole Saint Luc, Brussels, but his studies were interrupted by World War II. In 1944, he got a job in film animation at Studio CBA and when the studio closed in 1946, he was offered work at *Le Journal de Spirou* by Joseph Gillain (known as Jijé). Franquin, Jijé and friends visited the USA and Mexico in 1948/9.

Jijé entrusted Franquin with *Le Journal de Spirou*'s star attraction, a series called *Spirou et Fantasio*. Spirou was originally invented by Robert Velter (known as Rob-Vel) in 1938. Rob-Vel did not have time to develop Spirou before being conscripted, and passed Spirou over to Jijé; Jijé in turn passed Spirou on to Franquin.

Rob-Vel's Spirou, a hotel bellboy, was accompanied by Spip the squirrel. When Jijé took over, the importance of Spirou's job diminished and Fantasio, a human being, replaced the squirrel as Spirou's best friend. Those changes show Jijé modelling Spirou on Tintin: after

Tintin au Pays des Soviets Tintin's job was played down, and Haddock replaced Milou as Tintin's best friend after *Le Crabe aux pinces d'or*. Fantasio, like Haddock, raised laughs by falling down, knocking things over and so on.

To begin with, *Le Journal de Spirou,* like *Le Petit Vingtième* and *Le Journal de Tintin,* offered its readers firm moral guidance. The magazine ran a regular column by a scout-masterly figure called Le Fureteur; he encouraged readers to behave by pretending that Spirou really existed as their exemplary role model, rather like an invisible friend: 'Le Code d'honneur nous enseigne qu'un ami de Spirou est franc et droit'.[2]

Franquin took *Spirou et Fantasio* over during *Spirou et la Maison préfabriquée* (1946), which was a run of visual gags about a prefab house falling down.[3] The first story Franquin completed, *Le Tank* (1948), showed a Europe still overshadowed by World War II: Spirou and Fantasio buy an ex-US army tank, and they lose control when they drive it off. They cause all kinds of comical mayhem, but no one gets seriously hurt. When the tank stops, Spirou insists they repair all the damage they have caused. The humour is visual slapstick, and the action takes place against simple backgrounds.

In Franquin's second effort, *Radar le Robot* (1948), Spirou again struggles with a machine: a driverless car tries, unsuccessfully, to run people over. The murderous, driverless car was later used to more frightening and less humorous effect in John Carpenter's movie *Christine* (1982).

Franquin recalled that when his career began 'il n'y avait que deux grands noms: Disney et Hergé'.[4] Inevitably, young Franquin was influenced by both those artists, although stylistically he was much closer to Disney. Neither Disney nor early Franquin drew with carefully researched, 'clear line' realism. As with Disney, objects and speech-balloons were gently rounded, bulbous and elastic-looking, evoking a naive and innocent whimsy that was absent from Hergé. Like Mickey Mouse, Spirou wore red clothes with gold buttons. Disney and Franquin used more bright, jolly colours than Hergé, particularly orange, yellow and light blue. Like Disney, Franquin used shadows to create dramatic effects.

Over the course of his career Franquin adopted numerous devices popularised by Disney, though not necessarily invented by him. Examples include suddenly plunging the action into silhouette, motion-lines creating the illusion of objects moving through space, and brightly coloured onomatopoeic words. Disney's influence remained with Franquin until the mid-1970s but it gradually grew more attenuated. With time, Franquin evolved his own graphic style.

Despite differences between young Franquin and Disney on the one hand and Hergé on the other, our three artists' strips developed along similar lines. Franquin's first attempts, like early *Mickey Mouse* and *Tintin*, consisted of simple, visual gags. Later all three began drawing longer adventures, which were well adapted to serialisation in magazines. They all adopted the Proppian folktale structure discussed in Chapter 1; they all linked visual gags into the adventure, suspending the action to provide comic relief.

Franquin's first two full-length adventure stories fall between Disney and Hergé. In the first adventure, *L'Héritage de Spirou* (1948), Spirou is motivated by money: he braves a haunted house to obtain an inheritance. In the second, *Spirou chez les Pygmées* (1950), Spirou, like Tintin, is perhaps inevitably paternalistic towards the natives when he visits colonial Africa. Spirou stops a war between two pygmy tribes, one with black skin and one with brown skin, by teaching those with black skin how to wash; when the dirt comes off both tribes have the same colour skin, and the fighting ceases. Franquin later regretted *Spirou chez les Pygmeés*, saying, 'Je ne suis pas raciste moi-même ... Je dessine des Noirs ridicules autant que je dessine des Blancs ridicules.'[5]

Franquin's most original early adventure story is *Les Chapeaux noirs* (1952). Here, Spirou goes to the Wild West, where he gets involved in a gun-toting escapade. A gag where a cactus is shot by mistake and topples onto a bandit was lifted straight out of Disney, according to Franquin.[6] Finally Spirou is cornered by bandits, and is about to be killed. But the reader has been tricked: Spirou was only acting in a movie, and his action-packed adventure was not for real.

Les Chapeaux noirs provides the first example of Franquin's tendency humorously to subvert the conventions of adventure stories: traditionally, the hero's exploits are exemplary and meaningful, but *Les Chapeaux noirs* is nothing but a false adventure, a sham. Franquin's tendency to subvert the conventions of the genre became more pronounced over the course of his career, distancing him from Disney and from the Hergé of the 1950s.

'Style atome' and the Rise of Spirou

Spirou and Fantasio were not invented by Franquin, but he soon brought his own characters into their adventures. In *Il y a un Sorcier à Champignac* (1951) Franquin invented the village of Champignac and peopled it with new protagonists, notably the mayor and the count.

The Mayor of Champignac's verbose speeches, which are full of comically confused metaphors, introduced a new level of verbal humour. In a later adventure, *Le Voyageur de Mésoïque* (1960), the mayor says, 'Agriculture, commerce et tourisme sont les deux mamelles qui sèment le pain dont il abreuve ses enfants' (p. 1014). The mayor had no precedent in comic strips, but his nonsensical pomposity recalls a famous figure from French literature, Henri Monnier's character Joseph Prudhomme, who is best known for having said 'Ce sabre est le plus beau jour de ma vie'.[7]

The Count of Champignac, an offbeat, scientific genius, became even more indispensable to Spirou's adventures than the mayor. Eccentric scientists like Franquin's count recur frequently in twentieth-century popular culture. In French-speaking countries, such characters were first popularised by Jules Verne's protagonists, Professor Lidenbrock and Captain Nemo in *Voyage au centre de la Terre* (1864) and *Vingt mille Lieues sous les mers* (1870); Hergé's Tournesol is a later influential example. Franquin's count differs from his predecessors in that his miraculous discoveries involve serums made from mushrooms. Franquin's count is original: in Spirou's later adventure *Le Voyageur du Mésozoïque* (1960), the count brought a dinosaur back to life over thirty years before Steven Spielberg's *Jurassic Park* (1993).

In *Il y a un Sorcier à Champignac*, where Spirou meets the mayor and the count, nature seems bewitched (for example, pigs turn blue), and the mayor blames the strange happenings upon gypsies. The plot is a series of false clues that put everybody on the wrong track, until Spirou discovers that the count's serums are behind it all. As Sadoul points out, *Il y a un Sorcier à Champignac* may have influenced Hergé.[8] Hergé's *Bijoux de la Castafiore*, like *Il y a un Sorcier à Champignac*, is structured by misleading clues; moreover, both stories involve gypsies wrongly accused of a crime.

By the early 1950s, Franquin's graphic style was becoming more visually realistic: there were detailed street scenes with recognisable makes of car. Observant readers like the young Tardi noticed that the street-fittings in Spirou's home town looked rather more Belgian than those in Tintin's Moulinsart. As Tardi recalled, 'il y avait quelques petits élements qui font savoir qu'on est en Belgique'. Franquin combined such visual realism with colours reminiscent of Disney; for example, the count's castle is purple with yellow doors.

Spirou et les Héritiers (1952) introduced the Marsupilami, a loveable, yellow-and-black spotted creature. Spirou and Fantasio go to Palombia, a fictitious South American country, where they capture and befriend the Marsupilami, who returns with them to Champignac. Like the unicorn and the phoenix, the Marsupilami is a mythological creature with exceptional properties. The only equivalents of the Marsupilami in earlier comics are two equally fantastic animals: the Giff Wiff (*The Katzenjammer Kids*) and Jeep (*Popeye*).[9] Unlike the Giff Wiff and Jeep, the Marsupilami is an egg-laying mammal with a tail 25 feet long. He uses his tail for self-defence and for locomotion, bouncing along on it like a spring. Although small, the Marsupilami is incredibly strong, and in *Le Voyageur du Mésozoïque* he knocks the dinosaur unconscious. The Marsupilami was hugely popular with *Spirou* magazine's readers, and the funny little animal frequently accompanied Spirou on his adventures.

Seccotine, the first female character, arrived in *La Corne de rhinocéros* (1955), another African adventure. Unlike most female secondary characters in 1950s adventure comics, Seccotine has a strong personality. She is a brave, intelligent professional journalist; Seccotine is far cleverer and far more competent than Fantasio. On returning from Africa, Spirou and Fantasio obtain the 'Turbotraction', a 1950s dream-car complete with chrome and wraparound windscreen. The 'Turbotraction' combined pure imagination with contemporary notions of modern styling.

As Sadoul noted, *La Corne de rhinocéros* contains the first example of Franquin directing subtle irony at Spirou: when an Arab salesman encourages Spirou to buy a present for his fiancée back home, the suggestion that Franquin's chaste hero has a girlfriend must be a joke.[10] Franquin's humorously ironic treatment of the hero, which would be unthinkable in Disney and Hergé, became more overt in Spirou's later adventures.

Palombia, where Fantasio's cousin Zantafio emerged as the local dictator, received a political dimension in *Le Dictateur et le champignon* (1956). Spirou's adventures became less innocent and more hard-edged with this portrait of Third World fascism. In Palombia, oppression is everywhere: the Palombian national symbol (a parrot) parodies the Nazi eagle, and a man is kicked by soldiers for failing to salute Zantafio with sufficient enthusiasm. However, the story ends happily because Spirou uses one of the Count's serums to melt Zantafio's military hardware, and prevent war.

Spirou's evident delight in melting Zantafio's weaponry gives *Le Dictateur et le champignon* anti-war undertones which were almost unknown in 1950s adventure comics, where war was far more likely to be glamourised. In contemporary comics, *Le Dictateur et le champignon* is comparable only to strips in Harvey Kurtzman's non-humorous EC Comics magazine *Frontline Combat* (1951), which depicted warfare through the ages with a grimly accurate realism.

By the late 1950s Franquin's graphic style was losing its bulbous, Disneyesque elasticity, without becoming grimly realistic. With his friend and assistant Willy Maltaite, Franquin helped popularise the newly emerging 'style atome', a style he also adopted in his next comic, *Modeste et Pompon*. In 'style atome', shapes became more angular, more geometric, and they were drawn with bolder, straighter lines. In 'style atome' cities, elegant buildings of steel and glass, filled with shiny, ultra-modern gadgets, suggested financial security and material comfort; sleek, American-looking vehicles (like the 'Turbotraction Mk II') suggested hi-tech dynamism and effortless speed (Figure 5). 'Style atome' glorified the mass consumerism and the technological optimism of a Europe emerging from post-war austerity.[11] It also matched Spirou's rising living standards: by the mid/late 1950s, Franquin's one-time boy scout had a very expensive car and a modern, comfortable home. Incognito City in *Les Pirates du silence* (1958), an adventure where Spirou outwits bank-robbers, provides numerous examples of 'style atome'.

Franquin's 'style atome' was akin to Hergé's 'clear line': both styles depicted a safe, clean, prosperous world, where goodness always triumphs; there was no pollution, no urban blight, no unemployment and no social or moral decay. Like 'clear line', 'style atome' was peculiar to *bandes dessinées*. American artists such as Stan Lee and Jack Kirby were drawing adventures influenced by America's, not Europe's, post-war preoccupations: the space race, atomic secrets and Cold War angst. The atomic bomb and tensions with the Soviet Union meant that ultra-modern technology inspired fear as much as optimism in the USA. The space monsters, evil

Figure 5. The Turbotraction Mk II, with the Marsupilami, Fantasio, Spirou, and Spip, *La Foire aux Gangsters* © 1960 Dupuis 1960

commie spies and darkly menacing atmosphere of Lee and Kirby have no place in the reassuring Franco-Belgian world of 'style atome' and 'clear line'.

Spirou Undermined

As the 1950s drew to a close, Franquin tired of Spirou. He departed radically from conventional tales of adventure in *Le Nid des Marsupilamis* (1960), which became the biggest seller of the entire *Spirou et Fantasio* series in France.[12] In *Le Nid des Marsupilamis* roles are redistributed when Seccotine sidelines Spirou: the story consists of Seccotine's documentary about the life, habitat and courting rituals of the Marsupilami, filmed by her in the Palombian jungle. Spirou is merely a spectator in the crowd, having lost the initiative to a woman. Superman, Mickey and Tintin could never be treated so ignominiously.

Franquin's belittling of Spirou weakened Spirou's status as an exemplary hero. Spirou's moral status became still less clear with the arrival of Zorglub in *Z comme Zorglub* (1962). Conventional wisdom holds that true heroes need worthy opponents, but Zorglub is simply pathetic. Zorglub flies to Champignac in a menacingly futuristic 'Zorgocopter'. He makes a pompous speech and promptly falls down a ladder. Zorglub wants to rule the world, but his main achievement is writing 'Coca-cola' backwards on the moon. Depressed and lonely, he exits ingloriously on an old bicycle.

There is an ironic contrast between Zorglub's failure and the glittering modernity of his equipment. Unlike any of his contemporaries, Franquin used 'style atome' futurism to question prevailing post-war optimism in *Z comme Zorglub*: Zorglub's state-of-the-art technology merely provides incitements to consume, and even then it goes wrong.

In *L'Ombre du Z* (1962) Zorglub is more dangerous: aided by Zantafio the thuggish dictator, Zorglub enriches himself by hypnotising poverty-stricken Palombians into buying absurd quantities of toothpaste. Franquin's humour turns corrosive when the Palombian army, chanting Zorglub's advertising slogans, beats up its own citizens and tries to grab all the toothpaste for itself. Naturally Spirou thwarts Zorglub's plans, but the disturbing suspicion remains that insatiable consumerism conspired with fascism in Palombia. Franquin's disquieting association between rampant consumerism and oppression in developing countries was not found again in comics until artists such as Robert Crumb emerged with the US Underground.[13]

By the mid-1960s, Franquin was tiring of Spirou and wanted to concentrate on his new character, Gaston Lagaffe. Franquin's weariness with Spirou expressed itself through parodies of the genre and through ever more ironic treatment of Spirou. In *QRN sur Bretzelberg* (1966) Spirou restores freedom to a starving east European country. Soldiers shoot at him, but their grenades are nothing but cans of beans. Spirou triumphs over villainy so easily that his victory seems ridiculous.

The last Spirou adventure that Franquin drew, *Panade à Champignac* (1969), collapsed the adventure narrative. Nothing really happens: the opening pages are set in the offices of *Spirou* magazine and depict Gaston Lagaffe's antics; the Count is old and tired; Fantasio is a depressive neurotic; Zorglub has a baby's mind but a man's body, a notion that borders on the obscene, as he needs to be washed and fed; Spirou has exchanged his glamorous 'Turbotraction' for a humble little Honda; there is a chase in which Spirou hotly pursues Zorglub's runaway pram.

Full-length send-ups of adventure stories were unusual in *bandes dessinées* before Franquin's later *Spirou et Fantasio* stories, although in the USA Harvey Kurtzman's *Mad* (1952) had already parodied Superman (Superduperman) among others. But Franquin's parody was not exactly the same as *Mad*'s. In *Mad*, lampooned heroes

> became self-conscious commentators on their own formats, which they talked over with themselves, their peers, and the readers. They were aware of the fact that they existed in a narrow frame, and seemed to resent it.[14]

Spirou never became a resentful, 'self-conscious commentator' on his own format. Quite the reverse: humour arose because Spirou persistently acted the virtuous hero, blissfully unaware that the adventure narrative was collapsing around him.

Franquin was renowned for his modesty, and he was a notoriously harsh judge of his own work: he later claimed to be dissatisfied with all of the *Spirou et Fantasio* stories. Apparently forgetting that he had undermined the hero's position before Hergé, Franquin even called Spirou an old-style hero, who was too much like Tintin.[15] Although Spirou's setting was more Belgian than Franco-Belgian, *Spirou et Fantasio* struck a chord with the French public. By the mid-1950s, *Spirou* magazine was one of the most successful *bande dessinée* magazines in Europe, selling over 150,000 copies per issue.[16]

Younger artists imitated Franquin. The Marsupilami, in particular, inspired a number of fantastic animals. One comic, *Cha'apa et Group Group*, shows how hard French publishers of the 1950s and 1960s were struggling to keep up with Belgium.[17] Group Group looks like the Marsupilami, except that he has green-and-black stripes and a squirrel tail. Like the Marsupilami, Group Group lives in a South American jungle, and he accompanies a human back to civilisation.

Over the years, the Marsupilami has gone from strength to strength, eventually becoming more popular than Spirou. The Marsupilami has spawned innumerable cuddly toys and various other spin-off products, including a hit record.[18] A statue of the Marsupilami was erected in Charleroi, Belgium in 1988, and in Brussels the *Musée des sciences naturelles* dedicated an exhibition to him in 1996. The Marsupilami's fame even crossed the Atlantic. Walt Disney Company made a cartoon film about the Marsupilami in 1992, although Franquin was unenthusiastic.[19] New Marsupilami comics, signed by 'Franquin et Batem', are still being published today by Marsu Productions (Brussels).

'Style atome' Suburbia: *Modeste et Pompon*

Modeste et Pompon was the result of a short-lived financial dispute between Franquin and Editions Dupuis.[20] Dissatisfied with his publisher, Franquin briefly went over to *Le Journal de Spirou*'s rival, Hergé's *Journal de Tintin*, who commissioned the strip for five years. *Modeste et Pompon*, unlike *Spirou et Fantasio* and *Les Aventures de Tintin*, consisted of short, self-contained gags lasting about eight panels. Franquin recalled that in Europe, adventure comics were the norm, and that few *bande dessinée* artists were drawing short gags during the 1950s.[21] Short gags had chiefly been popularised in Europe by George McManus' *Bringing up Father*, which was about a *nouveau riche* American family. Gags make readers laugh by flouting expectations, and they generally have a three-stage structure: the first stage presents a fairly neutral situation; the second develops the action towards a logical outcome; the third suddenly delivers the unexpected ending. Much of the humour in *Modeste et Pompon* and *Bringing up Father* arises from domestic concerns, and jokes turn on the hero's desire for a quiet life being thwarted. Like Donald Duck, Modeste is often disturbed by his three mischievous nephews.

Some gags in *Modeste et Pompon* are very similar to those in *Bringing up Father*. For example the hero, be he Jiggs or Modeste, sets off to an engagement.[22] On the way, he becomes embroiled in an argument with a passer-by. When he arrives at his engagement, the hero discovers that the passer-by is none other than the person he is scheduled to meet.

Although it clearly shows Franquin's influences, *Modeste et Pompon* is not plagiarism. The society depicted in *Modeste et Pompon* is less matriarchal than that of *Bringing up Father*; Modeste's female companion Pompon, unlike Maggie (Jiggs' wife) is not a domineering snob. Pompon is wiser than Modeste but she exerts a calming, moderating influence. Félix the incorrigible salesman, who tries to sell up-to-date gadgets to Modeste, has no equivalent in *Bringing up Father*. Anticipating later technology, Félix even touted a remote

Figure 6. Pompon, Modeste and Félix, in a 'style atome' interior, *Bonjour Modeste* by Franquin © 1973 Editions du Lombard, Brussels

control zapper for changing TV channels, ten years before the zapper was first marketed in Europe.[23]

Both *Bringing up Father* and *Modeste et Pompon* are very much of their time. *Bringing up Father* depicts America in an art deco style that evokes the pre-war era. *Modeste et Pompon* depicts post-war French/Belgian suburbia with 'style atome': clean streets, prosperous villas, neat gardens, comfortable interiors and domestic gadgetry (Figure 6).

Modeste et Pompon is not Franquin's most original creation, but it has a certain period charm. *Modeste et Pompon* allowed Franquin to try his hand at short gags, and he was soon to exploit the potential of such gags more fully in his next comic, *Gaston Lagaffe*.

Gaston Lagaffe, an Original Hero

Gaston Lagaffe, Franquin's most commercially successful comic, was signed 'Franquin et Jidehem' until 11 April 1968. The strip continued, with various interruptions, until 1990. Thirty-five million Gaston albums have been sold world-wide, Gaston has been translated into 11 languages, a statue of him was erected on the Boulevard Pacheco, Brussels in 1996, and a restaurant was named after him.[24] Gaston became the second Belgian after Tintin to appear on a French postage stamp, during *La Fête du Timbre* (2001).

Franquin originally intended Gaston to be a moronic anti-hero: 'Contrairement aux héros, il n'aurait aucune qualité, il serait con, pas beau, pas fort. Ce serait un "héros sans emploi", un héros dont on ne voudrait dans aucune bande dessinée tellement il était minable.'[25] Gaston made his entry in *Spirou* magazine on 28 February 1957 wearing a smart jacket and tie.[26] When asked what he was supposed to be doing, he mumbled that he did not know. On 14 March 1957, Gaston swapped his jacket and tie for clothes more indicative of his personality. For the next forty years he wore a slovenly, ill-fitting pullover and threadbare jeans. In December 1957, Gaston was given a job in *Spirou* magazine's office. To begin with, Gaston committed gaffes around the office in single-picture cartoons. As his popularity grew, he was given half a page in *Spirou* magazine from 24 September 1957, and a full page from 14 July 1966.

At first Fantasio accompanied Gaston, but soon Fantasio was replaced by new secondary characters: Jeanne the office secretary, who loves Gaston madly; de Mesmaeker, a businessman whose attempts to sign contracts with *Spirou* are nearly always involuntarily thwarted by Gaston; Prunelle, Gaston's boss, who exasperatedly cries 'rrogntudjuu!' in response to his subordinate's blunders; Longtarin the dim-witted policeman, who has occasional run-ins with Gaston on the street.

As *Gaston Lagaffe* developed, Gaston began to change. His face became more expressive and his stiff, upright posture slumped. He remained gaffe-prone, but he became less moronic. A philanthropist, Gaston recycled bottles to raise money for sick children.[27] He was good with his hands, and he became an inventor of some talent. One of his first creations, a rocket, aroused the interest of the Pentagon.[28] Gaston was also anti-war: he showed his disapproval of the war toys advertised in *Spirou* magazine by building a model warplane that bombed his colleagues at work.[29] Gaston had a flair for music. He made the 'Gaffophone', an eight-stringed musical instrument, whose sound knocked down walls and disrupted over-flying aircraft.[30] Gaston often causes explosions, gives himself electric shocks or gets a punch on the nose from irate colleagues. However, Gaston's inventiveness shows he does not lack a spontaneous, natural intelligence.

Gaston had an extraordinary ability to communicate with animals; he displayed an interest in animal rights and in environmental issues long before they became fashionable. Gaston rescued a lobster from a restaurant, and trained it to sort his mail; he sabotaged a hunt with a gun that fired carrots, enabling rabbits to avoid hunters by seeing better.[31]

Despite his strongly held convictions, Gaston remained an ambiguous, contradictory hero. As Franquin said, 'On a dit que Gaston était écologiste avant la mode mais il empeste la ville avec sa voiture'.[32] Gaston's dogged insistence in parking his filthy old jalopy wherever he pleases hardly makes him a Green.

Gaston Lagaffe has been called the first of many anti-heroes, although the anti-hero, who simply reverses the traits of the conventional hero, is as old as comic strips themselves.[33] The diabolical Katzenjammer Kids are early anti-heroes. Gaston certainly has some of the anti-hero's traits: he is eminently fallible and he is afflicted by grave defects; he is incorrigibly lazy and criminally irresponsible. Gaston never questions his own actions, however destructive. Sometimes he is selfish, sometimes plain daft. However, Gaston genuinely cares about other people, and he tries to make them happy. He does not relish violence, and if he provokes catastrophes, he generally does so unintentionally. Catastrophes often happen precisely because of Gaston's concern for others: worried about pollution, he attached a large balloon to the exhaust-pipe of his car; the balloon burst, asphyxiating the entire street (*Des Gaffes et des dégats*, p. 423).

With *Gaston Lagaffe*, the clear-cut distinction between heroes and anti-heroes was humorously broken down, making Gaston quite unlike any *bande dessinée* hero who had gone before. Arguably, that humorous breaking down had already begun in pre-war France with the illustrated story *Bécassine* whose heroine, a good-natured servant girl, committed serial blunders. But Franquin created the first morally ambiguous *bande dessinée* hero, and since then there have been plenty of others, as we shall see below. One among many is the Frenchman Frank Margerin's Lucien, who is a lazy, amiable, would-be tough guy; Margerin was among the famous French *bande dessinée* artists who dedicated a cartoon to Franquin when he died.[34]

Regarding the American strips, a certain similarity exists between Gaston and Charles Schulz's hapless loser Charlie Brown in *Peanuts*: both heroes are exceptionally unfortunate, and yet despite all odds they persevere and never give up hope entirely.[35] However, although we can feel sorry for Charlie Brown, it is impossible to feel sorry for Gaston. Charlie Brown's ability to engage our pity gives him a moral dimension, which Gaston lacks. Charlie Brown's moral aspect is attested to by his sobriquet 'Good ol' Charlie Brown', as well by the 1967 Broadway play *You're a Good Man Charlie Brown*.[36]

Like Hergé and Schulz, Franquin fostered the illusion that the imaginary hero actually existed, abetted by the comic strip form; thus, they all eased the hero's passage into popular mythology. In each case, the effect was different. Schulz authenticated Charlie Brown by referencing the American way of life (baseball, Halloween, summer camp etc.); Hergé and Franquin authenticated Tintin and Gaston by referencing their own publishers. However, Tintin never visited the offices of *Le Petit Vingtième*, and his adventures almost invariably took him abroad; Gaston, on the other hand, 'worked' in and around *Le Journal de Spirou*'s office. The gap between reality and fantasy disappeared entirely when readers wrote to Gaston at work. One day two genuine readers sent Gaston a new pair of shoes, which he duly wore in the strip the following week.[37]

Franquin took the office joke further by bringing his own colleagues into Gaston's imaginary world. De Mesmaeker was Jidehem's real surname. Franquin himself appeared twice, and Monsieur Dupuis, head of Editions Dupuis (*Spirou*'s publisher) made his presence felt in the office; usually, Monsieur Dupuis stayed just out of sight behind a door or on the phone, although readers once saw his feet.[38]

Before *Gaston Lagaffe*, a genuinely existing publisher had already been used to authenticate fiction in some American comics, notably *Weird Fantasy*.[39] Franquin is unlikely to have read those strips, as *Weird Fantasy* was not translated into French. Again, the effect produced in *Weird Fantasy* is not exactly the same as in *Gaston Lagaffe*. In *Weird Fantasy*'s office, staff write science fiction stories, which unexpectedly come true; the inference is that the real world mirrors their fantastic stories. But Gaston does not write stories or gags. In *Le Journal de Spirou*'s office, funny things happen because Gaston's presence blurs the line between reality and fantasy.

Verbal and Visual Humour in *Gaston Lagaffe*

Gaston Lagaffe's workaday office setting was very different from Tintin's and Spirou's globe-trotting adventures. The structure of *Gaston Lagaffe* was also very different. From now on, Franquin only used short gags which, rather than bringing comic relief to an adventure story, were an end in themselves, and gave the strip meaning.

As we have seen, Franquin recalled that short gags were rare in 1950s *bandes dessinées*. Contemporary American humorists, following *Peanuts*, were mostly using short gags to generate humour based on character study. The new conventions in American gags, which Schulz pioneered, are neatly summarised by Richard Marschall:

> The sarcastic punch line; the upturned-eyes response; eye-contact with the reader in the final panels; the primal scream as reaction to a situation; an entire gag relaying one character's reflections rather than an interchange between two; the gag payoff in the penultimate panel; and a comment in the last balloon.[40]

Franquin reinvented the gag in Europe just as Schulz did in America, although Franquin did not take gags in the same direction.

The first gags in *Gaston Lagaffe* were visual slapstick, with Gaston causing disasters around *Le Journal de Spirou*'s office. Soon Franquin introduced verbal humour. Gags using verbal humour often began with humdrum office conversation and ended with a visual payoff: a picture of Gaston taking a figurative expression used in that conversation literally; this technique had previously been used in *Bécassine*.[41] For example Fantasio, tired of seeing Gaston loafing around the office, says, 'Ayez du ressort'. Gaston slouches out of the room but soon bounces back in again, scattering Fantasio's paperwork everywhere, with two enormous springs attached to his shoes (*Gala de gaffes*, p. 79).

In later gags, verbal humour became more varied. As befits an ambiguous, equivocal hero like Gaston, verbal humour frequently arose from punning word-play. Sometimes, dialogue consisted entirely of double meanings. When Gaston goes for an interview for a part-time job as nightwatchman in a porcelain shop, the word-play is particularly funny: an abundance of puns about fragile objects and breakages are incorporated into a coherent conversation between Gaston and his prospective employer. This is an extract:

> *Shopkeeper*: Je suis brisé depuis que mon veilleur de nuit m'a laissé tomber.
> *Gaston*: Pourquoi … Il n'était pas bien dans son assiette? … Faut pas en faire un plat.
> *Shopkeeper*: Ca vous fait rire?
> *Gaston*: Aux éclats![42]

In the final panel Gaston produces a racket and ball, and readers are left to wonder whether his words will be translated into actions.

Figure 7. Gaston Lagaffe and Longtarin, *Un Gaffeur sachant gaffer* by Franquin © 2002 Marsu, www.gastonlagaffe.com.

As Gaston became more of an inventor, visual humour arose from his ingenious creations. Gaston's inventions were amusing because, although they were utterly fantastical, they were made from simple, everyday materials, and they looked as if they could work in reality. Franquin said, 'Si Gaston invente une machine, je dois l'étudier pour que le lecteur n'y puisse rien détecter qui devrait l'empêcher de marcher, sinon, je ne serais pas content'.[43]

Our illustrated example shows how Franquin was combining verbal and visual humour to craft subtle, cleverly constructed gags twelve years into *Gaston Lagaffe* (*Un Gaffeur sachant gaffer* p. 515; Figure 7). Although the setting is supposedly Belgium, the street could easily be French: trees with circular grilles round their base and houses with window shutters are common sights in any French town. Unlike the Gaston gags cited above, the humour here begins with the pictures, and then it moves to the words. First, Gaston's car-hoist looks funny, because it combines outrageous fantasy with the technically feasible. Secondly, humour arises from the unexpected reversal of roles: when Gaston is arrested by Longtarin we expect Gaston is going to be punished but instead, Longtarin ends up in trouble, thanks to Gaston's word-play.

The first thing Gaston says to Longtarin is a pun that plays with the similarity of sound between 'souffle' and 'sifflet'. 'Ça vous coupe le souffle' means 'it takes your breath away'. 'Ça vous coupe le sifflet', Gaston's invented expression means, by analogy, 'it takes your whistle away': a reference to the policeman's whistle, one of his tools for maintaining public order. Gaston's pun both looks ahead to Longtarin's failure and blocks meaningful communication by making words interchangeable. In the same panel, just before Gaston's word-play makes the legal status of his car uncertain, the car itself changes colour from yellow to white.

In panel seven, when Gaston suggests that his car is not parked illegally as it is off the ground, his logic breaks the rules governing the context in which the word parking is generally understood. At that moment, words become totally unstable: they break free from the confines of speech-balloons, anarchically invading the picture.

The ending of this gag is especially powerful because readers do not know the punchline. We must imagine for ourselves the extremes of absurdity to which Gaston's flawed logic leads Longtarin, because we cannot see what question Longtarin asks his superior at the police station between the last two panels. Judging by his superior's reaction, one can guess that Longtarin said something like: 'How far off the ground can a car be parked before it becomes illegal?'

Our example shows how far Gaston had come from the blundering imbecile of his earlier gags. By diverting language away from meaningful communication Gaston subverts Longtarin's thought, and so he can park where he wants to. Gaston successfully blurs the distinction between mundane reality and pure fantasy with his original behaviour, his word-play and his inventions. In so doing, he dreams up new and interesting ways of negotiating everyday problems, such as where to park one's car.

*   *   *

Over the course of *Gaston Lagaffe* Franquin evolved a graphic style which differed from 'style atome' yet which was also distinct from Hergé and from American comics. While Gaston was becoming popular, Hergé was perfecting his detailed, 'clear line' realism. Hergé's lettering remained sober and neutral. American funnies, influenced by Schulz's *Peanuts*, were mostly adopting an economy of line, stripping images down to the essentials and reducing backgrounds to the minimum. The uncluttered décor in *Peanuts* and others focused attention on the witty dialogue.

Franquin's graphic style contrasted with the clarity and sobriety of Hergé and Schulz, becoming increasingly complex and chaotic-looking during *Gaston Lagaffe*. The first *Gaston Lagaffe* gags were simply drawn, generally depicting Gaston and colleagues against a yellow or blue background. From *Gare aux gaffes* (1966), drawings became more animated: letters bursting out of speech-balloons; exaggerated, inventive onomatopoeia (like Prunelle's 'rrogntudjuu!'); long, elaborate motion-lines as objects hurtle around *Le Journal de Spirou*'s office. Franquin's early interest in Disney and in film animation resurfaced: events are accelerated, often with only a split second between panels, as wildly gesticulating characters race in and out of the office. Very tight graphic organisation underlies the apparent chaos, for images flow smoothly from one to the next. Often for example, a character exits right from one panel through a door; in the next panel he enters left, with the same door now behind him.

From the mid-1960s, colour was increasingly varied. Franquin set more gags outside *Le Journal de Spirou*'s office, depicting night scenes, country scenes and street scenes. He drew objects half-glimpsed through mist with the help of a vaccinostyle, a medical instrument used to prepare the skin prior to injections, which looks like a pen with a diamond-shaped tip. Franquin used his vaccinostyle to blur objects by scratching at the ink; the more distant the object, the more he scratched it away. A good example of this effect appears in *Gare aux gaffes* (p. 303).

Like Hergé, Franquin was using ever more detailed backgrounds. Unlike Hergé, Franquin delighted in exaggerated caricature. Gaston's recognisable but unreasonable world has absurdly cluttered desks, street-lamps bent at odd angles, shops with punning names (like 'sec shop', the dry cleaner), a passing biker with 'fragile' on his crash helmet (*Gaffes bévues et boulettes*, p. 285; *Un Gaffeur sachant gaffer*, p. 512). By the early 1970s some of Franquin's outdoor scenes have such an abundance of background detail that subtleties are not immediately noticeable. When Gaston drives a depressed friend out to the country to cheer him up, the scenery looks attractive at first glance; but on closer inspection, we notice that the landscape is full of half-hidden rubbish (*Gaffes bévues et boulettes*, p. 849). Sadoul comments that readers see this scene twice: first through the eyes of cheerful Gaston, and secondly through the eyes of his depressed friend.[44]

In Gaston's last albums, growing numbers of incidental, background characters add discreet touches of verbal and visual humour. When Gaston causes a traffic jam, a driver behind shouts and sounds his horn in a speech-balloon which reads: 'Quel est le fils de TUUUT!'[45] Here, Franquin is both concealing the obscene insult 'fils de pute', and using the speech-balloon in an original way: as the driver's voice and the sound of the horn are both encapsulated by the same balloon their meaning is equivocal. Is the car speaking, or is the driver making the noise of the horn?

Like all good cartoonists, Schulz, Hergé and Franquin each adopted a graphic style that fitted their protagonists' behaviour. Schulz's mock-reasonable style suits gags about children and a dog naively imposing adult rationality on their surroundings. Hergé's 'clear line' matches Tintin's perfect clarity of thought. Gaston's mere presence undermines adult rationality. As Gaston plays with everyday language, sometimes making rational thought impossible, his behaviour is matched by Franquin's pictures: deceptively disorganised-looking panels reflect Gaston's chaotic, unbridled intelligence; extreme caricature counteracts the effect of reality created by the profusion of everyday objects, placing Gaston's world at the interface between banality and utter fantasy.

With *Gaston Lagaffe*, Franquin exploited the visual and verbal potential of comic strip gags to the maximum, using elaborate slapstick, intelligent word-play and jokes where readers imagine the punchline. Franquin established his own, distinctive brand of humour, as well as creating an original character. *Gaston Lagaffe*, like *Les Aventures de Tintin*, had enough knockabout fun to sustain a child's interest, yet enough sophistication and subtlety to please the adults. By the early 1960s Franquin was second only to Hergé in stature; French and Belgian artists influenced by Franquin are far too numerous to be listed in full. A few examples follow.

Inventive, likeable, blundering Gaston spawned innumerable morally ambiguous imitators. One is Marc Lebut who drives a Model T Ford and makes life impossible for his neighbour with his imaginative but hare-brained schemes; another is Désiré, a scatter-brained, musically minded hero, who also drives a quaint, unusual car.[46] Gags about gaffe-prone heroes with cars like Gaston's almost became a cliché in 1960s *bandes dessinées*. *Les Petits Hommes*, an amusing yarn about a meteorite that falls on a village causing the inhabitants to shrink, has an energetic, caricatural style, whose playful mix of detailed, everyday reality with pure fantasy recalls Franquin.[47] Renaud, the ingenious main protagonist, resembles Gaston physically; but serious, courageous Renaud is a more conventional hero than Gaston.

Following Gaston's success in *Le Journal de Spirou*'s office, other artists drew gags about heroes working for *bande dessinée* publishers. The best-known is Achille Talon, published in René Goscinny's French magazine *Pilote*; in the comic, Achille works for a magazine called *Polite*.[48] The graphic style of *Achille Talon* recalls Franquin; but unlike Gaston, Achille is a fat, pompous suburbanite, who talks much but says little. Finally, *Le Gang Mazda* has a 'clear line' style similar to Hergé, and depicts three artists who, like Gaston, work for *Le Journal de Spirou*, while the strip itself appears in *Spirou*.[49]

Idées noires and Beyond

By the early 1970s Franquin had more than proven his talent. In 1974 the first annual French *bande dessinée* festival at Angoulême awarded him its Grand Prix. Yet, despite growing international acclaim and huge sales, he was increasingly depressed. Franquin later spoke frankly about how he had needed medical treatment in the early 1980s for depression.[50] *Idées noires*, Franquin's next comic, showed his darker side.[51]

Idées noires consisted of short gags, but it was very different from *Modeste et Pompon* and *Gaston Lagaffe*. Whereas Modeste and Gaston were surrounded by friends, characters in *Idées noires* are marooned in a universe that does them harm. Throughout *Idées noires*, black humour arises from the pointless, unheroic deaths of the protagonists by electrocution, decapitation and shooting, to name but a few. This unrelenting gallows humour is particularly grating because, ironically, characters often die precisely at the moment they believe they are saved: a man lost in the snow sees lights ahead, and thinks he has reached civilisation; but the lights turn out to be the eyes of a wolf-pack (*Idées noires* I, p. 51).

Some gags in *Idées noires* use ideas previously found in Franquin (such as anti-militarism and green issues), but Gaston's cheerful, imaginative subversiveness is replaced by cynicism of cosmic proportions: goodness does not exist and faith in goodness is laughable. For example, a supertanker is shipwrecked and the survivors are covered by an oil-slick. They pray that God, in his infinite goodness will save them; immediately after their prayer, feathers come down from heaven, sticking to everybody. Why? Because an aeroplane carrying feathers for making eiderdowns spontaneously explodes overhead (*Idées noires* II, p. 127).

Franquin's graphic style changed radically with *Idées noires*. Drawings are in black and white, and all traces of Disneyesque wholesomeness have gone. Franquin's new style in *Idées noires* recalls painters of fine art, the Flemish painters Hieronymous Bosch and Pieter Bruegel, and Spaniard Francisco de Goya, rather than previous comic strip artists. *Idées noires* contains no vast, allegorical tableaux, and the comic lacks the Christian morality underpinning Bosch's *Garden of Earthly Delights* (1504). Yet *Idées noires*, like Bosch's painting, depicts a swarming, dangerous world, where people are deformed by their own folly; Franquin's gag in which a hunter negligently shoots off part of his own head is one particularly grotesque example (*Idées noires* I, p. 45). The hideous, skeletal shapes, desolate landscapes and scenes of carnage in *Idées noires* recall Bruegel's *Triumph of Death* (1562) particularly as Franquin, like Bruegel, paints death as the ultimate victor. Like Goya's *Madhouse* (1794) or *Third of May 1808* (1814), *Idées noires* depicts mentally confused characters with exaggeratedly distorted expressions and glaring, frightened eyes; Franquin's squad of soldiers, like Goya's madmen or the victim in *Third of May 1808,* are both terrified and terrifying (*Idées noires* II, p. 70). Yet, unlike Bosch, Bruegel and Goya, Franquin refused to draw anything moral, noble or aesthetic from catastrophes. He extracted black humour and took ugliness to extremes.

Franquin's combination of despairing humour with hallucinatory, deliberately ugly drawing bears some resemblance to American Underground artists, notably to Robert Crumb, whose work Franquin knew.[52] Crumb and Franquin both set their characters in a morally bankrupt world. Like Crumb, Franquin was unconvinced by religion, was anti-war and was worried about the environment. But Crumb was also very different from Franquin: Crumb subversively drew with rounded, mock-Disneyesque sweetness, giving numerous depictions of humanised animals. Moreover, Crumb's characters can rebel, and they salvage some pleasure through sex and drugs. Franquin's characters in *Idées noires* are denied rebellion and pleasure; Crumb's psychedelic influences and sexually explicit drawing are entirely absent from Franquin. Crumb is laughing at America, but Franquin is laughing at hope.

Franquin's pessimism in *Idées noires* exceeded that of the Underground. When *Idées noires* came out in the mid-1970s, the idealism of the 1960s had already been overtaken by disillusionment. The aggressive cynicism of *Idées noires* parallels the 'no future' bleakness of its contemporary: punk. Franquin did not listen to punk music, but he called the punk slogan 'no future' an expression which is 'dure mais c'est formidable … elle exprime les gens enfermés dans une société qui commence à ne plus aller du tout'.[53] Punk rock and *Idées noires* both articulated that depressing vision.

Franquin took pessimism to extremes. The punks proposed anarchy as a solution and rebelled, like their Underground forebears, with sex, drugs and loud music. In *Idées noires* there is neither revolt nor any solution. There is only lonely and futile death, without hope of resurrection.

*　*　*

In his later years, Franquin became less prolific. His reputation grew, and he won the Adamson prize in Stockholm (1980). Franquin was becoming ever more concerned about international problems. He drew advertisements for UNICEF and Amnesty International (1979) and for Greenpeace (1982). In 1979 *Cauchmarrant*, Franquin's collection of pictures of grotesquely humorous monsters, was published by Bédérama (Paris). In 1990 Franquin drew *Tifous* for Belgian television with Yvan Delporte, marking a return to the gentler humour of the past. On the eve of his death, Franquin was working on little abstract pictures that he called 'doodles'. According to Sadoul: 'Chez André Franquin ça prenait des proportions purement apocalyptiques. C'était des œuvres d'art. Il en a fait des centaines.'[54]

Franquin died in the South of France on 5 January 1997, just after his seventy-third birthday. Tributes flowed in, including an article by the French Minister of Culture Philippe Douste-Blazy, and cartoons by the French artists Frank Margerin, Jean Giraud and Philippe Druillet.[55] Such accolades prove that Franquin had built strong cultural links between France and Belgium; as such, his strips inevitably assert a sense of Franco-Belgian cultural togetherness. They do so in various ways: Franquin used urban and pastoral décor, which could either be in France or Belgium; he explored the punning possibilities of the shared French language extensively; rather less frequently, he referenced a common, Francophone history and culture. However, Franquin's most original contribution to the ninth art lies in changing the position of the hero, thereby creating moral ambiguity.

Spirou began as a model of heroic virtue like Superman, Mickey and Tintin; then, by treating Spirou ironically, Franquin questioned the triumphant goodness that conventional heroes exemplified. Gaston Lagaffe is neither good nor bad, unlike 'good ol' Charlie Brown'. *Idées noires* has no exemplary heroes at all; it makes us laugh at pointless catastrophes in a godless universe. Franquin makes the distinction between good and evil fall away (*Spirou et Fantasio*), disappear (*Gaston Lagaffe*) and become meaningless (*Idées noires*). Franquin's legacy lives on. Since Gaston, morally ambiguous heroes have become a recurring feature of both humorous and non-humorous *bandes dessinées,* as we shall see below.

A pessimistic vision lurks beneath Franquin's amusing and often colourful comic images. Taken as a whole his body of work evokes a world gone adrift, having lost its moral bearings; from the mid-1970s, he became distinctly darker. Yet for all Franquin's implied pessimism, he was a great humorist. His expertly drawn comics are very funny. André Franquin succeeded in making French and Belgian people laugh together for over fifty years; he deserves greater recognition in the English-speaking world.

CHAPTER THREE

A Hero for Everyone: René Goscinny's and Albert Uderzo's Astérix the Gaul

Goscinny's and Uderzo's Sources

Astérix is the ninth art's best-known hero. Surpassing even Tintin in popularity, he has attained a level of international renown comparable to Mickey Mouse, Superman and Charlie Brown. Astérix is particularly popular in Europe but, unlike most BD heroes, he has also found his niche in America. Nowadays, Astérix is the ninth art's most widely recognised face and an invaluable asset to Franco-Belgian cultural identity. Although he is a pre-Christian Gaulish warrior, Astérix is nonetheless a hero with whom almost everybody can identify, wherever they come from.

The adventures of Astérix the Gaul were a collaboration between the script-writer René Goscinny (1926–1977) and the artist Albert Uderzo (b. 1927).[1] Goscinny, a Frenchman who grew up in Argentina, moved to America in 1945. He met Uderzo, who was of Italian descent, while they were both employed by Harvey Kurtzman in New York. By the 1950s Goscinny and Uderzo were back in Paris, working with the American publisher World Press. There they befriended a fellow artist, Jean-Michel Charlier. Goscinny, Uderzo and Charlier all rebelled against World Press's policy towards its artists. Goscinny recalled,

> Les éditeurs exerçaient un véritable pouvoir de droit divin. Un éditeur pouvait mettre un dessinateur à la porte, simplement parce qu'il était malade ... Il pouvait faire dessiner sa série par quelqu'un sans lui payer la moindre redevance.[2]

The three artists desired greater freedom and more control over their own work; they wanted to operate 'selon le principe europeén', which had been established by the Belgians Hergé and Franquin. According that principle, 'l'auteur est l'unique propriétaire de son oeuvre, l'éditeur en étant le locataire'.[3] In order to protect artists' rights, Goscinny, Uderzo and Charlier set up a 'Syndicat des dessinateurs'. In 1958 Goscinny and Uderzo left World Press to found their own magazine, *Pilote*.

Pilote was aimed at the growing number of adolescent *bande dessineé* enthusiasts. The magazine set out to provide readers with clear moral leadership. However, its tone was more secular, and it was less directly influenced by *scoutisme* than *Le Petit Vingtième*, *Le Journal de Tintin* and *Le Journal de Spirou*. *Pilote*'s first editorial read:

> Pourquoi 'Pilote'? Oh! C'est bien simple. Un pilote, c'est celui qui conduit les autres ... Pour être un vrai pilote, il faut d'abord des connaissances. Mais il faut également beaucoup de travail et beaucoup de courage et notre souhait, c'est que vous soyez, avec nous, de vrais pilotes.[4]

Prior to *Pilote*, Goscinny and Uderzo had collaborated on a humorous strip called *Oumpah-Pah*, which was about a Native American who resisted the colonising Europeans.[5] However, the pair wanted a more typically French hero for *Pilote*. In August 1958, they ran through the different periods of French history in chronological order, looking for inspiration. They eventually settled on a Gaulish hero, because 'les Gaulois, c'est notre western à nous'.[6] Comic strips about the Gauls were unusual before *Astérix*; the only previous one of note, *Alix*, was strongly influenced by 'clear line'.

Goscinny remembered that, in the late 1950s, 'il fallait faire du Tintin ou du Franquin', and *Astérix*'s adventures reflect both those influences, as well as that of Disney, whom Goscinny and Uderzo admired.[7] Following the example set by *Les Aventures de Tintin*, *Spirou et Fantasio* and Disney, *Astérix* combined humour with Propp's traditional, folktale structure. *Astérix* was the exemplary hero and the villains were the Roman legionaries who were occupying Gaul. Like Mickey Mouse, Tintin and Spirou, *Astérix* had a gaffe-prone sidekick, Obélix, who raised slapstick laughs. Clumsy, likeable Obélix was funny in much the same way as Donald Duck, Captain Haddock and Fantasio.

Uderzo's caricatural graphic style recalled Disney and Franquin rather than Hergé: everything was drawn with rounded, elastic-looking lines and bright, cheerful colours; *Astérix*, Obélix and the others had bulbous noses and exaggeratedly large feet. *Astérix* himself resembled Mickey Mouse: he was an unusually small hero who was not exactly handsome, but what he lacked in brawn he made up for in brain.

Astérix's adventures are set in 50 BC, when Gaul was part of the Roman empire. Astérix and the other Gauls live in a little village on the north coast of Armorica (present-day Britanny), and they refuse to submit to Julius Caesar (Figure 8). The Gauls hold out against Rome with the aid of a magic potion, brewed by their druid Panoramix, which gives them superhuman strength.

André Stoll notes that Astérix's indomitable village has no basis whatsoever in fact, as history records that the Romans pacified the region fairly easily. Stoll quotes a passage from Caesar's *Commentaires sur la Guerre des Gaules*, which reads 'Les autres cités, situées aux confins de la Gaule, touchant à l'Océan, et qu'on appelle Armoricaines … remplissent sans délai, à l'approche de Fabius et de ses légions, les conditions imposées'.[8] Goscinny's and Uderzo's choice of Armorica as a setting for Astérix's village was not historically correct, but neither was it arbitrary. Their choice is in line with the popular French-speakers' perception of Britanny, which comes from Arthurian legends and Grail romances. Britanny is a mysterious land, rich in legends and folklore; it is the perfect setting for tales of magic and heroic exploits. Britanny is also widely regarded as a rebellious region which strongly opposes interference by outsiders, following its long-standing separatist tradition.[9]

Although Goscinny and Uderzo were not primarily concerned about historical accuracy, they researched their Gaulish setting carefully. Goscinny said, 'Je me documente à toutes sortes de sources, dont la clé de voûte est, bien entendu, *La Guerre des Gaules*. Mais quand je travaille, je ferme mes bouquins. Mon boulot, c'est le pastiche.'[10] Goscinny and Uderzo used Gaulish history to make people laugh. The fact that many Gaulish names ended in 'ix', the best-known being the warrior chieftain Vercingetorix (d. 46 BC), gives rise to punning names such as Astérix, Obélix and Panoramix. The Romans have funny names ending in 'us'. In the first adventure, *Astérix le Gaulois* (1961), the Roman commander is 'Bonus' and his deputy is 'Sacapus' (or 'sac à puces', meaning 'fleabag').

Astérix's adventures are doubly amusing because they playfully masquerade as the truth, despite being grossly inaccurate. Parodying Ernest Lavisse's widely read school textbooks, *Astérix le Gaulois* recounts Rome's victory over the Gauls: 'En 50 avant J.C., nos ancêtres les Gaulois avaient été vaincus par les Romains, après une

Figure 8. Astérix and Obélix in the Gaulish village by Goscinny and Uderzo © 2005 Les Editions Albert René/Goscinny and Uderzo, *www.asterix.com*

longue lutte'.[11] Lavisse's schoolmasterly phrase, 'nos ancêtres les Gaulois', is instantly recognisable to generations of present-day French-speakers: Lavisse was first published in the nineteenth century, but his textbooks were commonly used in French schools well into the twentieth. Lavisse's words are immediately followed by a comic surprise: Vercingetorix concedes defeat by throwing his weapons onto rather than at Julius Caesar's feet, making the mighty emperor suddenly look ridiculous.

The opening sets the tone for the rest of the adventure: roles are reversed and the victors vanquished. The Romans who subjugated Gaul come off worst from the punch-ups, yet the violence is funny and stylised. Nobody suffers life-threatening injuries in battle, still less dies. Panoramix is kidnapped by the Romans, and the village runs low on magic potion. Astérix goes to a Roman fortified camp to rescue Panoramix, outwits his opponents and brings the druid safely back. Once order is restored, the village warriors gather for a feast; a warriors' feast invariably rounds off each subsequent Astérix adventure.

Goscinny and Uderzo replaced Gaulish history with their own comical version of events; in so doing, they reworked the old into the new, thus creating a distinctive brand of *bande dessinée* folklore.

Their comedy of anachronism makes Astérix's adventures quite unlike any previous strip; the only American equivalents are Johnny Hart's *B.C.* and William Hanna and Joseph Barbera's *Flintstones*.[12] However, there are also sizeable differences. Hart's short, prehistoric gags resembled *Peanuts*: like Schulz, Hart drew with great economy of line and emphasised dialogue. *The Flintstones'* energetic, exuberant graphic style is closer to Uderzo's, but *The Flintstones* transposed an all-American, consumer model family onto the Stone Age.

Goscinny's and Uderzo's humour attaches Astérix to a venerable tradition in Francophone jesting, rather than to the American funnies. This tradition dates back at least as far as Touchatout's burlesque parody of French history, *Histoire de France tintamarresque*.[13] Touchatout, like Goscinny and Uderzo, humorously combined a specifically Gaulish history with anachronisms. For example, Touchatout states that when a child was born in ancient Gaul, '*papa Gaullois* l'embrassait avec effusion et allait de suite le déclarer à la mairie de son arrondissement'.[14] Touchatout established an amusing parallel between ancient Gaul and contemporary France, just as Goscinny and Uderzo were to do throughout Astérix's subsequent adventures.

Astérix Triumphs

Soon Astérix and Obélix began travelling away from their Gaulish village. In *La Serpe d'or* (1962), their second adventure, the pair go to Lutèce (Paris), to buy Panoramix a new sickle. While they are in Lutèce they defeat a criminal cartel, which has fixed sickle prices. *La Serpe d'or* contains more anachronisms than *Astérix le Gaulois*: Lutèce/Paris is the Gaulish capital, despite having been a settlement of lesser importance in Gallo-Roman times. Astérix and Obélix criticise modern architecture (a Roman aqueduct), and they pass through Suindinum/Le Mans, where a 24–hour chariot-race is going on (p. 10).

In *Astérix chez les Goths* (1963), Astérix and Obélix go to Germany. On this, their first foreign escapade, humour arises from national stereotypes: the Goths are a warlike, goose-stepping people with square heads, who speak in gothic script. *Astérix chez les Goths* alludes to the long-standing Franco-Belgian unease about German military muscle; in particular the story evokes the frequent border clashes that soured relations between the three countries until 1945.

Astérix chez les Goths particularly recalls *Les Pieds Nickelés s'en vont en guerre*, which was published by the Parisian magazine *L'Epatant* in 1915.[15] Like the Pieds Nickelés, Astérix and Obélix dress up in German uniforms and cross the border incognito; like the Pieds Nickelés, they secretly infiltrate the imperial palace where they sow disorder among the Goths, thereby preventing an invasion.

In *Astérix Gladiateur* (1964) Astérix and Obélix hitch-hike to Rome; there, they enlist as gladiators at the Colisseum to rescue their village Bard Assurancetourix, whom the Romans want to throw to the lions. Assurancetourix has a cacophonous voice. He sings 'ils ont les casques ailés, vive les Celtes', which parodies the folksong 'ils ont les chapeaux ronds, vive les Bretons' (p. 6).[16]

By this time, Uderzo was establishing a graphic style that combined Disneyesque caricature with accurate, historical details. *Astérix Gladiateur* has elegant, Roman buildings and animated, authentic-looking street scenes. Documented realism coexists, of course, with anachronisms. The blocks of flats (or 'insulae'), which genuinely existed in Ancient Rome, are called 'Habitations Latines Mélangées' (p. 22), a reference to French social housing, which is known as 'Habitations à Loyer Modéré' (or HLMs).

The title of *Le Tour de Gaule d'Astérix* (1965), the next album, recalls the annual 'Tour de France' bicycle race. In order to win a bet with the Romans, Astérix and Obélix go round Gaul, collecting a speciality from each place they visit. This adventure has numerous jokes to do with the different French regions. The Normans refuse to commit themselves to anything whatsoever, answering questions with 'réponses de Normand': 'Je n'dis pas qu' c'est impossible, mais j'dis pas oui!' (p. 11). The southern Gauls speak with a southern French accent, saying 'Luteciengs' instead of 'Luteciens' (p. 28). The Roman road number 7, which Astérix and Obélix take southwards, is jammed with Luteciens heading for the seaside, an allusion to the mass exodus of Parisians down the arterial Route Nationale 7 that marks the start of the French holiday season each August.

Some of the humour is subtle to the point of being incomprehensible to those who are unfamiliar with French history and culture. Astérix and Obélix arrive at the harbour district in Marseille; they go to a quayside tavern where a card game is taking place, and the landlord tells them 'Je suis César mais je suis pas Jules' (p. 31). The landlord is referring to Marcel Pagnol's film *César* (1935), in which a man of that name also owns a quayside tavern in Marseille where card games are played. When he heard about the scene, Pagnol quipped, 'Maintenant, je sais que mon oeuvre est éternelle'.[17] There is an even more obscure joke about 'l'affaire du courrier de Lyon', a miscarriage of justice in which an innocent man was executed for robbing a mail-coach in 1796.[18] In *Le Tour de Gaule* a Roman requisitions a cart, which bears the French post-office logo. He then says, 'On n'a pas fini d'en parler de l'affaire du courrier de Lugdunum', 'Lugdunum' being the Roman name for Lyon (p. 24).

In *Astérix et Cléopatre* (1965) Astérix, Obélix and Panoramix leave Europe for the first time. They go to Egypt, where they use their superhuman strength to help Cleopatra win a bet with Julius Caesar. The exotic Egyptian location with its ships, buildings and monuments is carefully researched; jokes arise from Egyptians speaking in hieroglyphs. More humour comes from interplay between the characters than in previous adventures. One particularly funny example is when a sheepish Caesar is nagged by Cleopatra in front of his soldiers (p. 44). There are also oblique, jocular references to French history. When Obélix is unimpressed by the pyramids, Panoramix says, 'Du haut de ces Pyramides, Obélix, vingt siècles nous contemplent' (p. 23). Panoramix is echoing Napoleon's speech to his troops at the Pyramids in 1798: 'Soldats, songez que du haut de ces Pyramides, quarante siècles vous contemplent'.[19]

Fittingly the next album, *Le Combat des chefs* (1966), coincided with the French presidential elections: in this adventure, a pro-Roman Gaulish chief challenges Abraracourcix to single combat, but, despite dirty tricks by the Romans, Abraracourcix wins. Abraracourcix gave a press conference in the style of General de Gaulle to publicise *Le Combat des chefs*.[20]

In *Astérix chez les Bretons* (1966) Astérix, Obélix and Panoramix cross the channel to help the Ancient Britons resist Rome. Although *Astérix chez les Bretons* pokes French fun, the portrait is not entirely unflattering. In line with contemporary French myths about the UK, the Ancient Britons have bad food, dreary weather and absurdly stiff upper lips; but they are a brave, hospitable people, with exciting football and a flourishing pop culture. There is even a caricature of The Beatles (p. 19). English food, in particular, has long been a source of merriment to French-speakers. Touchatout, for one, wrote, 'Notre pays ne serait probablement, à l'heure qu'il est, qu'un immense plum-pudding, sans l'intervention d'une jeune fille de Domremy, nommée Jeanne d'Arc'.[21]

Unlike Touchatout, Goscinny and Uderzo introduce humorous word-play deriving from anglicised French. Typically English grammatical constructions, like question-tags, sound very funny when translated literally into French: for example, the Britons say 'il est, n'est-il pas?' (p. 6). The Britons also put adjectives before nouns saying 'la magique potion' (p. 9) and 'un breton repas' (p. 15). Some English-language expressions sound amusing when translated literally. Examples include 'goodness gracious' ('bonté grâcieuse', p. 6) and 'a piece of luck' ('un morceau de chance', p. 8).

In its first two weeks of sale alone, *Astérix chez les Bretons* sold 600,000 units.[22] Astérix was rapidly becoming widely recognised all over France, and was even being compared to General de Gaulle. Jean-Noel Gurgand commented:

> Le mercredi 31 août, à Phnom Penh, le général de Gaulle disait au monde ce qu'il pensait de la puissance américaine. Le même jour, à Paris, les éditions Dargaud lançaient en librairie «Astérix chez les Bretons» ... Succès pour de Gaulle, triomphe pour Astérix ... César peut-il faire régner la paix romaine sur son empire à coups de pilums et de sesterces? C'est la question que posait de Gaulle à Phnom Penh. Pour les Gaulois, la réponse ne fait pas de doute: c'est non, tant que ... le druide saura préparer la potion.[23]

Just over a decade later, Alain Peyrefitte made an almost identical comparison:

> Ce phénomène est le fondement même de la pensée politique du général de Gaulle pour lequel les Français devraient toujours rester des Français ... C'est cet invariant national que Goscinny a caricaturé plaisamment dans le personnage d'Astérix.[24]

De Gaulle, himself an Astérix fan, gave other politicians nicknames ending in 'ix'.[25]

For many people in the mid-1960s, Astérix, like de Gaulle, was perceived to assert French national identity. At a time when French identity was increasingly challenged by Anglophone influences, the General and the Gaulish warrior were both putting up a robust resistance. As Irène Dervize said, Astérix 'concrétise les aspirations du Français moyen qui rêve d'assommer James Bond à coups de cuissot de sanglier'.[26] Dervize added that, by 1966, 95 per cent of parents had heard of Astérix.

During the late 1960s, Goscinny and Uderzo reiterated their winning formula. Among other things, Astérix and Obélix joined

Caesar's legions to rescue a press-ganged Gaul (*Astérix Légionnaire*, 1967); they also went to the Olympic games (*Astérix aux Jeux Olympiques*, 1968). There was still plenty of slapstick fun, and Goscinny's verbal humour was ever more ingenious. *Astérix aux Jeux Olympiques*, for instance, has a series of puns about the athletes' places of origin: 'Les athlètes entrent dans le stade ... Ceux de Milo sont venus aussi; ceux de Cythère viennent de débarquer ... ceux de Macédoine sont très mélangés ...'(p. 38). 'Ceux de Milo son venus' refers to the *Venus de Milo*, an ancient Greek statue of Aphrodite in the Louvre (150 BC). 'Ceux de Cythère viennent de débarquer' calls to mind Antoine Watteau's painting *Embarquement pour l'Ile de Cythère* (1717), which hangs in the Louvre. 'Ceux de Macédoine sont très mélangés' alludes to a French dish, 'la macédoine', which consists of a mixed assortment of chopped vegetables in a vinaigrette dressing.

Astérix's rise to fame during the late 1960s attracted the attention of the business newspaper *L'Entreprise*, which called him the 'héros de la plus vaste opération de *merchandising* jamais réalisée en France'.[27] However, trouble unexpectedly flared up at *Pilote* in May 1968. When Goscinny rejected a strip by Nikita Mandryka (*Le Concombre masqué*) for publication, his authority was challenged by *Pilote*'s rebellious younger artists, who included Jean Giraud and Claire Bretécher. Goscinny, for his part, could not see why his artists were turning on him. Uderzo recalls that May 1968 was a turbulent time in *Pilote*'s offices, just as it was on the streets of Paris outside:

> Le petit monde de la bande dessinée voulait faire sa propre révolution culturelle. Il s'agissait de démolir les positions établies. Des questions de jalousie professionnelle et de concurrence entre auteurs s'y sont mêlées. Tout cela m'a fait sourire, m'a un peu chagriné aussi. Le succès d'Astérix a tout de même favorisé l'essor d'une profession si longtemps décriée. On oubliait de le dire.[28]

Goscinny prevailed, but some of his younger artists started to leave *Pilote* in order to set up their own magazines in competition: Gotlib, Mandryka and Bretécher founded *L'Echo des savanes* (1972), which carried adult oriented/humorous strips; Giraud and Druillet launched the science fiction magazine *Métal hurlant* (1975).[29]

Despite problems at *Pilote*, Astérix's adventures still sold exceptionally well. Among other things Astérix visited Spain, where he helped a proud, passionate, fiesta-loving tourist destination resist

Rome (*Astérix en Hispanie*, 1969); he foiled Roman property-developers, who tried to urbanise his village (*Le Domaine des dieux*, 1971); he also saw off a fortune-telling charlatan (*Le Devin*, 1972). As Stoll notes, *Le Devin* recalls Jean-Jacques Rousseau's play, *Le Devin du village* (1752): Goscinny's fortune-teller, like Rousseau's, dupes naive villagers by flattering them.[30]

Although Astérix was hugely popular, *Pilote* was gradually losing its hold over the *bande dessinée* market. *Pilote*'s adolescent target audience was growing up and rival publications, catering more specifically for adults, were appearing on the newsstands. So, in the mid-1970s, Goscinny and Uderzo decided to concentrate exclusively on Astérix. They set up Studios Idéfix in 1974, and Goscinny resigned as *Pilote*'s editor in 1975.

Although Astérix mostly travelled around Europe, occasionally visiting the Middle East, he did eventually find his way to the New World. In *La Grande Traversée* (1975), Astérix's ship is caught in a storm, which blows him across the Atlantic to America. He is befriended by the Native Americans, who (unlike the Ancient Britons) do not speak his language. There is less anachronistic humour in *La Grande Traversée* than in the other adventures: America is not a superpower and, in the absence of white Americans, the scope for lampooning national stereotypes is limited. The natives do, however, eat 'chien chaud', and Astérix strikes a pose that resembles the Statue of Liberty (pp. 29 and 35).

The last adventure Goscinny completed, *Obélix et Compagnie* (1976), is a very funny account of a Roman attempt to sap the Gauls' will by making them rich and decadent. The plan is devised by one Caius Saugrenus, who looks like the Mayor of Paris (and later the French President) Jacques Chirac. Saugrenus pays the Gauls handsomely to make menhirs, giving them no time to fight. Following the law of supply and demand the Roman Empire is saturated with menhirs, their price collapses, and the Roman plot comes to nothing: the Gauls remain indomitable. *Obélix et Compagnie* sold 1,350,000 copies.[31]

Goscinny died on 5 November 1977, while he was working on *Astérix chez les Belges* (1979). This adventure, more than any other, directly addresses questions of Franco-Belgian identity. The Belgians, like the French, are descended from the Gauls; France and Belgium, together known as Gaul, were part of the Roman empire. Julius Caesar, no less, is on record as having said that 'of all the Gauls, the

Belgians were the bravest'.[32] In *Astérix chez les Belges,* Caesar's famous remark prompts Astérix to arrange a competition with his Belgian neighbours to see who really is the bravest. The result is a draw and, as Astérix puts it, 'les Belges et nous sommes à égalité' (p. 48).

The Belgians and the Gauls are brothers-in-arms: they fiercely resist Rome, their names end with 'ix', they appreciate good food and their houses look similar. They also speak the same French language, albeit slightly differently: like the present-day Belgians, Astérix's Belgian friends say 'ça est pas' not 'ce n'est pas', and 'septante' rather than 'soixante-dix' (pp. 14 and 32); they also use Belgian slang words such as 'carabistouille' meaning 'stupidity' or 'foolishness' (p. 22). Obélix jokingly comments, 'Si nous parlions la même langue, nous pourrions vraiment nous croire chez nous' (p. 20).

Throughout *Astérix chez les Belges,* the parodies of Belgian culture are affectionate. The disparaging 'histoires belges' (a French equivalent of Irish jokes) are only told by the Romans, never by the Gauls. There are references to Belgian cultural and sporting achievements, which the French respect and admire: the Belgian chief's wife looks like the Belgian actress/singer Annie Cordy; Eddie Merckx, the Belgian winner of the Tour de France in 1969 appears, as do Hergé's Dupondts (pp. 39 and 31); Astérix meets a character who resembles the Mannekinpis, a famous statue in Brussels (p. 33); the farewell dinner that the Belgians offer Astérix is a parody of the Flemish painter Bruegel's *Peasant Wedding* (1567, p. 47).

Astérix's appeal to feelings of empathy between France and Belgium is well summarised by Nelly Feuerhahn:

> Avec *Astérix chez les Belges,* la question porte sur la troublante proximité d'un Nous que l'histoire et ses frontières stupides voudraient tenir à distance. Le sort fait aux histoires dites belges met l'accent sur le peu d'intérêt à décider de la supériorité d'un peuple sur un autre que même la langue ne sépare pas.[33]

After Goscinny's death Uderzo continued *Les Aventures d'Astérix* alone, and new Astérix albums are published to this day. By the 1980s Astérix was outselling *Les Aventures de Tintin.*[34] Astérix's familiar face has advertised Amora Mustard, Lessive Skip and Fromages Bel. In September 1985, an Astérix exhibition was held at the Eiffel Tower; in 1989 an Astérix theme park opened near Paris, which receives an average of two million visitors per year.[35]

Astérix-mania shows no signs of fading. Uderzo was awarded the Grand Prix at Angoulême in 1999. Claude Zidi's film starring Gerard Depardieu, *Astérix et Obélix contre César*, was released the same year, and a related computer game, *Astérix and Obélix take on Caesar*, was marketed by Playstation in 2000. Astérix is now recognised all over Europe: new Astérix theme parks may soon be opening outside France; a Spanish journalist recently compared the Catalan politician, Jordi Pujol, to Astérix, saying 'Pujol aparecía como un Asterix al frente de una tribu de irreducibles'.[36]

What Makes Astérix so Popular?

How can we explain Astérix's unprecedented success? Astérix's initial popularity could well have stemmed from the fact that, like de Gaulle, he gave France a positive self-image at a time of a messy retreat from empire, waning global influence and growing US dominance. Jean Lartéguy wrote, 'Je sais pourquoi j'aime Astérix. Il refait une histoire à ma convenance ... Mon chauvinisme s'en trouve agréablement chatouillé.'[37] Anne-Marie Thiesse noted that Astérix 'jouait du comique d'anachronisme en projetant sur "nos ancêtres les Gaulois" la "check-list" identitaire nationale'.[38] Goscinny himself called Astérix 'la caricature du Français moyen ... c'est l'homme raisonnable'.[39] Bruno Frappat summed up the link between Astérix and French national pride:

> La correspondance ... existerait entre le nationalisme des Gaulois et le sentiment de 'fierté nationale' et d'indépendance des Français, encouragé par le gaullisme. Astérix, pensait-on, représente le petit Français débrouillard qui fait le pied de nez aux grands – qu'ils soient romains ou américains. A la force brutale de la bêtise, il oppose la finesse du petit malin; au nombre, la puissance de l'individu volontaire; à l'impérialisme culturel, militaire et économique, la revendication de l'autarcie et la fierté chauvine. Au fond, il ne manquait qu'un béret à Astérix pour être vraiment français. Astérix gagnait toujours, pour nous.[40]

Astérix can embody what is best about France very easily. Comparisons between the Gauls and the Free French and between the Nazis and the Romans are perfectly obvious: like the French Resistance, the Gauls refuse to collaborate with a bullying, occupying army; the Gauls are individualistic, freedom-loving *bons viveurs*; like the *maquis,* they organise to form an effective fighting force when necessary.

Alternatively the Romans can be the Americans from whom de Gaulle, and many other French-speakers, desired greater independence. According to that reading, the magic potion is a product of Gaulish genius, like the French independent nuclear deterrent; the Americans, like the Romans (and the Nazis) have an eagle as their symbol; the pro-Roman Gaul has 'Rome sweet Rome' on his wall because English threatens French (*Le Combat des chefs*, p. 8). Plenty of other evidence can be found to suggest that Astérix is a French David to America's Goliath.

However, to see Astérix's adventures as glorifying the French national narrative is to overlook an important aspect of their humour: namely that, except for Astérix and Panoramix, the Gauls are remarkably like the Romans they resist. Much joking arises precisely from the fact that the two opposing sides resemble overgrown children: the Romans and the Gauls are gullible and quarrelsome; they sulk, they cry easily and they get over-excited by trivialities; they make playful bets with each other. The difference between the heroes and villains is played down, and it is far from irreducible. A Roman government official is even invited to the Gaulish warriors' feast at the end of *Astérix chez les Helvètes* (1970). Besides, if Astérix and his village simply embody the proud spirit of French resistance, then why bother with the Gaulish setting at all? Why not, for instance, set his adventures in World War II, with Astérix a hero in the *maquis*?

Ultimately, the Gaulish setting frustrates attempts to reduce Astérix to a flattering portrait of 'la belle France'. After all, occupied Gaul is a remote, non-contentious historical period, which few people know very much about, even in France and Belgium. As a result, freed from loyalties, prejudices and other historical baggage, people of all nationalities and all political persuasions read whatever they like into the Gaulish warrior's exploits. Meanwhile, Goscinny's repeated references to 'le petit village que nous connaissons bien' invite everyone, whoever they are, to identify with the Gauls.

Consequently people the world over, holding radically different opinions, claim that Astérix speaks for them. Goscinny recalled, 'Toutes les formations politiques m'ont demandé d'utiliser "Astérix" pour leurs campagnes!'[41] Astérix has no problem whatsoever championing mutually exclusive points of view. Among much else, Astérix has been called both a social conservative and supporter of the May 1968 uprising. Henri Bordillon thought that during the May revolt, 'on a pu écrire qu' "en 1968, c'est Astérix qui est descendu dans la rue"'.[42] Bruno Frappat thought the opposite, calling Astérix 'un conservateur'.[43]

Although they contradict each other, Bordillon's and Frappat's readings are equally well founded. Astérix's village, like the rebels on the May barricades, holds out against a patriarchal, money-making, technologically advanced society. Astérix's village has the makings of an environmentally friendly hippy-idyll: the long-haired inhabitants live simple lives in harmony with nature; their communal, counter-society turns its back on Rome's corrupt, urbanising rat-race, military-industrial complex and irresponsible consumer culture; magic potion is the drug of choice. The Gauls disapprove of Romans felling trees and spoiling the landscape; they could be eco-warriors, camped out in the forest years ahead of their time.

Yet, following Frappat's reading, Astérix's village simultaneously represents everything opposed by May '68 and its descendants: the village looks cosily petit bourgeois with portly shopkeepers, pretty houses and smooth lawns; there are brawls aplenty, but the chief's authority is not seriously challenged; moreover, the woman's place is firmly in the home. In Astérix's Utopia the women do the shopping, or else they cook and clean for the men. Unlike the female partici-pants in May '68, the Gaulish womenfolk show scant interest in breaking into male preserves: women are routinely excluded from the warriors' feasts, except to serve as uncomplaining waitresses and occasionally as dancers; they do not participate fully in the festivities until *La Rose et le glaive* (1991).

Astérix can support other opposing points of view. When President Pompidou visited Britanny, separatists held up banners saying 'Astérix est contre!', but if Astérix really is a Breton separatist, then why is his village the only place in Gaul where everyone speaks perfect Parisian French?[44] The most bizarre effort of all to co-opt Astérix was surely made by the German magazine *Lupo*, which turned him into a right-wing extremist, 'dans une ambiance revancharde de pure teinte néo-nazie'.[45]

None of the many attempts to make Astérix the vehicle for one single, clear-cut moral or political view has ever been entirely success-ful; almost invariably, he simultaneously represents a completely different viewpoint. Astérix is a cipher, with little or no objective meaning. Thanks to Goscinny's and Uderzo's comic genius, Astérix can be whoever his readers want him to be, and therein lies the secret of his success.

Beyond France and Belgium Astérix's adventures have been very elegantly translated, enabling readers from many different countries to appreciate the verbal jokes. National characteristics are stereotyped, but they are not stigmatised as being 'other'. Such good-natured lampooning is easily understood in an age of *rapprochement*, European integration and mass tourism. With the exception of the early *Astérix chez les Goths*, Astérix encourages good neighbourly relations. He helps other countries but only when asked, and he never imposes his will. Astérix's village could turn itself into a superpower and set out to dominate the world, given its overwhelming force in the shape of magic potion; yet the Gaulish village shows no inclination to do so. Astérix and friends do not even try to kick the Romans out of Gaul once and for all; they would rather stay at home, having fun.

Although he has penetrated the American market, Astérix is particularly popular in Europe, including the UK. In post-war Europe Astérix has become a hero for everyone; as such, he necessarily asserts a strong sense of common, European identity. Astérix binds Europeans together, as they put their long-standing differences behind them and cooperate within a community of nations of roughly equal strength. Astérix exorcises the ghosts of conflicts past through shared laughter: Goscinny and Uderzo hold up an amusingly deformed mirror in which various nationalities, after centuries of bloodshed, look at themselves and their neighbours, and laugh out loud.

Putting aside the various meanings that have been read into Astérix, the fact remains that his adventures are, above all, funny. They have something for every taste in humour: historical pastiche, joking cultural references, exuberant slapstick, tongue-in-cheek stereotyping, anachronisms and word-play. Like Hergé and Franquin, Goscinny and Uderzo struck the perfect balance between boisterous fun and more sophisticated humour. Yet no other comic strip exploits the form to generate verbal and visual humour more fully than *Astérix*.

We should leave the last word on what Astérix supposedly means to his creators. Goscinny said, 'Nos intentions étaient beaucoup plus simples que toutes celles qu'on nous prête. Nous voulions seulement tenter d'amuser les lecteurs.'[46] Uderzo said, 'Nous n'avons qu'un but: nous marrer et faire marrer les autres'.[47]

Tintin, Gaston and Astérix: Three Heroes of Classical Mythology

By the 1970s the ninth art had given France and Belgium a triumvirate of shared mythological heroes: Tintin, Gaston and Astérix. As all cultures produce myths, mythology's role in constructing cultural identity cannot be exaggerated. Cultures produce myths because they satisfy a deep-rooted human need: the need to make sense of life. Myths are appealing because they reduce the complexity of experience, by making things seem simple and absolute; myths define popular realities which are accepted readily, even uncritically.

The reasons why comic strips give birth to mythological heroes, which we have touched on only lightly thus far, require closer scrutiny. Comics lend themselves exceptionally well to mythological production for three reasons. First, as noted above, readers give life to the hero by reading, and so they must want him to exist. Secondly, comics use attractive imagery that is easily understood: both myths and comics tend to express the moral and the abstract through physical actions. Finally, adventure stories and gags ease the hero's entry into the collective consciousness by reiterating similar structures over the years. Comic strip heroes are truly mythological once they are more universally recognised than their creators.

When Hergé, Franquin and Goscinny died, the reaction of the press across the social and political spectrum proved that all three artists had become myth-makers: in France, newspapers identified them as the fathers of their respective characters.[48] The journalists concerned all knew that Tintin, Gaston and Astérix were imaginary but, endowing the three heroes with an unusual degree of reality, they wrote as though they genuinely existed in flesh and blood. Tintin, Gaston and Astérix had crossed national boundaries, giving people from all walks of life a common cultural reference. They had taken their place alongside Mickey Mouse, Superman and Tarzan in the gallery of contemporary mythological heroes.

An important difference between mythological heroes in comic strips and those in Antiquity has been pointed out by Umberto Eco. Heroes in Antiquity became mythological through a story that 'has taken place and can no longer be denied'; myths in Antiquity told of 'something which had already happened and of which the public was aware'.[49] In comics, on the other hand, events happen while the strip is being read. How then can one reconcile the mythological hero, who 'must be in part *predictable* and cannot hold surprises for us ... he must necessarily become immobilized in an emblematic and fixed nature which renders him easily recognizable', with the hero whose future is unknown, and who is passing through time before our eyes?[50]

The answer lies in the nature of the adventures and gags: 'To begin a story [or gag] without showing that another had preceded it would manage, momentarily, to remove Superman [Tintin, Gaston and Astérix] from the law that leads from life to death through time'.[51] Beginning a new story or gag where the previous one ended would make the heroes age; not doing so breaks up time and immobilises the heroes in an eternal present.

The comic strip 'classics', like those of Antiquity, tell of godlike figures with powers beyond the lot of mortals. Mickey, Superman, Tintin, Gaston and Astérix are typical figures of myth: they are eternally youthful, indestructible and unbound by the laws of physics or of human society. Even Gaston, the office boy in a humdrum location, has mythological powers: no matter whether he gets a black eye, blows up his office, antagonises the police or bounces up into the stratosphere, he will never be fired or jailed, let alone killed. In his ever-fixed present, Gaston neither plans ahead nor faces the consequences of his past actions. Gaston renews himself after every gag, just as the other heroes renew themselves after every adventure.

If, like Greek gods, mythological heroes from our comics embody popular ideas in human and/or animal forms, then what are these ideas? Superman, Mickey Mouse and Tintin sent out a clear moral message: good triumphs over evil. Superman and Mickey were America's invincible champions; Tintin grew into a more human, politically unaligned French-speaker, but he remained virtue personified until *Tintin et les Picaros*. In the Europe of the late 1950s and the 1960s a rising ambivalence obscured the moral clarity, despite Le Fureteur's proclamations and *Pilote*'s early editorial. Gaston Lagaffe is morally ambiguous: he is not just another anti-hero, and yet neither is he 'Good ol' Charlie Brown'. Sometimes Gaston succeeds, sometimes he does not, just like the rest of us. Gaston embodies clever, but fatally flawed humanity.

Astérix, like the US superhero comics, is more optimistic than *Tintin et les Picaros* and most strips by Franquin: the hero always wins and order is restored. Astérix obviously represents some kind of a triumph, but what kind? As Astérix is a post-war European, he does not operate at superhero level. Astérix is no match for Superman, even with his magic potion. Moreover, we have seen how Astérix's adventures separate the hero from any clear-cut message. Consequently Astérix introduces a new subjectivity and moral relativism into Propp's traditional adventure story. Astérix's triumphs easily lend themselves to a multitude of contradictory interpretations; over time, those multiple interpretations gradually rob his exploits of objective significance. No one reading of his adventures is more true than any other. Critics will search in vain for an unequivocal message. Astérix can mean anything his readers like; all we ask of him is that he make us laugh.

In 'classical' superpower mythology, comic strip heroes do not find themselves in such a subjectivised and morally relative position. Far from it: unquestioning allegiance to a well-rehearsed, perfectly explicit and clearly defined code of ethics makes a superhero combat evildoers.

Hergé, Franquin, Goscinny and Uderzo all wrote the ninth art's 'classical' mythology. In Part II 'Innovation and Renewal' we shall see how, with the generation that followed the 'classicists', the *bande dessinée* scene grew more fragmented: some artists followed the Old Masters, but others went on to achieve radically different results. Meanwhile heroes on the two sides of the Atlantic continued to diverge.

PART II

Innovation and Renewal

PART II

Innovation and Renewal

CHAPTER FOUR

A Challenge to Convention: Jean Giraud/Gir/Moebius

Lieutenant Blueberry and the Western

In 1960s and 1970s Paris, the next generation of *bande dessinée* artists came of age. Many of these young artists began their careers at Goscinny's and Uderzo's magazine *Pilote*. They had grown up reading Tintin, Spirou, Gaston and Astérix, but rather than simply copying the Old Masters, they departed from 'classical' tradition and they sometimes produced radically different results. Jean Giraud (b. 1938), otherwise known as 'Gir' and later as 'Moebius', was prominent among this generation (Figure 9).

Giraud's experiments took the ninth art into territories previously uncharted on either side of the Atlantic: he was among the first to break with 'classical' Hergéen realism, and to ask the *nouveau réaliste* 'question du réel'; moreover, some of his science fiction strips did away entirely with speech-balloons and coherent sequences of panels. But before looking at Giraud's SF and his *nouveau réalisme*, let us consider the Western, *Lieutenant Blueberry*, which first made his name in Europe.

Before Giraud's career began, Westerns had been popularised in France and Belgium by Marijac's strip *Jim Boum*, which recalled the American Fred Harman's *Red Ryder* comic: cowboys and Indians were drawn with bold, angular lines, their adventures taking place against simple backgrounds.[1] In 1956, the young Giraud drew a caricatural Western called *Frank et Jérémie* about a pair of fractious cowboys, which appeared in Marijac's magazine *Far West* (Paris).

By 1961 Giraud was helping Joseph Gillain (known as Jijé) draw the Western *Jerry Spring*.[2] Jijé and Giraud authenticated Spring's adventures by Hergéen means: the gun-slinging action was accompanied by carefully researched, well-documented pictures of animals, vegetation and Indian costumes. *Jerry Spring* also combined mimetic, Hergéen realism with a new device: subjective colours.

Figure 9. Photograph of Giraud taken by the author in Paris, 15 December 1998.

Subjective colours, rare in US comics and in *bandes dessinées*, involved surprising readers by using colours in deliberately unconventional ways that sometimes bordered on the irrational: for instance, Spring meets a Mexican who rides a pink donkey.[3] Jijé's subjective colours impressed young Giraud, who used them throughout his career, and he played an even greater role than Jijé in popularising them among later artists.

In 1963 Giraud, now calling himself 'Gir', started drawing *Lieutenant Blueberry* with Jean-Michel Charlier, who wrote the story.[4] Blueberry was a brave, rough-hewn cavalry officer. Stationed in an isolated fort 'aux confins de l'Arizona et du Nouveau Mexique' in the mid-nineteenth century, Blueberry was responsible for Indian relations. The first five albums form a cycle in which Blueberry makes peace with the Indians.

Early *Lieutenant Blueberry* was influenced by Western movies: the first panel generally depicted a panoramic view (the equivalent of a cinematic establishing shot); the second panel zoomed in on individual characters. The hero in Delmer Dave's film *Broken Arrow*

(1950), like Blueberry, was a soldier who tried to make peace with the Indians; Bascom, the Indian-hating officer who opposes Blueberry, had a predecessor in Robert Wise's film *Two Flags West* (1950).

At first, Gir's drawing resembled Jijé's: he mixed Hergéen realism with subjective colours. Gir also experimented with panels to produce new effects: when Cochise, an Indian chief, escapes from Bascom's tent by ripping the material, the tear closely follows the edge of the panel, and Cochise seems to spring out of nowhere (*Fort Navajo*, p. 44).

The second *Blueberry* cycle displayed a disillusionment with the way the West was won: Blueberry, having promised that the Indians would be fairly treated, fails to prevent their massacre by the US army.[5] The pessimism underlying *Blueberry*'s second cycle is lightened by touches of humour: a cowboy resembling John Wayne deposits his gun outside a town where weapons are banned, in a jocular reference to Howard Hawks' movie *Rio Bravo* (1959), a film with a similar scene (*L'Homme à l'étoile d'argent*, p. 29).

Blueberry's pro-Indian second cycle fits the pattern for Franco-Belgian comics; as we have seen, Hergé's BD *Tintin en Amérique* (1932) expressed sympathy for the Native Americans long before the American comic strips. Disenchantment with winning the West was, however, expressed more openly in American Western movies from the mid-1960s: in John Ford's *Cheyenne Autumn* (1964) the cavalry mercilessly harass the Indians; in Ralph Nelson's *Soldier Blue* (1970) the US army commits atrocities upon the Cheyenne. By the end of the second cycle, Gir's backgrounds were becoming more varied than those of Harman, Marijac and Jijé; *Blueberry* had detailed interiors and finely crafted depictions of the West's prairies, deserts and mountains.

The plot of *Blueberry*'s third cycle was inspired by James Curwood's novel *The Treasure Hunters*: Blueberry goes to an abandoned gold mine to rescue his kidnapped friend Jimmy McLure; the mine is guarded by a ghost who fires golden bullets at intruders.[6] The Western décor ceased to be a mere backdrop and started playing an integral role in the action: the story is set in a desert-like landscape, where Blueberry and his opponents are forced together by lack of water. Labyrinthine canyons, strangely shaped mountains, treacherous sand-dunes and shadowy caves contribute to an impression of hidden menace.

Chihuahua Pearl began the longest cycle, in which Blueberry falls from grace with the American authorities, but is later rehabilitated (Figure 10).[7] By now Gir was contributing to the scripting, and the plot is more complex and less derivative than before. In Hergéen fashion, it is lent credibility by a real, historical figure, Confederate General Edmund Kirby Smith (1824–1893), who fled to Mexico after the American civil war; Blueberry is recruited to track down the gold that Smith hid in Mexico.

By the fourth cycle, subjective colours were giving structure and continuity to the narrative; colours were less arbitrary and more functional, yet they lost none of their aesthetic appeal. When General Macpherson arrives, his strange shade of blue marks him out as an exceptional person (*Chihuahua Pearl*, p. 8). Macpherson court-martials Blueberry, who turns orange, then green. Macpherson secretly informs Blueberry that the court martial was a show trial, designed to fool rivals who also want Smith's gold. Macpherson explains Blueberry's delicate mission and turns green, like Blueberry. Macpherson's change of colour suggests complicity between the two men (*Chihuahua Pearl*, p. 15).

Blueberry goes to Mexico, and his adventures are recounted with powerful subjective colours. He returns to the US empty-handed, and is wrongly accused of stealing Smith's gold. Blueberry is jailed; his escape is then arranged by President Grant's opponents who try to assassinate Grant, successfully pinning the blame on Blueberry. Outcast by white America, Blueberry sides with the Indians. He helps them escape from a reservation, and accompanies them back to Mexico.

Gir's experiments grew more daring: when the Indians hold up a stagecoach, six characters are superimposed over the scene, discussing what happened after the event (*Nez cassé*, p. 7). Normally, each comic strip panel depicts one moment frozen in time. Here, no fewer than seven moments are frozen within the panel: the hold-up, and the moment at which each character speaks.

The rocky desert crossed by Blueberry and his 'frères rouges' en route to Mexico has a hallucinatory quality that is absent from Western movies: bizarrely shaped blue and pink boulders, orange mountains, yellow rivers, red lakes, scrubland changing from blue to orange. Blueberry's wilderness recalls Carlos Castaneda's, whose works Giraud enthusiastically read.[8] For example:

> There were endless valleys and mountains towards the north and a range of high sierras towards the west. The sunlight reflecting on

Figure 10. Lieutenant Blueberry court-martialled, extract from *Chihuahua Pearl* by Charlier and Giraud © Dargaud

the distant northern mountains made them look orange, like the color of the banks of clouds over the west. The scenery, in spite of its beauty, was sad and lonely.[9]

Similarities between *Blueberry* and Castaneda are not merely aesthetic: in Blueberry's wilderness, as in Castaneda's, hardship brings revelation. That desert fits with biblical tradition: the children of Israel spent forty years in the wilderness 'that you might learn that I am the Lord your God'; Jesus overcame temptation there by experiencing divine grace (Deut. 29.6 and Mark 1.12). Blueberry's wilderness brings pessimistic revelation: the Indians are doomed to extinction. A tragically beautiful desert defies the endeavours of Blueberry and the Indians, who are constantly under attack. The weary band eventually reaches Mexico, but nothing suggests that their plight will improve there.

As soon as Blueberry arrives in Mexico, he takes leave of the Indians. He then goes on to locate Smith's gold, and to save President Grant's life. Blueberry takes great pains to redeem himself in the eyes of the American authorities, even though the US government is exterminating his 'frères rouges'. Why does Blueberry switch his allegiance? Because the futility of the Indians' cause was revealed to him in the desert.

Lieutenant Blueberry is still hugely popular in Europe, and Giraud draws new stories about him to this day. When I interviewed Giraud he was starting a new Blueberry story, *Geronimo l'Apache*.[10] Over the years, Blueberry has followed Tintin, Gaston Lagaffe and Astérix into the pantheon of *bande dessinée* mythology, and his adventures are now a 'série classique'.[11] *Lieutenant Blueberry* spawned two related stories, *La Jeunesse de Blueberry* and *Martial Blueberry*, and it inspired other *bande dessinée* Westerns: *Jonathan Cartland* has detailed landscapes and subjective colours; *Capitaine Apache* tells of a settler who sides with the Indians; *Al Crane* depicts an anti-racist cowboy, with subjective colours.[12]

Lieutenant Blueberry took Western *bandes dessinées* into the 21st century, while the genre all but disappeared in its country of origin. American Western comics remained overshadowed by the movies, but Gir used devices peculiar to comics to produce effects that are impossible on screen. Hallucinatory, desert-like landscapes and experiments with panels, balloons and colours resurface repeatedly throughout his work, becoming Moebius trademarks.

Nouveau réalisme I: 'Cauchemar blanc' and 'la question du réel'

In the early/mid-1970s Giraud began re-using the pseudonym Moebius, a name inspired by the Möbius strip, which he had first seen in a science fiction magazine (either *Galaxie* or *Fiction*) during the late 1950s.[13] Giraud had previously used the name Moebius when drawing absurdly humorous strips influenced by *Mad* in the early 1960s.[14]

In 1974 a short, one-off strip called 'Cauchemar blanc' appeared under Moebius' name.[15] 'Cauchemar blanc' was radically different from *Lieutenant Blueberry*; its concise story and contemporary, urban setting gave it the look of a non-fictional *fait divers*; it was drawn in stark black and white with straight, cold-looking pen-strokes. 'Cauchemar blanc' depicts a racist attack, in which a gang of white youths in a car run an Arab off the road, and a fight breaks out. But this is just a dream from which the ringleader awakes. He then goes out in the car with his cronies, and they run the Arab down for real (Figure 11).

'Cauchemar blanc' did not evoke the racist's dream by means of the two conventional comic strip devices: thought-balloons with wavy, cloud-borders attached to the dreamer's head by chains of bubbles, and exaggeratedly unrealistic décor. These devices draw a clear boundary between the subject's dream and external reality; dropping them therefore blurs this boundary in 'Cauchemar blanc', producing disturbing effects. In 'Cauchemar blanc', uninterrupted urban banality provides continuity between the racist's dream and the real world; his dream occurs in everyday reality.

Everyday reality then turns dreamlike, once the racist has awoken: characters grimace nightmarishly, as though making intense efforts; the action is depicted from strange angles; dialogue disappears and the Arab, knocked off his bike, flies through the air in silence. 'Cauchemar blanc' shows a racist's violent, irrational fantasies mingling with everyday life; his dream is an extension of his waking life and vice versa. When Sadoul asked Moebius what had made him draw 'Cauchemar blanc', he could not remember: 'Je ne sais pas ce qui m'a pris de faire ça! Et il y a eu un énorme travail au niveau du scénario, du découpage ... Mais je ne comprends pas ce qui m'a poussé à faire cette histoire.'[16]

Although Moebius could not recall the source of his inspiration, he was not the first artist to have dropped the conventional devices for evoking dreams. In Hergé's *Sept Boules de cristal*, when the Inca-mummy comes through the bedroom window while Tintin sleeps, readers cannot be sure whether or not Tintin is dreaming (p. 32). Bruno Lecigne and Jean-Pierre Tamine mention that in the Italian Guido Crepax's strip *Valentina*, the heroine's mental images are barely distinguishable from the world outside her mind.[17]

Nevertheless, 'Cauchemar blanc' marked an entirely new departure: unlike Hergé and Crepax, Moebius used a short *fait divers* to confuse the boundary between dream and reality. That narrative structure was apposite, given the nature of *faits divers*. *Faits divers*, like 'Cauchemar blanc', exist at the very point where mundane reality meets the dreamlike: *faits divers* are items of news that appear in the media and are then imagined by the public; furthermore, *faits divers* often tell of irrational and nightmarish things happening in everyday life. As Georges Auclair wrote:

Figure 11. The racist has awoken, 'Cauchemar blanc' by Moebius © 2000 Les Humanoïdes Associés SA, Geneva

Significatifs, les faits divers ne le sont pas tant de la réalité statistique du crime que des fantasmes que la collectivité forme à son sujet ... Il suffit parfois de ne pas se laisser impressionner outre mesure par la « réalité » qu'ils prétendent resitituer pour y voir des récits de rêve ... [C'est] à une confusion du réel avec l'imaginaire qui'invite le récit d'un fait divers.[18]

'Cauchemar blanc' was the first of many *bandes dessinées* to fit the trend which Lecigne and Tamine defined as *nouveau réalisme* in *Fac-Similé*. The term *nouveau réalisme* was originally coined by the critic Pierre Restany, who applied it to experiments in the plastic arts during the late 1950s/early 1960s. Lecigne and Tamine take *nouveau réalisme* to embrace a wide range of strips, which appeared from the early/mid 1970s onwards. The *nouveaux réalistes* were a disparate group, who produced no manifestos and no shared statements of aims. Yet these artists were united by their desire to experiment: the *nouveaux réalistes* all discovered new uses for pictures of that which is real.

In 'classical' realist *bandes dessinées* (e.g. *Les Aventures de Tintin* and *Lieutenant Blueberry*) adventures had led, through a rationally linked sequence of developments, to the hero's triumph. Mimetic, Hergéen realism made the story plausible: it created the illusion that the hero's triumph was happening in the real world. In *nouveau réaliste* strips, realism no longer created that illusion; instead, artists used pictures of reality to ask where the real ends and where the imaginary begins. In so doing, they asked what Lecigne and Tamine termed 'la question du réel'.[19] Many *nouveaux réalistes* asked 'la question du réel' by drawing short, urban *faits divers*. *Nouveau réalisme* thus marked a move away from the traditional, Proppian folktale structure. There were no exemplary heroes in the style of Tintin, Spirou and Astérix, and few exotic adventures in foreign lands. Instead, *nouveau réaliste* strips tended to have mundane urban settings.

Other aspects of *nouveau réalisme* resembled 'Cauchemar blanc'. Like Moebius, *nouveaux réalistes* saw the city as constantly open to invasion by irrational fantasies, and as bereft of morality; revelling in aspects of everyday life that 'clear line' had tastefully filtered out (urban decay, sex, violence, swearing etc.), they replaced heroic exploits with a loss of innocence. *Nouveau réaliste faits divers* shattered Hergéen realism's clear, clean-cut, optimistic illusion.

Nouveaux réalistes asked 'la question du réel' in various ways.

Golo, Frank and Chantal Montellier were particularly similar to Moebius. Golo's and Frank's 'Sphinx de verre', like 'Cauchemar blanc', is drawn with cold, black-and-white pen-strokes.[20] On page one a scruffy man wanders through the Paris metro; he is then almost run over by a train and suddenly awakes, shivering and sweating. The man is a delirious junkie who needs a shot of heroin; the sequence in the metro was his waking dream.

Montellier also drew urban nightmares in black and white with cold, straight lines. Her 'Oscar Brown n'est pas un Espion' is a *fait divers* about racism, which was based on a real news report.[21] Because of media allegations, there is a clash between the false reality that everyone believes (Oscar is a black spy), and the truth (he is innocent). Montellier asks 'la question du réel' by using a *fait divers* to suggest that the media distorts reality.

Other *nouveaux réalistes* broke with Hergéen realism, but in different ways from 'Cauchemar blanc'. Jacques Tardi and Jean Teulé are two such artists. Teulé's 'Banlieue sud' defies conventions in comic-strip realism because the plot does not unfold rationally, and because the graphic style no longer provides sequences of panels with continuity.[22] Teulé juxtaposes hand-drawings with photographs which are crumpled, overexposed and bleached.

Teulé emphasises 'Banlieue sud's' *fait divers* aspect by opening with a precise date and time: 'Lundi 25 octobre 1980, au sud de Paris' (p. 47). On the next page, there is a photograph of a dilapidated house in a grim, Parisian suburb. 'Banlieue sud' then recounts a typically violent, *nouveau réaliste fait divers*: gang rape is committed in the house; the gang later extort money from Clarisse, an old lady who lives nearby. But there is uncertainty about what is actually going on: over the course of the story the rape recurs four times, rather like an obsessive fantasy. The second time, a photograph of the victim is reproduced back to front; the third and fourth times, a different photo of her coexists with exaggeratedly sketchy pictures of matchstick men. Towards the end, in what may be a parody of the conventional hero's triumph, Clarisse beats up one of the rapists and the house catches fire. On the very last page Clarisse and a child stare at a photograph of the house, which gradually becomes creased, crumpled and eventually unrecognisable (Figure 12).

The urban décor of 'Banlieue sud' takes on an allusive, metaphorical dimension. Perhaps the ugly house symbolises life in a rundown suburb. Perhaps the burning is a purifying fire that will allow Clarisse,

Figure 12. Clarisse, the child and the house, *Banlieue sud* © Jean Teulé.
Cliché Bibliothèque nationale de France

the rape victim and the child to make a fresh start. Whatever his photographs mean, we can see how Teulé is using them to play upon interactions between the urban environment and pure fantasy. Was serial rape committed? Did Clarisse avenge the victim? Are the rape and/or the revenge no more than fantasies? If so, whose fantasies are they? A gang-member's? Clarisse's? Or simply those of the artist?

Silvio Cadelo's *Envie de chien* also uses photographs to ask about relationships between the urban décor and sheer fantasy: a character awakes from a beautiful love-dream – or does he?[23] What may or may not be his return to reality is shown by a photograph of Parisian rooftops, where someone thinks 'un rêve d'après-midi'.

Nouveau réaliste experimenting went to extremes in the mid/late 1970s with the *Bazooka* group, which was centred around Olivia Clavel, Kiki and Loulou Picasso (Christian Chapiron and Jean-Louis Duprès), and José Perfección (Jean Rouzaud).[24] In keeping with *Bazooka*'s punk spirit, much of their work came out in ephemeral, do-it-yourself magazines. *Bazooka* called into question all of the artificial devices that, along with balloons and stylistic homogeneity, had been thought indispensable to Hergéen realism: with *Bazooka* there are few plots (not even *faits divers*) and the written texts contain numerous swear-words, misspellings, grammatical errors and crossings out. Instead of neatly dividing events up into panels, *Bazooka* artists put together sequences of different shapes, sizes and styles. *Bazooka* creations defy the laws of perspective and proportion: they mix in photographs, drawings, press-cuttings, graffiti and advertisements to create jarring effects of contrast.

Rouzaud's 'Verdadera del Tío José' is a good example.[25] The title calls to mind the long-running Belgian strip *Les Belles Histoires de l'Oncle Paul* (1951–1983), because 'tío' is Spanish for 'uncle', and 'verdadera' is Spanish for 'true' or 'real'. When I interviewed Rouzaud, he insisted that 'Una Verdadera del Tío José' was not a reference to *Les Belles Histoires de l'Oncle Paul*; even so, a comparison between the two strips sheds useful light.[26] Oncle Paul was an archetypal *ancien réaliste* hero. A kindly, pipe-smoking uncle who lived in prosperous suburban surroundings, he told his nephews 'true', morally stimulating accounts of historical events. For example, Oncle Paul ended his account of the sinking of *The Titanic* thus: 'Songez à tous ces gens qui moururent en chantant un cantique ... et à tous ceux qui se laissèrent couler plutôt que de surcharger des canots déjà trop pleins! ... Quelle leçon!'[27]

On page 1 of 'Una Verdadera del Tío José' a dissipated-looking man (José, one assumes) smokes a joint, not a pipe, in pleasant surroundings: there are trees, flying birds and a hilltop castle, which suggests a romanticised view of the past. The setting looks agreeably rustic, yet it is also apparently urban: however, José's city, unlike Oncle Paul's, is cluttered up with billboards advertising various consumer products. The caption reads: 'Tu te promènes dans la rue. Rien de spécial à faire.' In the picture below, José walks past a photo-montage which has advertisements for cigarettes, seedy cabarets and strip clubs. On the next page, a critique of sexist attitudes and of the ninth art's (mostly male) readership is implied, in gross language which is said to be that of the readers themselves:[28] a woman stands on a pedestal marked 'prix phallo 1976', while a text reads 'chatte, moule con, figue ... ces mots ont été les vôtres'; the text runs up the left-hand margin, making conventional left-to-right reading impossible.

On page 3 language loses its meaning. Pictures of people in the street and on the metro are accompanied by a text that says: 'Je m'suis acheté un costard en Alpaga, en Alpego, en Al Capone, en Alpages, en Alpoggi' etc. The last page is a huge, finely detailed picture of a crowd of people, drawn in a broad range of styles from Disney to photo-realism (Figure 13). The picture contains, among much else, a pregnant Brigitte Bardot, Yul Brynner with a shiny head of hair, and a woman who says: 'Bonjour Corto, c'est moi: la tentatrice chauve'. Her words are not gratuitous and they say much about Rouzaud's influences. The woman is referring to Hugo Pratt's adventure comic about a wandering sailor, *Corto Maltese*; she is also referring to the Absurdist playwright Eugène Ionesco's *Cantatrice chauve* (1950).

Prior to *Bazooka*, *Corto Maltese* had already asked 'la question du réel', when characters who might or might not be real appeared in Corto's adventures. As Dominique Petitfaux commented, *Corto Maltese* contains 'un mélange subtil entre personnages réels et personnages fictifs (il est parfois bien difficile de savoir dans quelle catégorie l'on peut ranger certains d'entre eux)'; one such character is the Russian monk Rasputin (1869–1916), who befriends Corto on the Pacific Ocean.[29]

'Una Verdadera del Tío José' also recalls Ionesco's *Cantatrice chauve*: both pieces depict people adrift in a city, where rational communication through language is breaking down. The hubbub on José's streets recalls Ionesco's dialogues: all traces of sense disappear

Figure 13. 'Una Verdadera del Tío José' © Jean Rouzaud. Cliché Bibliothèque nationale de France.

in a babble of words that are associated only by sound, not by meaning. For example:

> *Mme Martin*: Touche pas ma babouche!
> *M. Martin*: Bouge pas la babouche !
> *M. Smith*: Touche la mouche, mouche pas la touche
> *Mme Martin*: La mouche bouge.[30]

Above the huge picture that ends 'Una Verdadera del Tío José', an ironically self-congratulatory/self-deprecating text underlines the strip's commerciality and artificiality:

> Cette succession imagée vous a été vendue (!) grâce à la gentillesse et la compréhension d'Almonde presse et Bazooka production... le fait qu'elle soit prétencieuse, ringarde, de mauvais goût, pas claire pour tous et assez loupée dans l'ensemble, n'a rien à voir avec le fait de la lire ... Mieux vaut louper 1 coup beaucoup beau que réussir 1 coup triste ... ou le contraire, je sais pas. Votre: José Perfección. (L'Homme qui tout ça qu'il touche se transforme en Bon).

Rouzaud highlights the unbridgeable chasm between the *ancien réaliste* hero and the *nouveau réaliste* hero. Morally speaking, Oncle Paul was the one with the Midas touch: he turned everything into an uplifting, edifying lesson. Oncle Paul was the perfect, omniscient uncle. Tío José, on the other hand, is amoral and there is much that he does not know. José's claim to be perfect is unfounded, as is his claim to be a moral King Midas; nothing that José touches turns into goodness.

Instead of leading readers to an edifying conclusion, Rouzaud bombards them with images in which the imaginary and the real overlap: Bardot is pregnant; Brynner has the wrong hair-do; a real play and a fictional character are referred to in the same breath, and so on. Rouzaud is asking 'la question du réel' by superimposing the imaginary over the real and vice versa. He is operating a process similar to that of montage as described by Jean Baudrillard: 'Le procès contradictoire du vrai et du faux, du réel et de l'imaginaire est aboli dans cette logique hyperréelle du montage'.[31] Rouzaud's creations quite deliberately raise 'la question du réel'. As he himself said: 'C'est intéressant de dire aux gens: "qu'est-ce c'est que la réalité?"'

From Moebius to Rouzaud we can pick out three strands of *nouveau réalisme*. Moebius' 'Cauchemar blanc' started the trend towards experimentalism by dropping folktale structures and Hergéen realism in favour of an urban *fait divers*; Moebius also asked 'la question du réel' by confusing the boundary between dream and reality. Yet in 'Cauchemar blanc' readers can still tell reality from dream, because they see the racist awake to the real world. 'Le Sphinx de verre' also belongs to that strand of *nouveau réalisme*, because readers see the junkie awake; so too does 'Oscar Brown n'est pas un Espion', because readers know that Oscar is innocent. In each case, we can distinguish what is real from what is not.

With Teulé, Cadelo and some strips by Jacques Tardi, *nouveau réalisme* enters a second phase: the subject's irrational dreams and fantasies are utterly indistinguishable from external reality; causal links between events are weak and/or impenetrable. Was serial rape committed in 'Banlieue sud'? Did Cadelo's hero awake in *Envie de chien*? We cannot be sure. Rouzaud pushes 'la question du réel' to the limit: plot-structure disappears, along with most of the other elements that convention had deemed essential to comic strip realism; meanwhile, the real and the imaginary are superimposed. *Bazooka* took *nouveau réalisme* as far as possible before it ceases to be a *bande dessinée* phenomenon and becomes something else instead.

Nouveau réalisme II : Modernism meets May '68

To discover *nouveau réalisme*'s origins we must leave the realm of 1970s *bandes dessinées* and go back to early twentieth-century Paris. The artistic movements which emerged at that time can be grouped loosely under the heading 'Modernism'.[32] Put briefly, European Modernism began with Cubism, which then gave rise to Dada, Surrealism and Absurdism. Let us first consider what the circumstances were prior to Modernism's emergence. The broad outlines are as follows.

From the Renaissance up to the beginning of the twentieth century, most European artists had adopted approaches that dated back to Classical Greece. René Bray succinctly defines Classical aesthetics:

> L'instruction morale assignée comme but, ... la foi dans l'art et dans la règle, le culte de la raison, les dogmes de l'imitation de la nature et de l'imitation des Anciens, voilà le credo de l'esthétique classique, les fondements de toute la doctrine.[33]

Of course, not everybody stuck rigidly to every single tenet of Classicism. The Classicists and the Modernists were loosely associated groups of artists with no single, consistent aim; yet in France just as elsewhere, Academies actively promoted the Classical aesthetics handed down by the Renaissance. Following the Classical credo, most pre-Modern artists copied examples set by Greek and Roman art: they imitated perceptible reality by obeying the laws of perspective and proportion; they delighted and instructed their audiences with exemplary heroes; they rejected indecency and things incompatible with reason; they cultivated harmonious, homogeneous styles; they told stories that unfolded rationally.

As befits a 'série classique', *Les Aventures de Tintin* were influenced by Classical aesthetics, albeit not selfconsciously. Despite occasional experiments with panels and balloons, Hergé stayed within tradition: he constructed plots that unfolded rationally, and Tintin was an exemplary hero. Hergé did not offend good taste, and he cultivated stylistic homogeneity. Hergé's mimetic depictions of the real world obeyed the rules of perspective and proportion.

When Modernism emerged, artists rejected those Classical ways of depicting reality. To quote Herbert Read, 'The aim of five centuries of European effort is openly abandoned'.[34] The split between Classicism and Modernism mirrors the split between Hergéen realism and *nouveau réalisme*. With Modernism, as with *nouveau réalisme*, reality is no longer an objective truth, which may be taken for granted and shared a priori. On the contrary: reality is subjectified, profoundly irrational and permanently open to question. *Nouveau réaliste bandes dessinées* and Modern artists point towards 'a crisis of reality'; they break down 'communal reality and conventional notions of causality ... the communal universe of reality and culture on which nineteenth-century art had depended [is] over ... all realities have become subjective fictions'.[35] Conversely, all subjective fictions have become realities.

Modernists and *nouveaux réalistes* have much in common: they stopped instructing the public with exemplary models; they deliberately destroyed the rational; they ceased reproducing the physical world by means of correct proportions and obedience to the rules of perspective; they welcomed 'the freedom to abandon the ancient duty of imitating reality more or less directly ... in order to present novel views of the world'.[36] Modernism and *nouveau réalisme* both substitute 'disorder for order, ugliness or distortion for beauty and proportion, obscurity often for predetermined clarity of meaning'; like Modernism, *nouveau réalisme* is 'a productive engagement with aspects of experience previously considered abnormal and not art-worthy'.[37] As Norbert Lynton suggests, Modernism is a product of its era. It fits the trend set by Dostoyevsky's novels, Nietzsche's philosophy and Freud's theory of the subconscious, all of which popularised the notion that people are motivated by needs and fears that have little to do with ideals of beauty, harmony and reason.

Let us now examine how *nouveau réalisme* connects to Cubism, Dada, Surrealism and Absurdism in greater detail. We shall take each movement in chronological order.

Some early Cubists introduced stylistic disharmony. Pablo Picasso's *Bottle, Glass and Violin* (1912–13), for instance, juxtaposed hand-drawn pictures with advertisements, signs and newsprint. Picasso and Georges Braque, like Teulé, Cadelo and Rouzaud, used frag-mented graphic styles when depicting the twentieth-century city. Cubist writer Guillaume Apollinaire's comment on Picasso and Braque, made in 1913, fits Rouzaud in particular:

> Picasso et Braque introduisaient dans leurs oeuvres d'art des lettres d'enseignes et d'autres inscriptions, parce que, dans une ville moderne, l'inscription, l'enseigne et la publicité jouent un rôle artistique très important et parce qu'elles s'adaptent à cette fin.[38]

Dada and the avant-garde took stylistic fragmentation one stage further. Artists such as John Heartfield and Max Ernst made montages by arranging pictures and photographs in unexpected ways. With Dada, as with *nouveau réalisme*, taking everyday objects out of their normal context made the public see new significance in the mundane. Dada montages raised 'la question du réel' in the same way as Teulé's photographs and Rouzaud's constructions: they asked 'what is and is not reality'.[39] Rejecting Classical notions of decency and propriety, Dada and *nouveau réalisme* both attacked twentieth-century society with unprecedented ferocity: 'Through photomon-tage Dada periodicals could make use of all aspects of contemporary life. The images could be subverted to expose the hypocrises and idiocies of that existence.'[40]

In the late 1920s and the 1930s, Surrealism sought to free artists from rules and conventions; Surrealism also emphasised the reality of the subject's irrational mental images, just as the *nouveaux réalistes* were to do. André Breton's second Surrealist manifesto (1930) contains an early echo of *bande dessinée nouveau réalisme* and 'la question du réel': 'Tout porte à croire qu'il existe un certain point de l'esprit d'où la vie et la mort, *le réel et l'imaginaire* ... cessent d'être perçus contradictoirement.'[41] In paintings such as *La Durée poignardée* (1939), which depicts a steam locomotive emerging from a fireplace, the Belgian Surrealist René Magritte used an everyday setting to blur the boundary between the real and the imaginary; in so doing, Magritte asked 'la question du réel'.

In Paris in the late 1950s/early 1960s a small group of sculptors and painters appeared who were named *nouveaux réalistes* by the critic Pierre Restany. Like their successors in the ninth art, Restany's earlier *nouveaux réalistes*, such as Yves Klein and Jean Tinguely, sought new meanings for urban trivia: they gave ordinary objects original, expressive power; they used mundane reality to produce unusual effects, by operating a 'singularisation du banal' that triggered '[de] nouvelles approaches perceptives du réel'.[42]

Modernism is also apparent in the twentieth century's narrative art forms, notably in Absurdist theatre, the *nouveau roman* and films. I have already pointed out the parallel between *La Cantatarice chauve* and 'Una Verdadera de Tío José'. It could be added that in Ionesco's plays, just as in *nouveau réaliste bandes dessinées,* the subject's irrational fantasies and obsessions invade the outside world; moreover, like his descendants in *bandes dessinées*, Ionesco rejected Aristotelian plots that had a beginning, a middle and an end; he also dispensed with logical sequences of events.

Moebius' 'Cauchemar blanc' was the first *bande dessinée* to link the ninth art into the twentieth-century tradition of European Modernism. During our interview, I asked Moebius about Modernism. He confirmed that he was, of course, acquainted with the great Cubist, Dada and Surrealist masterpieces, as well as with Ionesco, but added that he was unfamiliar with Klein's and Tinguely's branch of *nouveau réalisme*. Yet any connections Moebius makes with Modernism are purely intuitive, not rationally thought out. On the subject of 'Cauchemar blanc', Moebius emphasised that he had not been knowingly inspired by Modernist and avant-garde experimenting, and he repeated what he had told Sadoul: he had simply no idea what had made him draw 'Cauchemar blanc'. Rouzaud, on the other hand, was more consciously inspired by Modernism: he spoke at length of his interest in Dada, Surrealism and the avant-garde, saying 'on fait partie d'une tradition, mais on évolue'.

Whether the artists themselves noticed it or not, the Modernist tributary flowed into the ninth art with 'Cauchemar blanc' and spread wider with *nouveau réalisme*. Modernism had been present since at least the early twentieth century in Paris, and one wonders why it took so long to surface in *bandes dessinées*. Tintin's success surely encouraged imitations of Classical aesthetics; Franco-Belgian publishers, with their eyes on sales figures, would certainly have encouraged artists to repeat the successful formulas.

Modernism eventually appeared in *bandes dessinées* during the mid-1970s, shortly after the events of May '68 had challenged the reigning aesthetics, values and authorities. Significantly, 'Cauchemar blanc' first came out in *L'Echo des savanes*, a magazine founded by the breakaway artists Gotlib, Mandryka and Bretécher; like Giraud they rebelled against *Pilote* in May 1968 when they perceived Goscinny's editorial policy to be too conservative. Other *nouveaux réalistes*, notably Golo, Frank, Teulé and some *Bazooka* artists, also published experimental work in *L'Echo des savanes*.

What, then, is the link between Modernism, *nouveau réalisme* and the May '68 revolt? The link between the avant-garde, Dada, Surrealism and May '68 has already been analysed.[43] Modernism and May '68, like *nouveau réalisme*, all rebel against established tastes, aesthetics and conventions: none of them sees much goodness in the twentieth-century city; they are all fascinated by the irrational; they display great interest in 'la question du réel'. May '68's anti-authoritarian slogans suggest that the boundary between the real and the imaginary can be erased; as a result, they attest to the uprising's keen interest in 'la question du réel'. Moebius himself recalled that, although he was not politically involved in May '68, 'tout le verbiage révolutionnaire me séduisait'.[44] Lastly, ideologically speaking, Modernism, May '68 and *nouveau réalisme* all imply hostility towards the bourgeoisie as defined by Ionesco:

> That aspect of humanity which accepts and cultivates the illusion of material realism as being the equivalent of the whole of reality, which renounces the perception of 'total reality' (the 'inner life') and prefers the superficial comfort of rational logic as displayed in the visible forms of social order.[45]

May '68 did not bring down the French government; arguably, the movement failed to achieve its immediate political objectives. Yet despite that, May '68 scored an undeniable cultural success. The

May uprising marked a turning point: it dragged Modernist tendencies, once confined to the fringes, centre stage. Post May '68, Modernism erupted into mainstream popular culture. As Bernard Brown comments:

> The ferment expressed by the May Revolt has seeped through all of French society. It is everywhere ... Themes of the May Revolt – in particular denunciation of the consumer society and the insanity of modern civilization – have been especially prevalent, even dominant, in the world of cinema and the theater.[46]

Nouveau réalisme adds *bandes dessinées* to Brown's list. It is no accident that *nouveau réaliste* experiments should have come to the fore during a phase of widespread political, moral and artistic questioning in the aftermath of May '68. As Rouzaud said: 'Il y avait un désir général après '68 d'élargir notre conscience et de voir la réalité autrement'.

Brussels, like Paris, saw serious unrest in May 1968. As Serge Govaert put it, '*Lorsqu'on s'enrhume à Paris, on éternue à Bruxelles. La phrase est bien connue.*'[47] However, Govaert clearly spells out the Brussels uprising's chief preoccupations: university overcrowding and the French/Flemish language question. *Bande dessinée nouveau réalisme* never caught on in Belgium as it did in France. *Nouveau réalisme*, for all its originality, thus continued the trend away from Belgium and towards France that had started with *Pilote*.

Like France and Belgium, the USA experienced socio-political turmoil in the late 1960s, which was reflected in popular culture; for that reason, the Underground provides *nouveau réalisme* with a point of comparison. Even before their European counterparts, Underground artists had turned away from traditional tales of adventure to tackle social issues such as drugs, sexism and urban violence. Like *nouveau réalisme*, the Underground frequently gave dreamlike depictions of everyday life; the Underground and *nouveau réalisme* both pointed uneasily towards a moral vacuum beneath the consumer society's rising prosperity.

Yet *nouveau réalisme* is peculiar to *bandes dessinées*, with no direct equivalent in American comics. In particular, Underground artists did not share *nouveau réalisme*'s predilection for *faits divers* and for 'la question du réel', being more preoccupied by American concerns: Vietnam, LSD, Haight-Ashbury, flower power. Moreover, Underground artists used different graphic styles from *nouveaux réalistes*. Robert Crumb (who frequently parodied Disney) drew with grotesque, caricatural exaggeration; his luxuriant, psychedelic visions were far removed from the straight, cold lines of Moebius, Tardi, Teulé and others.

Photographs are far less evident in Underground comics than in *nouveau réaliste* strips. Sally Stein points out that the USA, unlike France, has no strong, long-standing tradition in artistic photo-montage; that cultural difference may account for the relatively late arrival of photographs or montages in English-language comics; when Alan Moore incorporated photographic images into the comic *Rocks and Hard Places* as late as 1999, Geoff Klock referred to it as 'radical stylistic experimentation'.[48]

Nouveau réaliste bandes dessinées were different from all comics that had gone before: they neither copied everyday reality after the fashion of Hergé, nor caricatured it like Crumb. Moebius' 'Cauchemar blanc' was a bold, successful experiment, but, perhaps regrettably, Moebius soon turned away from his contemporary society and its problems. After the mid-1970s, Moebius rarely ventured outside science fiction.

Experimenting with Science Fiction

In 1975, Moebius launched the science fiction *bande dessinée* magazine *Métal hurlant* with Philippe Druillet and Jean-Pierre Dionnet, which was to provide a forum for experimenting. Moebius himself was looking for new directions. In an editorial for *Métal hurlant* he questioned the comic strip's conventional narrative structures, such as adventure stories and gags, humorously adding:

> Il n'y a aucune raison pour qu'une histoire soit comme une maison avec une porte pour entrer ... On peut très bien imaginer une histoire en forme d'éléphant, de champ de blé, ou de flamme d'alumette souffrée.[49]

To appreciate Moebius' innovations in the domain of science fiction *bandes dessinées*, it is instructive to consider SF prior to *Métal hurlant*. In the mid-1970s, science fiction *bandes dessinées* were still mostly dominated by American strips, particularly Alex Raymond's *Flash Gordon*.[50] Nonetheless, a distinctively European Francophone tradition was slowly beginning to emerge.

The first notable SF *bande dessinée* was *Futuropolis* by Pellos (René Pellarin), a black-and-white strip in the style of *Flash Gordon*: muscular heroes had space adventures in a fantasmagorical universe that combined prehistory, mythology, medievalism and futurism.[51] Despite Raymond's obvious influence, Pellos was no plagiarist. Unlike *Flash Gordon*, *Futuropolis* implied an ecologically sensitive critique that was unknown in previous SF comics: the story tells of a smug, technologically advanced society, which is at war with nature. Moreover, Pellos' page layout was extremely unusual:

> The layout of the panels, unique in the international comic strip field … is a disconnected and chaotic layout in which the pictures, separated by circles, lightning flashes, and oblique lines, whirl or burst into a fireworks display that no longer has anything in common with the prim succession of the usual squares and rectangles. The copious but minuscule text is integrated with the pictures and swept up into the chaos.[52]

Pellos' innovations with page layouts were later built upon by Moebius, Druillet and others.

After World War II, Roger Lécurieux and Raymond Poivet's *Pionniers de l'Espérance* again had a style reminiscent of *Flash Gordon*, yet once more there were differences.[53] Rather than featuring an American-style superhero, *Les Pionniers de l'Espérance* depicts a multiracial group of travellers, including a Chinaman, a Martiniquais, a Russian and a Frenchman as well as an American. Such depictions of racial harmony and ideological cooperation were very unusual in contemporary American SF comics. Moreover, unlike its American counterparts, *Les Pionniers de l'Espérance* was decidedly left-wing in its message: the crew of the *Espérance* oppose a group of ruthless capitalists, who are plundering a planet's natural resources.[54]

At *Pilote*, new science fiction strips emerged in the late 1960s/ early 1970s. *Valérian* combined Hergéen 'clear line' with a caricatural mock-realism reminiscent of Franquin. The hero was a time-travelling 'agent spatio-temporel', who patrolled the cosmos. In Valérian's adventure *Bienvenue sur Alflolol*, materialistic, colonising earthlings found a technologically advanced, ecologically unfriendly society on a beautiful planet, rich in natural resources.[55] The earthlings rob the planet's nomadic natives of their ancestral hunting grounds, confining them to reservations. The parallel with the USA's treatment of the native Americans could hardly be clearer. *Valérian* continues the strongly pro-Indian Franco-Belgian trend, discernible in *Tintin en Amérique* and in *Lieutenant Blueberry* among others; such criticism, even veiled, would have been highly unusual in contemporary American SF strips.

Also at *Pilote,* Moebius' friend Druillet published *Les Six Voyages de Lone Sloane*, in which an intergalactic traveller battles with space pirates, bloodthirsty warriors and demonic magician-priests.[56] Druillet took the tradition of experiments with page layouts to extremes: he drew geometric, highly complex pictures of colossal idols, gigantic machines and huge space-cities, some of which take up an entire page, or even two. Druillet's cities display a bewildering array of Grecian columns, gothic arches, Venetian balconies, Arabian minarets and more.

Despite the innovations by his compatriots such as Pellos, Druillet and others, Moebius felt the need to breathe new life into mid-1970s science fiction. He said,

> Je crois jusqu'à maintenant que la plupart des bandes de SF n'ont fait que broder sur des thèmes littéraires connus et éprouvés … Moi je pense que la SF dans la BD sera sauvée le jour où on aura vraiment des œuvres authentiquement nouvelles et où on aura l'impression d'avoir changé d'atmosphère.[57]

Moebius' *Arzach* is such a work.[58] It consists of four episodes in which Arzach flies above a world full of wonders and dangers on a pterodactyl. Like many SF comics from *Flash Gordon* to *Valérian*, *Arzach* mixes in different periods of history. Arzach's world has dinosaurs, a gorgon, rudimentary weapons, sophisticated machinery and more. However, any resemblance between *Arzach* and previous SF comics ends with its setting: *Arzach* has no balloons, no captions and no explanatory text. It challenges the idea that the *bande dessinée* is a text/image form.

Suppressing written words has far-reaching implications for comics. In previous strips, words locked time into the sequence of unmoving panels; each panel lasted the time needed to say/think the words in the balloons. But *Arzach*'s silent panels appear to exist outside time. Their air of timelessness suggests that Arzach's journey is a symbolic quest, evoking atemporal, universal truths. The feeling of timeless universality is reinforced by the heterogeneous objects surrounding the hero: Arzach is not tied to one particular place and time.

If *Arzach* is symbolic, then the key to the symbolism is not given, and various meanings are possible. *Arzach* lacks the specificity written words provide, nothing is explained and all is unresolved. Arzach is mysterious: we do not know who he is, where he is from or where he is going. Moreover, his name is spelt differently in each episode's title.

Arzach's lack of text focuses attention on the pictures, which are totally different from those of *Lieutenant Blueberry* and 'Cauchemar blanc'. Using an airbrush, Moebius drew exotic, fantastical landscapes and colourful, outlandish architecture. *Arzach*'s panels have a polished, aesthetic quality that makes them look like independent compositions, particularly as some take up an entire page. Panels are not immediately subordinated to the demands of a narrative, yet they cannot easily be isolated from those coming before and after. Resonances between panels do suggest some kind of a story: Moebius appears to be inverting superhero convention. Herculean heroes such as Flash Gordon, Batman and Superman rout evil and save the world, but Arzach is unusually vulnerable.

In one episode, a man drives a vintage car across a desert to a somewhat Mayan-looking building (p. 37). He struggles past attackers, and enters a room full of futuristic apparatus; on a screen we see Arzach and his pterodactyl, which is apparently dead. The man fiddles with a machine, the pterodactyl is revived and Arzach flies off (Figure 14). This reads like a short episode lifted from a longer story, but readers must imagine what took place before, and what happens next. What was wrong with the pterodactyl? Who are the attackers? What is the relationship between Arzach and the other man? Is the other man Moebius himself, struggling to bring his drawn character to life?

The Moebius who drew *Arzach* can only be compared to two contemporary artists: Philippe Druillet and Richard Corben.[59] Druillet's *Lone Sloane*, like *Arzach*, has pictures filling an entire page; however, Druillet's graphic style is more grandiose, more geometric and more detailed than that of Moebius. Moreover, Druillet's panels are supported by written words. American Richard Corben drew colourful science fantasies in a shiny, airbrushed style that recalls *Arzach*, but Corben, like Druillet, told stories using text.

Moebius' experiments with unusual page layouts continue a tradition that is peculiar to Franco-Belgian SF comics. Yet Moebius went even further than the other experimentalists by stripping SF

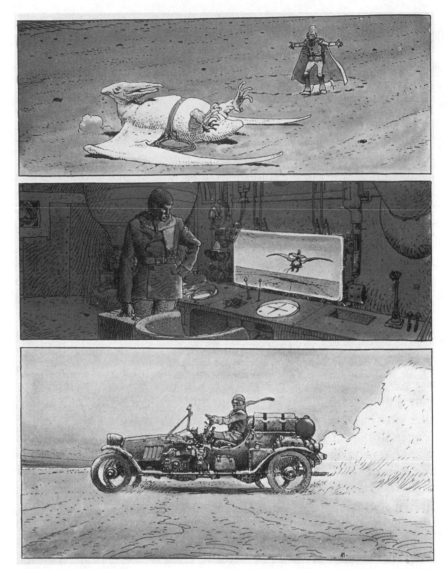

Figure 14. Arzach revived, *Arzach* by Moebius © 2000 Les Humanoïdes Associés SA, Geneva

comics of text and coherent plots. *Arzach*'s dreamlike aspect, combined with its sense of mystery, its power of suggestion and its symbolism, gave SF comics a new, poetic dimension.

The SF Narrative Deconstructed: *Le Garage hermétique*

Moebius' *Garage hermétique* is a science fiction story set at an undefined point in the future.[60] The plot hinges on the technologically innovative 'générateurs expenseurs à effet Grubert'. This innovation allows the hero, Major Grubert, to build his own complex, three-levelled universe on an asteroid called 'Fleur'. Moebius improvised the story over 33 episodes:

> Le *Garage* est donc l'exemple type d'une bande dessinée, sans scénario préétabli ... Chaque fois que la tentation me prenait de durcir la ligne de l'histoire et qu'un but se profilait, je cassais tout et je repartais à l'aventure.[61]

Le Garage hermétique deconstructed the science fiction narrative. It defied the traditional rules by which comic strips usually function. According to tradition, panels make up a coherent sequence of events: each panel develops from the previous one, and prepares for the following one. Artists suggest links between panels, connecting them by cause and effect, using captions and so on; guided by the artist, readers imagine what happens in the white spaces between panels.

Le Garage hermétique defies those rules because links connecting panels are often illogical, and the suggestive power of the white spaces is taken to the limit; readers must work exceptionally hard to discover/imagine what happens between panels, and thus piece the story together. We have come a very long way from Proppian folk-tales: on a first or second reading, *Le Garage hermétique* is a series of arbitrary developments and baffling red herrings; on further readings, a plot gradually emerges. A labyrinthine story underlies the apparent nonsense. Here is a brief, perhaps over-simplified summary.

On Fleur, an engineer named Barnier damages a machine. Grubert sends out a robot-spy to find out what is happening. Learning that Jerry Cornelius is among his enemies, Grubert investigates himself.[62] Dalxtré searches for Cornelius' brother, Eric; he visits various 'terres aléatoires', one of which resembles the Wild West. Cornelius conquers

Fleur's second and third levels, but he unites with Grubert against the superhuman Bakalite, who also seeks control. Barnier befriends Yetchem the archer, who reveals that Grubert has discovered the secret of immortality. Yetchem shoots down an 'aeroplane de la destinée' (Figure 15). Fleur disintegrates into political turmoil. Grubert and Cornelius escape to Fleur's first level. Grubert appears before various characters from the story, including the Bakalite, 'le maître de la vie et la mort', who judge him. The Bakalite reveals that, by damaging the machine, Barnier had inadvertently created anti-time, thereby allowing the Bakalite into Grubert's creation. Grubert runs away and suddenly finds himself in the Paris metro.

It should be stressed that *Le Garage hermétique* does not unfold in the linear fashion described above. The narrative is dislocated because panels frequently jump between the various characters (Barnier, Yetchem, Dalxtré, Grubert and more), without any explanation. Grubert does not appear until the third episode, he gets lost in his own labyrinthine creation and he shares the limelight with other characters he never even meets.

Each episode of *Le Garage hermétique*, following convention for serialised comics, begins with a brief summary of the story so far; but in *Le Garage hermétique* summaries often recount trivialities, or even events not previously depicted at all. Readers do not learn about Grubert's 'générateurs' until the summary to episode 15 (p. 83). The summary to episode 21 is a quotation from Saint Luke (12.2): 'Il n'est rien de caché qui ne doive être découvert, rien de secret qui ne doive être connu' (p. 99).

Le Garage hermétique's deconstructed narrative suspends meaning. Seemingly pointless things happen whose significance is only revealed much later: Barnier damaging the machine appears to have no bearing on the story until the very end. Everything is unstable and changeable. Grubert's appearance alters; he loses his spiked, Prussian helmet to don a superhero's cape, and finally he wears everyday clothes; Barnier turns into a woman.

The narrative is broken up still further by abrupt shifts between science fiction and humour. When Grubert sends out the robot-spy, it appears to argue with itself schizophrenically:

- VOUS! Je ... je vous avais pourtant interdit de me suivre.
- Parce que vous interdisez maintenant ?
- Vous mériteriez une bonne correction.
- Espèce de brute (p. 53).

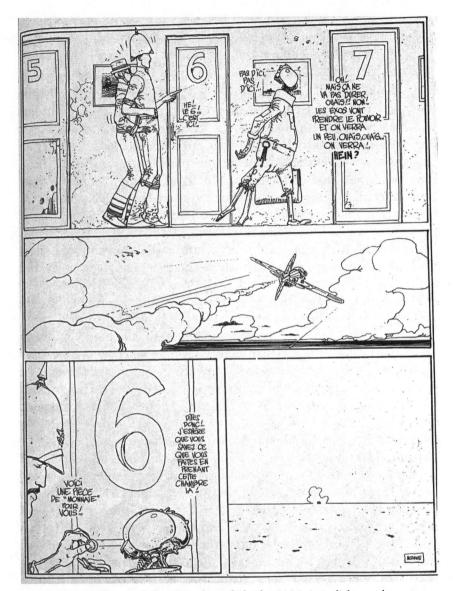

Figure 15. Grubert and the 'aeroplane de la destinée', in a dislocated sequence of panels by Moebius © 2000 Les Humanoïdes Associés SA, Geneva

We then see two human beings arguing inside the robot's massive head.

Before *Le Garage hermétique* and *nouveau réalisme*, the Underground artists Victor Moscosco and Rick Griffin, whose work Giraud told me he liked, had already deconstructed the narrative by drawing comics in which panels were not arranged in logical sequences.[63] The result was different, because Griffin and Moscosco drew short series of images, not long complex SF adventures. Their exaggeratedly psychedelic drawing was much more obviously drug-influenced than that of Moebius. Moreover, *Le Garage hermétique* took narrative deconstruction further than the Underground by introducing an as yet unknown fragmentation into the graphic style.

In Griffin and Moscosco, as in *Lieutenant Blueberry*, 'Cauchemar blanc' and *Arzach*, the graphic style still had a conventional function, which conformed to Classical aesthetics: it provided unity and continuity. But Grubert's world is closer to Tío José's, despite the science fiction setting: there is no continuity and disunity reigns. In *Le Garage hermétique*, panoramic scenes of Fleur's futuristic capital, complete with minutely detailed monuments, machines, buildings and roads, jostle with perfunctory-looking sketches, childishly drawn animals, Blueberry-style cowboys and superheroes. *Le Garage hermétique*'s lack of stylistic homogeneity and its fragmented plot linked *bande dessinée* SF to the Modernist tendencies discussed above.

Le Garage hermétique questions well-defined conventions of the form by disrupting the narrative's linear flow; the story, which is of considerable length, requires an unprecedented degree of reader-participation to generate meaning. Moebius' approach recalls the *nouveau roman* as exemplified by Alain Robbe-Grillet more than it does any previous comic. Similarities between Moebius and Robbe-Grillet are reinforced by the latter's habit of writing in the present tense: in Robbe-Grillet's novels, as in a comic, events happen while the work is being read. Giraud told me he was aware of Robbe-Grillet's experiments with narratives, but that he had not read any *nouveaux romans*. Nonetheless, Ben Stoltzfus' description of Robbe-Grillet's *nouveau roman* fits *Le Garage hermétique*:

> The dislocation of narrative sequence in time-space ... in terms of a continuous present, is not always easy to follow or anticipate. The reader must contribute actively to the elaboration and metamorphosis of thought and emotion. The fact that everything is

happening in the present, which the reader is actively interpreting, gives the narrative an immediacy and impact absent from the traditional past tense story.[64]

A further parallel exists between *Le Garage hermétique* and French new wave films, as exemplified by Jean-Luc Godard's *Week End* (1967). Godard and Moebius both create unusual effects by disrupting the narrative flow; they both tell stories which jump from one narrative strand to another without explanations; they both introduce new characters unexpectedly, and for no apparent reason.[65]

Even after several readings *Le Garage hermétique*, like Robbe-Grillet's novels and Godard's films, remains enigmatic; but despite their similarities, Robbe-Grillet, Godard and Moebius deconstructed the narrative by different means. Robbe-Grillet, of course, wrote prose texts; Godard used jump-cuts; Moebius combined words with sequences of panels. He placed so much emphasis on readers imagining what happens in between panels that various interpretations are possible.

Perhaps *Le Garage hermétique* is nothing but a superbly drawn shaggy-dog story. Alternatively, perhaps it reworks the ancient theme of the man who would be God, and who is punished for his ambition. Grubert raised himself to the level of the godhead by creating his own universe. The narrative is dislocated with good reason: human presumption throws creation into disorder and blocks clear communication, as with the story of the Tower of Babel (Gen. 11.1–9). Following biblical tradition Grubert is judged, and he must go back to being a normal human.

Le Garage hermétique may also be a cautionary tale for the technological twentieth century: Grubert built a new world using fantastic technology, but scientific knowledge is not an agent of his salvation, and he cannot control what he made. His works turn against him, and cause confusion.

Moebius called Grubert a 'projection symbolique de moi-même',[66] a point elaborated upon by Jacques Goimard:

> Le vrai créateur de Fleur, l'inventeur de cet univers imaginaire, ce n'est pas Grubert, c'est Moebius … Quand cet univers se révolte et exige d'accéder à l'existence, l'auteur est pris entre deux feux: d'un côté, le désir passionné de faire exister son rêve; de l'autre, la conscience de ne pas pouvoir lui donner la vie autrement qu'à coups de crayon. Voilà pourquoi il a cherché … à multiplier les surprises, à nourrir son récit d'enchaînements aléatoires qui, espère-t-il, lui

feront perdre le contrôle des événements ... Voilà pourquoi, vaincu, il comparaît devant tous ses personnages ... Dès lors il ne lui reste plus qu'à fuir, à se réfugier dans la réalité la plus banale – le métro de Paris.[67]

By the late 1970s, Moebius' international reputation was growing. In 1977 *Métal hurlant* was successfully published under the title *Heavy Metal* by Marvel Comics (New York). Moebius also attracted the attention of US film-makers: he co-designed costumes for Ridley Scott's *Alien* (1977), and contributed to the story-board for Walt Disney's *Tron* (1980). Moebius drew other volumes about characters from *Le Garage hermétique*, including two with the Americans Eric Shanower and Jerry Bingham.[68] Moebius was awarded the Grand Prix at the Angoulême BD festival in 1981.

Jean Giraud is the most Americanised master of the ninth art whom we have studied so far: Westerns and SF are staples of popular culture in the USA. What is more, unlike Hergé, Franquin and Goscinny, Giraud hardly ever plays directly upon notions of Franco-Belgian identity: he rarely draws inspiration from the two countries' shared histo ry, culture and geography; he does not make humorous, punning use of their shared French language. Yet paradoxically, no artist could have done more than Giraud to give the ninth art a new identity, distinct from that of American comics.

Giraud's contribution to the ninth art is manifold: he experimented with Westerns, realism and science fiction, and he produced previously unimaginable effects; other BD artists then followed his example. Giraud reinvented Western comics for French-speaking readers; he also broke out of Propp's traditional folktale structure and introduced 'la question du réel' to *bandes dessinées*, linking the ninth art to Modernism. Furthermore, Giraud continued the Franco-Belgian trend away from superheroes, which been started by the 'classical' BD artists: Blueberry and Arzach are fallible; 'Cauchemar blanc's' racist is no embodiment of triumphant goodness; Arzach and Grubert (like Astérix) can have various meanings, or none whatsoever. Giraud made a further contribution to the ninth art: in 'Cauchemar blanc', *Arzach* and *Le Garage hermétique*, he broke down the barriers between *bandes dessinées* and more traditional art forms such as poetry, paintings and novels; this achievement encouraged Giraud's French-speaking public to take *bandes dessinées* seriously as an art form.

Giraud is one of the ninth art's great innovators. He has a high international profile, and he enjoys the respect of numerous American artists. As we shall see in Chapter 7, Giraud continued to play a prominent role on the *bande dessinée* stage into the 1980s and beyond.

CHAPTER FIVE

New Visions of the Past: Jacques Tardi

History and Irony

Jacques Tardi, like Jean Giraud, began his career at Goscinny's and Uderzo's *Pilote* before becoming established in his own right. Today Tardi is one of the ninth art's most prolific, original and influential masters. In this chapter, we shall consider three aspects of Tardi's vast body of work: his World War I comics of the 1970s and 1980s, which engage directly with the shared, Franco-Belgian history; his distinctive brand of *nouveau réalisme*, which uses historical settings and the voice from beyond the grave to ask 'la question du réel'; and his unusual tendency towards irony. We shall see how Tardi strengthens folklore and consolidates Franco-Belgian cultural identity; he also distances the ninth art still further from American comics

Jacques Tardi (b. 1946) studied at the Beaux Arts, Lyon (Figure 16). His first published *bande dessinée* in *Pilote*, a black-and-white collaboration with Giraud, was called 'Un Cheval en hiver'; it was inspired by Anthony Mann's Western movie *Winchester 73* (1950), in which an ill-fated rifle kills each of its owners.[1] Tardi and Giraud grafted the story onto Napoleon's retreat from Moscow in 1812, and replaced the rifle with a horse: every soldier who rides the horse dies. Tardi's visually realistic horses recall those in *Lieutenant Blueberry*. Nonetheless, 'Un Cheval en hiver' shows a budding originality: Tardi's light pen-strokes leave expanses of white, making the soldiers look isolated and lost in the snow. Tardi's second strip, 'La Torpédo rouge sang', is similar to 'Un Cheval en hiver': a jinxed car causes each of its owners to die; one owner, Archduke Ferdinand, is assassinated at Sarajevo on 28 June 1914, plunging Europe into World War I.[2]

From the beginning of his career, Tardi displayed an interest in nineteenth- and early twentieth-century European history, and he was strongly influenced by writers and artists from that period. His early adventure story, *Le Démon des glaces*, recalls both Jules Verne

Figure 16. Photograph of Jacques Tardi taken by the author in Paris, 2 September 2001

and George Roux, whose engravings illustrated Verne's novels.[3] Tardi imitated Roux's technique 'en utilisant les mêmes instruments que les graveurs, c'est-à-dire des petits peignes aux dents plus ou moins écartées et qui donnent donc des gris différents'.[4] The period style produced by Roux's methods perfectly suits Tardi's detailed, meticulously drawn nineteenth-century interiors, steam locomotives and sailing ships.

Le Démon des glaces begins on 3 November 1889. Sailing in the Arctic, passengers on a ship called *L'Anjou* discover another ship that has been wrecked on an iceberg. The hero, Jerome Plumier, goes to explore the shipwreck and *L'Anjou* explodes, leaving him stranded. Eventually Plumier is rescued and returns to France. When other ships mysteriously explode in the Arctic Plumier goes back in order to investigate. He sails on a ship called *Le Jules Vernez*. This ship explodes too, and Plumier is thrown overboard. He regains consciousness in a palatial, artificial iceberg built by his uncle, a scientist called Charpontier. Charpontier plans to destroy civilisation with biological warfare, and he is sinking ships because he feels his scientific genius is unrecognised. Plumier joins in with Charpontier's scheme, which is thwarted when Simone Pouffiot attacks the iceberg stronghold, forcing them to flee.

Verne's influence over *Le Démon des glaces* is easy to see. Tardi's title echoes Verne's *Sphinx des glaces*, another story about a ship wrecked on an iceberg; the name Jules Vernez recalls both Jules Verne and also, as Thierry Groensteen points out, the marine painter Joseph Vernet (1714–1789).[5] Charpontier is an eccentric genius with a grudge against humanity, who constructs a luxurious, submarine dwelling; he resembles Verne's Capitaine Nemo, who built the Nautilus in *Vingt mille lieues sous les mers*.

Despite these similarities, Verne and Tardi differ, as *Le Démon des glaces* has no virtuous heroes. Plumier seems brave and generous at the start, but he enthusiastically joins Charpontier's murderous project. Pouffiot opposes villainy, but she only wants to defeat Charpontier so that she will be 'reçue à l'Elysée' (*Démon des glaces*, n. pag).

Unlike Verne, Tardi ends on a note of irony:

En somme, les méchants triomphent. Mais soyons rassurés, de tels individus n'existent pas, n'existeront jamais et de semblables inventions sont irréalisables. De plus l'homme a à cœur de mettre ses connaissances et la science au service du bien. Bien entendu il ne saurait les employer à des fins destructrices.

The moral of the story cannot be taken literally: the twentieth century saw bio-terrorism on a scale which Verne never imagined.

In *Le Démon des glaces*, 'La Torpédo rouge sang' and 'Un Cheval en hiver', an unsettling discrepancy between narrative fiction and historical fact produces irony. 'Un Cheval en hiver' asks us to believe that Napoleon's soldiers died because of fatalism associated with a horse; 'La Torpédo rouge sang' eerily implies that World War I was started by an unlucky car; *Le Démon des glaces* has a reassuring moral conclusion which does not correspond to the truth. In each of these three strips Tardi is working within the French-speaking tradition, established by Touchatout and continued by Goscinny/Uderzo: the artist replaces European history with his own, fabricated version of events. However, Tardi's vision of the past is marked by dark, disconcerting irony rather than boisterous humour.

World War I and 'la question du réel'

Tardi first heard about World War I from his grandmother, and her stories told of a conflict in which nightmares meet everyday reality. When I interviewed Tardi, he recalled,

> C'était mon premier cauchemar d'enfant. Ma grand-mère m'en faisait des récits terrifiants. Mon grand-père était tombé dans un mort en décomposition. Ma grand-mère me racontait les difficultés qu'il avait à se laver les mains et à retrouver de l'eau. Quand on est enfant, c'est une chose horrible. Plus horrible que tous les films d'horreur imaginables … et ça avait un rapport avec la vie quotidienne.

Tardi has used World War I as a setting throughout his career. 'Knock Out', one of Tardi's first World War I strips, is a short, fairly simple story; its precisely drawn pictures of early warplanes recall an American strip, Joe Kubert's and Bob Kanigher's *Enemy Ace*, which Tardi told me that he liked.[6] *Enemy Ace* depicted World War I fighter pilots as gallant knights of the air.

In 'Knock Out', jousting between an American airman (Stacy) and a German (Karl) comes unexpectedly to an abrupt end. Stacy suddenly flies away because he imagines Karl to be a German boxer called Hermann, whom he had fought in the ring and befriended before the war. Yet Karl is really a complete stranger, and he thinks that Stacy has flown away out of cowardice.

'Knock Out', which appeared the same year as Moebius' 'Cauchemar blanc' (1974), is an example of the ninth art's nascent *nouveau réalisme*: like Moebius, Tardi blurs the boundary between the real and the imaginary; in so doing, he asks 'la question du réel'. In 'Knock Out', Stacy's vivid memories of the boxing match are not held exclusively within thought-balloons: instead, they blend with the external reality of the war; panels jump between the boxing match and the dogfight, without explanatory captions; the two parallel dramas eventually converge in the same panel, as the memories flood into Stacy's mind. Meanwhile, Stacy's monologue unites his present with his past, as he makes comments appropriate to both a dogfight and a boxing ring, eg: 'Il va revenir à gauche, mais quand? … A NOUS DEUX'.

In his longer World War I strip, 'La Fleur au fusil', Tardi develops 'la question du réel' further.[7] 'La Fleur au fusil' depicts a 'saloperie de guerre' that is being fought out in a no-man's land somewhere in

Belgium or northern France. Soldiers are at the mercy of enemy fire and bullying officers. Lucien Brindavoine, the soldier hero, is so traumatised that he appeals to both sides to stop the carnage: 'Arrêtez de vous battre! Soldats allemands, soldats français, vos chefs vous envoient à l'abattoir! Ne leur obéissez pas! Rentrez chez vous!' (p. 52). Unusually for a war comic, Brindavoine's appeal posits a moral equivalence between the opposing sides: both the French and the German officer-class are using the common soldiers as cannon-fodder.

Of course, Brindavoine's appeal goes unheeded; he is caught in the crossfire, losing consciousness. Brindavoine then has a jumble of delirious visions, and Tardi's pictures become gentler and more wholesome-looking, as Brindavoine leaves the war behind (Figure 17). He joins his girlfriend and relives his conscription. Brindavoine then sees France's national symbols stripped of all their glory: in a desolate landscape an ugly statue of Marianne, symbol of the French Republic, stands on a war memorial. Marianne tells Brindavoine to keep fighting because 'la cause est juste' (p. 56). Marianne tells the Gaulish cock, another emblem of French nationhood, to chase Brindavoine. Brindavoine enters a ruined church. The cock attacks Brindavoine and he regains consciousness to find himself inside a church full of Germans, who are also taking shelter. Brindavoine befriends a German, who is shot in the back, unarmed, when French soldiers storm the building.

Brindavoine's World War I is no place for courageous actions and glorious feats of arms. Quite the opposite: war triggers the hero's moral collapse. In 1917 Brindavoine deliberately injures himself to avoid fighting; after the war he is shot by the police, because of an 'affaire de proxénétisme' (p. 50).

The graphic style of 'La Fleur au fusil' is more elaborate than that of 'Knock Out'. Bombed-out buildings and soldiers in accurately drawn World War I uniforms mingle with Brindavoine's delirious fantasies. Colour makes a greater contribution to the narrative, by producing contrasts between the reality of the war and the unreality of Brindavoine's mental images: the sky is a dirty grey during the war scenes; it turns a pleasant green when Brindavoine is with his girl-friend; it then turns an angry red during his surreal confrontation with Marianne.

Tardi produced a large number of other World War I comics, many of which also raise 'la question du réel'. One of the most harrowing is *C'était la Guerre des tranchées*, which takes well-

Figure 17. Brindavoine's visions, extract from 'La Fleur au fusil' by Tardi
© Casterman SA

researched documentation even further than Hergé by including a lengthy bibliography.[8] *C'était la Guerre des tranchées* again takes place in a war-torn Franco-Belgian no-man's land that is strung with barbed wire. As one soldier comments, 'C'était un des premiers jours de la guerre, du côté de la Belgique, peut-être même était-ce en Belgique' (p. 56). As in *Les Aventures de Tintin*, albeit in a totally different context, geographical differences between Belgium and France are played down. Tardi's French, Belgian and German soldiers, drawn with thick, heavy lines, are brothers in misfortune. The war sets neighbour against neighbour, but everybody is fighting for a cause that they neither understand nor care about. Soldiers die ingloriously, blown to pieces, caught on barbed wire, screaming for their mothers. The horror of the trenches contrasts with the militaristic propaganda of the day, which Tardi ridicules by quoting genuine examples, such as '"Il était temps que vînt la guerre pour ressusciter, en France, le sens de l'idéal et du divin", Général Rebillot, *Libre parole*, 13 December 1914' (p. 31).

   C'était la Guerre des tranchées raises 'la question du réel' with grim irony: it highlights discrepancies between the reality presented by official propaganda and the reality that is lived out on the ground. Authenticating their stories with their name, rank and regimental number, the men tell of a war that is turning them into brutes, cowards and madmen. One soldier remembers that the Germans used Belgian civilians as human shields; the French shot their way through, because 'nous, nous étions français, il ne s'agissait pas des nôtres' (p. 62). Another soldier loses his mind after shooting an unarmed woman, and he deliberately wanders into enemy fire. Individual tragedies and official versions of events are followed by a chilling statistic, that combines compassion for the victims with a history book's objectivity: 'Si tous les morts français défilaient en rangs par quatre pour le 14 juillet, il ne faudrait pas moins de 6 jours et 5 nuits avant que le dernier ne nous montre sa face livide' (p. 112).

   'La Fleur au fusil' and *C'était la Guerre des tranchées* are highly unusual war comics. The very few American artists who dealt with the Great War, such as Kubert, mostly drew strips which tended towards romanticism, not towards 'la question du réel'. The reasons for American romanticism about World War I are evident: the USA was far removed from the battlefields; it lost relatively few men (114,097 compared to France's 1,358,000), and it joined the fray late (6 April 1917).[9] To many Americans, World War I was a distant, exciting conflict, whose moral underpinnings were perfectly clear: 'America clearly represented all that was good, and the quest was to eradicate the Hun from Europe so that the good Europeans ... could be uplifted by American democracy'.[10]

Some strips in Harvey Kurtzman's *Two-Fisted Tales* and *Front-line Combat* are set in World War I and, like Tardi, they refused to romanticise the conflict. Kurtzman's 'Old Soldiers Never Die!', for example, tells the tragic story of an allied soldier, shot by the Germans on Armistice Day.[11] John Severin's and Will Elder's 'Zero Hour' also recalls 'La Fleur au fusil' and *C'était la Guerre des tranchées*: young men are bullied by their officers and traumatised by warfare; as in *C'était la Guerre des tranchées,* one soldier in 'Zero Hour' dies caught on barbed wire; another goes mad and deliberately wanders into enemy fire; a third asks himself 'What kind of a thing was this war where grownup men called for their mommas? ... War! What an ugly name! The ugliest disease we men were cursed with!'[12]

Yet differences with Tardi's war comics remain. Neither Severin, Kurtzman nor Elder see any moral equivalence between the opposing sides. Moreover, in the American war comics visually realistic weapons, uniforms and décor perform a more conventional function: they authenticate the fiction, rather than raising 'la question du réel'. In our interview, Tardi told me that he had read neither 'Old Soldiers Never Die!' nor 'Zero Hour', adding, 'C'est du côté littéraire que je suis allé chercher mes idées'.

Most American war comic artists rapidly forgot about World War I, although the irreducible moral opposition between the 'good' USA and her 'bad' opponents persisted. In the 1950s, for example, US strips depicted enemy soldiers in the Korean war as 'subhuman, monkey-like sadists'.[13] More recently, *The Nam* initially attempted to be balanced, but increasingly it depicted Vietnam as an American crusade against evil.[14] Like Tardi, some Underground artists combined anti-militarism with contempt towards officialdom, but Robert Crumb, Ted Richards and Michael J ignored World War I; instead, they ridiculed the H-bomb, the draft and the Vietnam War with short, satirical pieces.[15]

Tardi's war comics do not fit the pattern for *bandes dessinées* any more than for American comics. Most artists of Tardi's generation showed little interest in the war their grandfathers had fought. Some war comics, like *Les Trois Mousquetaires du Maquis*, told tales of patriotic resistance during World War II, a theme also apparent in post-war French cinema.[16] In the wake of May '68 some anti-militarist *bandes dessinées* emerged, but without a Great War setting. For example the Belgian strip *Sergent Laterreur*, about a bullying army officer, has a colourful, caricatural style.[17]

Tardi's World War I resembles depictions found in early/mid twentieth-century French-language novels rather than those in other war comics. Georges Duhamel suggests that French and German soldiers are united by their suffering; Roland Dorgelès evokes World War I with compassion balanced by harsh realism, and Tardi praised Dorgelès' *Croix de bois* in our interview.[18] But of all those who wrote about World War I, Tardi is closest to Louis-Ferdinand Céline, an author he admired greatly. Tardi called Céline

> L'écrivain qui bouleverse complètement la littérature française du XXe siècle... Céline propose des personnages qui sont foireux, qui, même s'ils ont des choses très simples à faire, ont très peu de chances d'y arriver. Mais moi, j'ai beaucoup plus de sympathie pour ces personnages là ... Je connais beaucoup plus de gens comme ça que de superhéros.[19]

Céline's *Voyage au bout de la nuit* (1932), which Tardi later illustrated, resembles 'La Fleur au fusil' and *C'était la Guerre des tranchées*.[20] It paints a bleak picture of a World War I that is fought out amid darkness and delirium. There are no superheroes here; instead, nightmare collides with everyday reality, just as it had done in Tardi's grandmother's stories. Lonely, futile death replaces camaraderie; effective action is absent, bravery is meaningless, soldiers are victims and/or moral degenerates, buffeted by events and incapable of rational thought. War is not based on an immovable distinction between good and evil. Quite the reverse. Erika Ostrovsky's description of Céline's war fits 'La Fleur au fusil' and *C'était la Guerre des tranchées*: war is 'brutality so great, absurd and grotesque that it brings about an attack of madness, followed by physical and mental collapse'.[21]

The similarity between Céline and Tardi does not stop there: *Voyage au bout de la nuit,* like Tardi's war comics, asks 'la question du réel'. In particular, Céline's hero, Bardamu, has a mysterious, phantom-like double, Robinson. Robinson's inexplicable appearances and disappearances during the story suggest that he may be a figment of Bardamu's imagination.

Of the American novelists who dealt with World War I, Tardi

most resembles Ernest Hemingway in *Farewell to Arms* (1929). Like Tardi, Hemingway questioned war heroism:

> I was always embarrassed by the words sacred, glorious, and sacrifice and the expression in vain ... Abstract words such as glory, honour, courage, or hallow were obscene beside the concrete names of villages, the numbers of roads the names of rivers, the numbers of regiments and the dates.[22]

Yet Hemingway's World War I still has romantic elements: war allows love to blossom for the hero, who has 'a lovely time' while he is in hospital.

War novelists Hemingway, Céline, Dorgelès and Duhamel all toned down gung-ho shoot-outs in order to give prominence to characterisation; they were interested in the war's impact on what went through the hero's mind. Tardi does likewise: his soldiers and airmen, with their vivid memories, dreams and fears, have a psychological depth which is common in war novels, but which is rare in war comics.

The Voice from beyond the Grave

Tardi's *Véritable Histoire du soldat inconnu* asks 'la question du réel' in a different way from his strips discussed above.[23] *La Véritable Histoire du soldat inconnu* is told in past tenses by a dishevelled-looking hero wearing civilian clothes. He wanders through a hallucinatory landscape of grotesque statues, dilapidated monuments, real buildings (e.g. the Passage Pommeraye in Nantes) and ornate, exotic constructions (a floating palace, a pyramid). The hero meets people who apparently recognise him, but he does not recognise them. Everyday objects and situations undergo bizarre, dreamlike metamorphoses: in one picture the hero takes a bath; on the next page he is standing in a lake; then he is in a rowing boat (pp. 3–5). The hero's mood swings arbitrarily between calm and panic, and he complains of a headache.

Understanding what is happening is peculiarly difficult, as the hero's thought is narrated in the first person by contradictory captions. One has the impression that the hero's statements are unreliable. For example, he says, 'Certes, je ne rêvais pas, mais à tout instant j'espérais émerger de ce cauchemar' (p. 15; Figure 18). Since when was a nightmare not a dream?

Figure 18. The novelist/soldier, *La Véritable Histoire du soldat inconnu* by Tardi © Editions Gallimard

The hero realises that he is a writer of pulp fiction, who is being confronted by situations from his own trashy novels. He also recalls that he is writing a story set in World War I, 'dans lequel je m'étais attribué le rôle du personnage central' (p. 15). On the last page he lies in a trench shot in the head, dressed in a World War I soldier's uniform. He declares that he was killed by a head-wound on 10 November 1918 (the eve of the Armistice); he also maintains that he was subsequently buried in the Tomb of the Unknown Soldier at the Arc de Triomphe, Paris: 'On m'inhuma sous l'Arc de Triomphe, rendant ainsi un hommage officiel à ma pitoyable oeuvre romanesque'.

La Véritable Histoire du soldat inconnu raises an unanswerable question: is the hero the Unknown Soldier? We cannot tell. Perhaps his death and burial are yet more imaginary scenes from his novels; but perhaps the hero really is supposed to be the Unknown Soldier. If that is so then he is dead, and his narrating voice is speaking from beyond the grave.

The voice from beyond the grave is a recurring narrative device. In Billy Wilder's *Sunset Boulevard* (1950), a film about an ageing movie star, the narrator recounts the events leading up to his own death. Joe Kubert also used the voice from beyond the grave: in 'Bonhomme Richard', a ghostly sailor, drowned during the American War of Independence, tells how he went down with his ship.[24] As Lecigne and Tamine note, 1950s American horror comics had already used the voice from beyond the grave occasionally: Reed Crandall's 'Carrion Death!' is told by a fugitive from justice, who is eaten alive by vultures in the desert.[25]

I asked Tardi where he had discovered the voice from beyond the grave, but he could not recall. He had never heard of 'Carrion Death!', nor, despite his fondness for Kubert, had he read 'Bonhomme Richard'. Tardi had seen *Sunset Boulevard*, although he said that he had not been consciously inspired by it.

Whatever Tardi's source, he used the voice from beyond the grave differently from Wilder, Kubert and Crandall. *Sunset Boulevard*, 'Bonhomme Richard' and 'Carrion Death!' do not call the narrator's death itself into question: within the context of the story, we are meant to believe that the hero has already died. But readers will never know whether Tardi's soldier-novelist actually died, or whether he merely imagined his own death.

*   *   *

'La Bascule à Charlot' again uses the voice from beyond the grave to ask where the imaginary begins and where reality ends.[26] Tardi told me that 'La Bascule à Charlot' was originally conceived as 'une bande contre la peine de mort', and it puts forward that most powerful argument against the death penalty: the wrong person may be executed. 'Charlot' is an old Parisian euphemism for executioners.

The story is told in the first person by a man called Choumacher. He comes home from World War I, in which he has won some medals, and an old man is waiting for him. Choumacher feels ill at ease and goes out drinking. A woman seduces him in a bar and they go back to her flat. Following what Choumacher calls 'un grand noir voluptueux et profound', he realises that the woman and a dwarf-like creature she lives with have been murdered. Confused, Choumacher wanders out into Paris, eventually ending up at his own house again. There the old man, the dwarf and a nurse are waiting for him. The old man gratuitously shoots the dwarf and the nurse, and Choumacher wanders out into the street again, confused. He is later arrested for murder, put on trial and guillotined before a jeering crowd.

The story, which inverts the traditional hero's triumphant homecoming, leaves several questions unanswered. How can the dwarf be murdered twice? If Choumacher has already been executed, then who is telling the story? Is Choumacher speaking from beyond the grave? As with *La Véritable Histoire du soldat inconnu*, the provenance of the narrating voice is mysterious.

The secondary characters are mysterious too. The nurse looks like the woman who seduces Choumacher. The old man and the dwarf wear the same clothes as Choumacher. Uncertainty about who those characters are encourages readers to speculate. Is the dwarf Choumacher's child, or Choumacher as a child? Is the old man Choumacher's father, or Choumacher in old age? Are they all just illusory figments of Choumacher's imagination, like Bardamu's Robinson in Céline's *Voyage au bout de la nuit*? Who knows?

'La Bascule à Charlot' is particularly puzzling because Choumacher's thoughts are narrated by captions that cannot be authoritative. Captions usually explain and organise the action, yet in 'La Bascule à Charlot', as in *La Véritable Histoire du soldat inconnu*, the captions are riddled with contradictions. When the old man inexplicably kills the dwarf and the nurse, Choumacher says, 'Cette fois, j'avais tous les éléments en main, c'était clair. J'étais fichu mais heureux, car enfin je comprenais ce qui m'arrivait' (p. 86).

Figure 19. Choumacher's wanderings through Paris, 'La Bascule à Charlot' by Tardi © Futuropolis

However, Choumacher's claim that he understands conflicts with the accompanying picture in which he wanders out into the street again, looking bewildered. On the next page Choumacher contradicts himself once more: 'Je savais à quoi m'en tenir ... N'importe quoi pouvait maintenant m'arriver' (p. 87). Choumacher resembles the Unknown Soldier: what he says is unreliable, and his attempts to rationalise events are unsuccessful.

Choumacher appears to suffer from a mental disorder that is affecting his perceptions and his emotions. Perhaps he is shell-shocked by trench warfare – we cannot tell. All we know is that nothing is explained, and that Choumacher cannot account for his own actions.

Unlike *La Véritable Histoire du soldat inconnu*, 'La Bascule à Charlot' has no luxuriant, baroque imagery. The story is set exclusively in early twentieth-century Paris. A recognisably Parisian backdrop appears to authenticate Choumacher's experience, after the fashion of Hergéen realism. However, for all its realistic detail, Paris is not an objective, external reality. The identifiable décor further undermines Choumacher's reliability, suggesting that he is a victim of delusions and hallucinations.

Choumacher's Paris has narrow, labyrinthine streets that seem to limit his freedom of movement. Buildings with gaping windows block out the sky. Lamp-posts barely shed light, shutting roads off in solid-looking darkness. Interiors have wallpaper covered with black lines like prison bars, dark corridors and ceilings full of oppressive shadows (Figure 19). Choumacher sees dead rats hanging in a shop-window. Is that a premonition of his own miserable, public death?

With 'La Bascule à Charlot', Tardi produced previously unknown effects: Paris and its people are seen as if by a character who cannot make much sense of what he perceives, and who may very well be dead anyway. One must look far beyond comics to find any sort of parallels at all. As Lecigne and Tamine point out, Tardi invented a completely new comic strip narrative in 'La Bascule à Charlot'; nonetheless, Tardi's new narrative form does recall 'la technique flaubertienne', because 'le point de vue du héros détermine le lieu et l'espace de la vision, si bien que le monde est une suite de découvertes visuelles, d'instantanés et d'impressions de réalité ... d'apparences et de simulacres'.[27]

Although it is written in the third person and has no voice from beyond the grave, Flaubert's *Education sentimentale* (1870) shows Paris and its inhabitants through the eyes of a hero who, like

Choumacher, tries unsuccessfully to explain what goes on around him. Jonathan Culler's description of Flaubert fits Tardi. Tardi and Flaubert both break with the tradition, in order to produce works

> whose major techniques are developed to set at a distance and undermine conventional modes of discourse and understanding and whose characters, caught up in this process, do little other than attempt to give meaning to their experience.[28]

Other aspects of Tardi resemble Flaubert: they both question whether the narrating voice is authoritative; they both cast doubt upon the hero's reliability by means of 'sentences which juxtapose and pretend to knit together items which our notions of appropriate human responses and behaviour render incongruous'.[29] The lack of any conclusive comment about Choumacher's guilt or innocence recalls Flaubert's famous maxim: 'la bêtise consiste à vouloir conclure'.

Of course, parallels between Flaubert and Tardi should not be overstretched. Flaubert wrote detailed descriptions of Frédéric's surroundings. Tardi combined words with detailed pictures. Tardi informed me that he had never read *L'Education sentimentale*, adding, 'Peut-être les influences seraient plutôt cinématographiques, plus à chercher dans les films de Fritz Lang, où il y a quelques petits éléments qui font vaciller le réel'. Lang's *Liliom* (1933), which Tardi praised particularly highly, bears some resemblance to 'La Bascule à Charlot'.[30] *Liliom* is set in early twentieth-century Paris. The hero, accused of murder, commits suicide in order to avoid arrest; he then goes to Purgatory, where he relives scenes from his own life. *Liliom*, like 'La Bascule à Charlot', asks to what extent the hero is responsible for what goes on around him, but leaves the question unanswered.

As for the visual aspect of Tardi's work, he drew inspiration from the turn-of-the-century artists Edvard Munch and Félix Vallotton, whom he admired. Like Munch, Tardi generated a feeling of unease by depicting solitary characters surrounded by menacing shadows. Munch's *Virginia Creeper* (1898), in which a disturbed-looking man walks away from an eerie house with blank, staring windows, recalls Choumacher's wanderings through Paris; the anguish is intensified because Munch's man, like Choumacher, is depicted head-on, 'drawing us into the main body of the painting and changing us from passive spectators into active participants'.[31]

The Parisian interiors of 'La Bascule à Charlot' recall those of

Félix Vallotton. Bernard Dorival's description of Vallotton perfectly fits the rooms Choumacher visits:

> Dans certains de ses intérieurs, les murs, l'enfilade des pièces, les objets si présents qu'ils en constituent une menace, l'atmosphère d'un univers clos, tout concourt à créer un climat étouffant, à la limite hostile, où rôde on ne sait quelle menace indéfinie, indéfinissable … Le monde platement bourgeois, en acquiert du coup une dimension insolite, on dirait presque dramatique et qui communique au spectateur son mal-à-l'aise.[32]

Vallotton's rooms, like Choumacher's, have dark corridors and bulky furnishings surrounded by all-engulfing expanses of black, which create a sense of unease. In Vallotton's *Mensonge* (1897), as in 'La Bascule à Charlot', wallpaper with black, vertical lines suggests claustration; in Vallotton's *Visite* (1887), a half-open door reveals another closed door just behind it; the effect is claustrophobic as the doors lead nowhere. Tardi produces a similar effect when Choumacher visits the woman's flat (p. 76).

* * *

Tardi's *bandes dessinées* studied thus far often have a well-documented, visual realism worthy of Hergé; nevertheless, Tardi's speculations about where the imaginary begins and where reality ends make him a *nouveau réaliste*, not a 'classicist' in the Hergéen tradition. Regarding *nouveau réalisme* and 'la question du réel', Tardi's strips fall into two categories. 'Un Cheval en hiver', 'La Torpédo rouge sang', *Le Démon des glaces*, 'Knock Out', 'La Fleur au fusil' and *C'était la Guerre des tranchées* belong to that strand of *nouveau réalisme* exemplified by Moebius' 'Cauchemar blanc': in each story the boundary between the real and the imaginary is blurred, but it is not erased entirely; readers can still tell the one from the other. Napoleon's soldiers did not die because of a jinxed horse ('Un Cheval en hiver'); World War I was not started by a car ('La Torpédo rouge sang'); the moral conclusion is incorrect (*Le Démon des glaces*); Karl is not Hermann ('Knock Out'); Brindavoine's visions exist only in his own mind ('La Fleur au fusil'); wartime propaganda has no basis in reality (*C'etait la Guerre des tranchées*).

La *Véritable Histoire du soldat inconnu* and 'La Bascule à Charlot' go one stage further: the difference between the real and the imaginary disappears entirely. Choumacher and the Unknown

Soldier are chronically unreliable heroes, who may very well be dead. They will never return to reality, because their mental images are indistinguishable from the outside world.

Tardi has published a large number of other strips. Among much else, he used the voice from beyond the grave again in *Griffu*, a detective story which has a later twentieth-century setting.[33] Since the mid-1970s, Tardi's experiments have exerted a huge influence over *bande dessinée* realism post-Hergé, both thematically and stylistically. A selection of artists influenced by Tardi's *nouveau réalisme* follow.

In the Belgian Didier Comès' *Ombre du corbeau*, dreamlike images mingle with World War I battlefields, until readers are barely able to distinguish reality from unreality.[34] Pierre Christin's and Enki Bilal's *Phalanges de l'ordre noir* uses the first-person narrative voice to raise doubts about whether the hero is alive or dead: the last page reads 'je me demande si je ne suis pas mort aussi'.[35] 'La Mort permissionnaire', by Enki Bilal and Dominique Grange, recalls 'La Bascule à Charlot', despite having a more contemporary setting: a mentally confused murderer, who speaks in the first person, wanders the streets aimlessly trying to make sense of what happens.[36] Michel Duveaux's 'Couperets de l'aube' is also strongly reminiscent of 'La Bascule à Charlot', although again with a more contemporary setting: Duveaux's story is a violent *fait divers* about a man who kills his partner and is guillotined; the tall, menacing guillotine resembles the one that executes Choumacher.[37] However, 'Les Couperets de l'aube' and 'Une Mort permissionnaire' lack the mysterious unease of 'La Bascule à Charlot', because readers know for sure that the hero is a murderer. As we have already seen, Jean Teulé's 'Banlieue sud', like 'La Bascule à Charlot', asks the 'question du réel' in the context of whether or not crimes (rape and extortion) were committed.

Other artists, notably Jacques Violeff and Chantal Montellier, are influenced by Tardi's graphic style. Violeff's thriller *Coup sur coup* depicts a late twentieth-century Paris that recalls Tardi's: street-lamps shed no light, and interiors have Vallottonnesque wallpaper with thick, black lines.[38] Montellier's 'Recours en grâce', a monologue by a condemned man, has a guillotine which closely resembles the one that beheads Choumacher; meanwhile, her 'So Fast in their Shiny Metal Cars' has a number of grotesque, dilapidated statues, like those in *La Véritable Histoire du soldat inconnu*.[39]

Adèle Blanc-Sec and *roman feuilleton* Tradition

Les Aventures extraordinaires d'Adèle Blanc-Sec is Tardi's longest running *bande dessinée*.[40] Adèle's adventures link the ninth art to a French literary genre: *romans feuilletons*. *Roman feuilletons* were popularised at the turn of the century by writers who included Gaston Leroux, Ponson du Terrail and Maurice Leblanc.

Adèle's adventures follow several of the *roman feuilleton's* conventions. They have elaborate plots that hinge on *coups de théâtre*: mistaken identities, impenetrable disguises, riddling clues, anonymous letters, hidden trapdoors, underground passages and so on. During her adventures, Adèle meets characters who have stepped straight out of *romans feuilletons*: amateur sleuths, corrupt politicians, incompetent policemen and shadowy members of secret societies.

Before Tardi, *romans feuilletons* had occasionally inspired *bande dessinée* artists: Georges Bourdin and Jacques Blondeau drew remakes of Leblanc's 'gentleman cambrioleur' Arsène Lupin, for example.[41] Unlike Bourdin and Blondeau, Tardi did not simply resurrect an old genre. He brought in elements unknown to *romans feuilletons*, such as monsters. Throughout Adèle's adventures, monsters invade Paris, clashing oddly with the *feuilletonesque* setting.

Adèle's adventures are set in a turn-of-the-century Paris, featuring Haussman architecture, gaslit streets, period interiors, veteran cars, steam locomotives and characters in contemporary costumes; all is drawn with an elegant, well-documented realism reminiscent of Hergé's 'clear line' (Figure 20). Adèle's city is much more obviously Parisian than Tintin's Franco-Belgian home town, but, paradoxically, a Belgian strip was what first inspired Tardi to draw Paris. Tardi told me that he had particularly enjoyed Edgar Jacob's *Blake and Mortimer* thriller *SOS Météores*, which had Parisian scenes drawn in 'clear line'.[42] He added, 'C'est certainement cela qui, chez moi, a déclenché l'envie de faire les choses typiquement parisiennes avec Adèle'. Tardi played up the effects of reality produced by Adèle's Parisian decor: he opened each album with a precise date and time; he also included real, historical events, as Hergé had done.

Adèle herself is an original heroine. Unlike most women in *romans feuilletons*, she is neither a passive victim nor a seductive, mysterious *femme fatale*. Maurice Dubourg noted that in *romans feuilletons*, 'la femme surtout est prisonnière de l'argent, car elle ne travaille pas, n'a ni métier, ni ordinairement grande instruction. Elle

Figure 20. Adèle Blanc-Sec in Paris, extract from *Adèle et la Bête* by Tardi ©
Casterman SA

s'est souvent mariée sans amour, mais pour des considérations de situation ou de fortune.'[43] Adèle, on the other hand, is strong-willed, unmarried and financially independent: she earns her living by writing detective stories.

Adèle also differs from other adventure comic heroines. Professional, financially independent BD heroines started appearing in the early 1970s (one example being the adventurous air hostess, Natacha), but such heroines tended to be pretty, short-skirted problem-solvers and/or righters of wrongs.[44] Unlike Natacha, Adèle is not exceptionally attractive, and she often seems to be overtaken by events. In her first adventure, she even admits that 'je ne contrôle plus la situation' (*Adèle et la Bête*, p. 29). Adèle resembles the male *feuilletonesque* heroes Arsène Lupin and Rocambole: she is likeable, but she is not above using dubious methods (notably kidnapping) to get her own way.

Following *roman feuilleton* convention, *Adèle et la Bête* has an almost absurdly complex plot. The story opens thus: 'Paris, 4 novembre 1911. Au Muséum d'Histoire naturelle du Jardin des Plantes. 23h. 45.' There are dinosaur skeletons and fossils in glass cases. Groensteen suggests that Tardi's gloomy opening scene recalls Victor Hugo's poem 'Le Jardin des Plantes' (1875), which is 'composé de splendeur et d'horreur'.[45]

Suddenly a huge, 136-million-year-old egg splits open and a red pterodactyl comes out. The pterodactyl terrorises Paris, and Inspector Caponi is called in. The pterodactyl has come to life because Boutardieu, an eccentric scientist, willed it to do so, using telepathy. When Boutardieu gets tired he loses control of the monster, and so it becomes dangerous. Meanwhile, Adèle kidnaps Edith Rabatjoie, because she wants Edith's father's flying machine, which looks identical to the pterodactyl. Edith escapes and, using the flying machine, she rescues a convict, who stole money-bags from a wealthy banker called Mignonneau. The first volume ends here.

Adèle's adventure takes the *feuilletonesque* convention of mistaken identities to extremes. Characters often dress up as each other, leaving readers to guess who is who. Adèle looks similar to Edith and they change places, fooling readers. In the final scene, several different characters wear bowler hats and dark glasses, which creates further confusion. There are two pterodactyls (the monster and the flying machine), and nobody is sure which is which.

Volume two, *Le Démon de la Tour Eiffel* (1976), continues the mixture of *roman feuilleton* and monster fantasy. The plot is even more complex, as it consists of four narrative threads: Mignonneau's bags, the secret Pazuzu sect, a murder committed at the theatre, and a series of unexplained disappearances on the Pont Neuf. Put very briefly, Adèle tracks down Mignonneau's bag, and in it she finds a statuette of an Assyrian demon called Pazuzu. Her investigations into the statue's origins lead her to a hidden trapdoor on the Pont Neuf that is being used by the Pazuzu sect; she goes through it and spies on one of their meetings. The sect's members claim that Paris 'pue de suffisance par toutes ses bouches d'égout', and that the city 'tente vainement d'égaler Babylone' (p. 25). *Le Démon de la Tour Eiffel* plays with ideas that preoccupied *fin de siècle* France. Raymond Rudorff notes an upsurge of orientalist sects at the time, as well as the fashionable notion that Paris was a latter-day Babylon; there were also widespread fears that France was in decline, and that 'sinister attempts were being made in secret to destroy the nation's social order and even its civilisation'.[46]

Adèle is caught spying and is overpowered, but Inspector Caponi arrives in the nick of time. He arrests everybody except the actress Clara Benhardt – a reference to the *belle époque* actress Sarah Bernhardt (1844–1923) – who manages to escape. The sect's leader turns out to be Caponi's boss, Chief Superintendent Dugommier.

Le Démon de la Tour Eiffel ends on a note of mockery aimed at the police. Caponi is demoted; Dugommier 'tira toute la gloire de l'arrestation des membres de la secte dont il était lui-même l'instigateur des crimes' (p. 48). *Romans feuilletons* sometimes ended by ironically mocking the police too. In *L'Evasion d'Arsène Lupin*, Arsène escapes from custody by disguising himself; he then cheekily explains his ruse to the authorities, who are far too embarrassed to re-arrest him.[47]

Adèle's Later Adventures

From *Le Savant fou* (1977) onwards, Tardi's parodies of turn-of-the-century popular fiction become increasingly overt. When a mad scientist brings a pithecanthropus back to life on a suitably dark and stormy night, Adèle comments on the hackneyed nature of the scene: 'C'est pour l'ambiance … la nature fait bien les choses … Avez-vous lu Mary Shelley?' (p. 11). Expectations are then humorously overturned because, instead of resembling Frankenstein, the pithecanthropus shyly asks for a cognac and cigar.

Following *roman feuilleton* convention (particularly that of Ponson du Terrail), the narrator intervenes to comment on the action, using the first person plural; but Tardi's interventions, unlike Ponson's, ironically draw attention to the genre's clichés. One night, for example, Adèle foils an attempt on her life by putting a dummy in her bed; this is a very old trick, which had previously been played by Arsène Lupin (*La Comptesse de Cagliostro*, I, p. 146). Tardi's caption inappropriately heaps exaggerated praise on Adèle: 'Dieu soit loué. Adèle est vivante! On remarquera par quel habile subterfuge notre astucieuse héroïne a déjoué son agresseur' (p. 18). Humour also arises from deliberately dreadful puns which would be quite out of place in a *roman feuilleton*. For example: 'Un jour, la vengeance de Pazuzu sera accomplie! Alors tu seras morte Adèle' (p. 46). Phonetically, the last phrase could say 'tu seras mortadelle'.

In the next volume, *Les Momies en folie* (1978), Tardi broke completely with *romans feuilletons*: the story consists chiefly of digressions, loose ends and false trails. A mummy comes back to life; it speaks of Edgar Allan Poe and claims to have been a nuclear physicist in ancient Egypt (pp. 45–46). Ludicrous attempts are made to murder Adèle: a clock-hand falls off a tower, just missing her; a steam locomotive inexplicably derails, almost crushing her (pp. 13–15). Adèle is given a free ticket to sail on *The Titanic*, which is sunk by Plumier and Charpontier (from *Le Démon des glaces*, p. 43). Adèle is finally cornered by her opponents and killed. However, with the mummy's help a scientist manages to preserve her body.

Like 'La Torpédo rouge sang', *Les Momies en folie* ironically suggests that our knowledge of history is wrong: readers are asked to believe that the ancient Egyptians had nuclear physics and that *The Titanic* was sunk deliberately. On the last page there is a harsh return to reality: World War I is declared (p. 48). The sobering reminder of the coming carnage suddenly puts Adèle's preposterous stories in a new light: each one of her adventures brought Europe a little closer to the outbreak of a terrible war. As Tardi said, 'Les histoires que je raconte dans *Adèle Blanc-Sec*, qui se déroulent en 1912, sont d'autant plus absurdes et dérisoires: on se tire dessus pour de sombres intrigues de sectes, de monstres et de momies, alors que deux ans plus tard, on va sombrer dans la boucherie'.[48]

Le Secret de la salamandre (1981) recalls the grim irony of *C'était la Guerre de tranchées*. The opening depicts soldiers returning home from the war: 'Ils gagnèrent des médailles et des morceaux de ferraille qui vinrent se ficher profondément dans leur chair, entraînant la mort ... Oui, mais une mort glorieuse pour la France' (p. 4). Much of the album consists of a flashback to the trenches. Brindavoine from 'La Fleur au fusil' reappears. Brindavoine, who found a statuette of Pazuzu in the trenches, is now a broken alcoholic. A series of clues connected with Pazuzu lead him to Adèle. He restores her to life in a scene that recalls the Sleeping Beauty fairytale (p. 47).

Adèle slept through a war that swept away the last vestiges of the *belle époque* and the world she wakes up to has changed. The villains are no longer members of esoteric, *fin de siècle* cults: rather, they are captains of industry and religious leaders, who are bent on world domination. At their meeting in New York, which is held beneath the American flag, the arch-villain makes his project clear:

> Il nous appartient d'organiser tel ou tel conflit pour assurer l'économie d'un pays et par là même de nous enrichir ... Il nous faudra créer une doctrine autoritaire qui planifiera les consciences, rendant toute opposition impossible et de nouveaux partis politiques, de manière à tenir en main les syndicats et la classe ouvrière (p. 42).

The following adventure, *Le Noyé à deux têtes* (1985), paints a pessimistic picture of a Europe in which World War I merely prepared the way for World War II. As one character says, 'Le Français déteste l'Allemand qui déteste l'Italien qui déteste l'Anglais qui nous haït ... Tous ces pays minuscules ... haïneux, prêts à s'étriper de nouveau à la première occasion! C'est ça l'Europe!' (p. 17). Adèle broods upon the future: 'J'ai peur pour ce siècle, pour la petite créature rose, irrémédiablement bornée, qui évolue à la surface du globe' (p. 12).

A better world has not emerged from the conflict, and France is a racist police state. One policeman involved in a murder prays for forgiveness with the words, 'L'homme que j'ai tué n'était qu'un nègre' (p. 8). Another beats Brindavoine up, because 'vous connaissez cette fille qui écrit des romans qui ridiculisent la police' (p. 35). Adèle is now completely submerged by events. She says, 'On s'ingénie à me faire perdre mon temps! Ne comptez pas sur moi pour tirer une quelconque "morale" à cette histoire' (p. 48).

Adèle's later adventures are funnier again. In *Tous les Monstres*

(1994), tentacled monstrosities sprout up all over Paris; characters cannot stop imagining monsters, some of which are borrowed from other *bandes dessinées*. One monster resembles the giant hand (or 'Manu Manu') from the humorous strip *Philémon* (p. 45),[49] another parodies the *bande dessinée* artist Marcel Gotlib (p. 38). Adèle spends much of the time saying that she wants to go to bed.

In *Les Aventures extraordinaires d'Adèle Blanc-Sec*, Tardi played with French-speakers' shared expectations, which popular novels had built up for almost a century. *Romans feuilletons*, however, were not a source of inspiration for American cartoonists, and US comics about monsters and detectives did not have Parisian settings. On the opposite side of the Atlantic, monsters stayed inside science fiction and horror comics, while villains were chased through (sometimes futuristic) American cities.

Tardi reinvented *romans feuilletons*. In Adèle's early adventures he brought in a self-conscious irony that later turned into parody. He introduced a new-style heroine and, as her story developed, he combined *roman feuilleton* clichés with acerbic comments about World War I, inter-war Europe and the growing might of the USA.

Les Aventures extraordinaires d'Adèle Blanc-Sec had a durable influence over the ninth art. As we shall see in Chapter 7, the 1980s witnessed a resurgence of historical dramas in which heroes and heroines, like Adèle, are frequently overtaken by events. Moreover, following Adèle's success, a number of other artists rediscovered *feuilletonesque* characters and period settings. Pierre Wininger's *Pyramide oubliée* is a mystery story, rich in historical detail, and set in early twentieth-century Paris, but Wininger's black-and-white graphic style is less elaborate than Tardi's. Annie Goetzinger's *Aurore,* about the life of novelist George Sand (1804–1876), has period settings similar to Tardi's, although her graphic style is also simpler. Chantal Montellier's *Fosse aux serpents*, a mystery based around the sculptor Auguste Rodin (1840–1917), evokes the Paris of yesteryear in a graphic style reminiscent of Tardi. Pierre Guilmard's *Java des Gaspards* has *feuilletonesque* settings and costumes, although the graphic style is more caricatural than Tardi's.[50]

The influence of Franco-Belgian history and culture runs deep in Tardi: his grandmother's stories about World War I inspired him with a lifelong passion for the subject. Tardi's World War I comics themselves call directly upon Franco-Belgian fellow-feelings: Tardi evokes the shared memories of two close neighbours, who have both been bloody theatres of war within living memory, and who are still coming to terms with their collective past. Tardi does not romanticise armed conflict. That is because he and his readers have learnt a harsh, historical lesson: war is not something noble that takes place in comfortably far-off lands.

Although Tardi breaks new ground, he simultaneously perpetuates and renews specifically Franco-Belgian cultural traditions. Building on 'clear line', Tardi opened up new directions for post-Hergéen realism: many of Tardi's carefully documented settings employ the voice from beyond the grave and/or ask 'la question du réel'; others generate irony and parody. Also, Tardi's innovations gave the ninth art a literary dimension comparable to French World War I novelists, *feuilletonistes*, Céline, Verne and (however coincidentally) Flaubert; Tardi's use of literary devices (e.g. characterisation and irony) moved the ninth art still further away from most US war comics and from superheroes. Finally, like Giraud, Tardi closed the gaps between comic strips and the more traditional art forms such as novels and painting; like Giraud, Tardi thus encouraged French-speakers to regard *bandes dessinées* as 'art'.

Tardi not only bridges the gap between mass culture and 'art', he also perfectly illustrates the folkloric process, which reworks the old into the new. Given the unbreakable bond between folklore and cultural identity, Tardi's place among the masters of the ninth art remains assured.

CHAPTER SIX

Laughing Together:
Humour and Shared Identity

Sending Up the Culture with Marcel Gotlib

One of the ninth art's great strengths is its ability to make French and Belgian people laugh together; as noted in Part I above, the humorous *bande dessinée* 'classics' played a prominent role in building cultural bridges between Belgium and France. This chapter examines later developments in *bande dessinée* gag humour, from the 1960s up to the 1980s. We shall look at three artists: Marcel Gotlib and Claire Bretécher (who both published with *Pilote*), and Régis Franc. Gotlib, Bretécher and Franc all satisfied the French-speaking public's shared appetite for laughter, by drawing gags inspired by French and Belgian history, culture and current affairs; they thus strengthened Franco-Belgian folklore in humorous counterpoint to Tardi.

Marcel Gotlib (b. 1934) studied at l'Ecole des Arts Appliqués (Paris); he first became known with the strip *Gai-Luron*, which was about a phlegmatic, anthropomorphic dog of the same name (Figure 21).[1] Gotlib frequently praised the American comic *Mad*, whose influence shows up very clearly in *Gai-Luron*.[2] Gotlib's light-hearted, caricatural style resembled *Mad* and, like *Mad*, Gai-Luron humorously imitated famous American comic strip heroes in short gags. Examples include Zorro ('Gai-Lorro', p. 126), Tarzan ('Gai-Lurzan', pp. 136–37), and Prince Valiant ('Prince Gai-Luron', pp. 156–57).

As an aspiring young French artist in the 1960s, Gotlib also lampooned 'classical' Belgian BD culture. Gotlib's title 'Gai-Luron rit de se voir si beau en ce Miroir' (pp. 113–62) echoes Bianca Castafiore's 'Jewel Song': 'Ah! Je ris de me voir si belle en ce miroir' (*Les Bijoux de la Castafiore*, p. 49). In 'Lotus et bouche cousue', Gotlib's allusion to Hergé is less direct (p. 204): Gotlib deforms the expression 'motus et bouche cousue' (or 'mum's the word') in the manner of the Dupondts, who say 'botus et mouche cousue' (*Le Temple du Soleil*, p. 5, *L'Affaire Tournesol*, p. 13 and *Coke en stock*, p. 10).

Figure 21. Photograph of Marcel Gotlib, taken by the author in Paris, 30 October 2001

'Les Belles Histories de l'Onc' Jujube' combines a send-up of *Les Belles Histoires de l'Oncle Paul* with an oblique reference to a French nursery rhyme (p. 90). The first line, 'il était une fois … une humble bergère qui gardait ses blancs moutons' recalls a children's song:

Il était une bergère,
Et ron, ron, ron, petit patapon,
Il était une bergère
Qui gardait ses moutons.[3]

In Gotlib's version a fox steals one of the little girl's sheep, and Oncle Jujube draws a singularly unfitting moral conclusion: 'L'intelligence et la ruse finissent toujours par triompher de la force brutale'.

Like *Mad*, *Gai-Luron* humorously referenced well-known charac-ters from outside comics. 'Les Raisins de la colique' has a title that echoes John Steinbeck's *Grapes of Wrath* (1939) or *Les Raisins de la colère*, as it is known in French; however, 'Les Raisins de la colique' is primarily a simple skit on La Fontaine's well-known fable about sour grapes, 'Le Renard et les raisins'. Gotlib's fox reaches the grapes but, as they are sour, eating them gives him a stomach ache (p. 22).[4] Other gags in *Gai-Luron* drew upon everyday childhood activities, particularly classroom situations. In 'Au Nom de tous les chiens' Gai-Luron goes to school, only to find that Lavisse's textbook phrase, 'nos ancêtres les Gaulois', is written up on the blackboard (p. 128).

Unlike *Mad*, *Gai-Luron* mostly poked innocent fun at stories, songs and situations recognised specifically by French-speaking children. The result was akin to a private in-joke between the hero and his youthful readers, which gave rise to an agreeable feeling of complicity: Gai-Luron lived in the same world as his readers and spoke directly to them. The dog and his public were in cahoots. The feeling of complicity was made stronger because, like characters from *Mad*, Gai-Luron addressed his readers as friends, calling them 'chers lecteurs', 'les copains' and so on. A sense of complicity with his public remained indispensable to Gotlib's humour throughout his career; indeed, it is an essential part of the fun. Readers must come to Gotlib's jokes able to recognise what he is sending up, otherwise, despite the undeniable pictorial humour, they are out of the loop. As Gotlib himself said, 'Tout le monde ne comprend pas forcément l'humour. Il exige ... une espèce de complicité avec les gens qui le reçoivent.'[5]

In 1965 Gotlib began working for Goscinny and Uderzo at *Pilote*. One of his first pieces for *Pilote* was a spoof history lesson, titled 'Le Clou à travers l'histoire'.[6] 'Le Clou à travers l'histoire' mines a similar vein to *Les Aventures d'Astérix* and Touchatout's *Histoire de France tintamarresque*: the humorist replaces historical fact with a funny, invented version of what happened. 'Le Clou à travers l'histoire' recounts European history back to Antiquity, maintaining that the humble nail had a decisive influence over the course of events. According to Gotlib, Archimedes trod on a nail in his bath, which prompted his famous cry 'eureka'; a nail tore a king's robe in 1337, sparking a war between King Philip VI of France and King Edward III of England; a workman removed a nail from the Tower of Pisa causing it to lean over; a horseshoe with a loose nail prevented Maréchal de Grouchy's reinforcements from reaching Napoleon at the Battle of Waterloo, and so on. 'Le Clou à travers l'histoire' is aimed less obviously at young children than Gai-Luron's school jokes: Gotlib is now assuming that his readers have a wider knowledge of history than before.

The next series for which Gotlib took sole responsibility was *Rubrique à brac*.[7] Suitably enough for a strip launched in Paris in May 1968, *Rubrique à brac* was more iconoclastic than *Gai-Luron*. In *Rubrique à brac* the importance of Gotlib's written texts increased; sometimes the white spaces between panels were crammed full of tiny letters. *Rubrique à brac* had no heroes who appeared every week, but it did have a number of frequently recurring characters. One is the English physicist Isaac Newton (1642–1727). Newton discovered the law of gravity by watching an apple fall from a tree. Gotlib made Newton ludicrous by exaggerating the anecdotal aspect of this discovery: the apple falls onto Newton's head and, over the weeks, a number of other objects also fall onto the unfortunate physicist.

Classroom situations still raised laughs, although the topics dealt with are more varied than before. 'Ah, si on l'avait aidé', which combines a history lesson with cod-psychology, is a joke at Napoleon's expense (*Rubrique à brac*, II, p. 12). Gotlib describes Napoleon's upbringing and schooldays, claiming that he was nagged by his mother, unpopular at school and unsuccessful with girls. Napoleon grew up bearing a grudge against humanity and so he took his revenge by becoming emperor. The gag concludes 'Napoleon? Rien d'autre qu'un petit mal-aimé. Voilà ce que je dis.'

'Der Rubrica of the Bracofsky' is a geography lesson about France for foreigners, which exaggerates the stereotypical views of the country. 'Der Rubrica of the Bracofsky' contains all of the gallic clichés about romance, accordions, pétanques, berets and cuisine (*Rubrique à brac*, II, pp. 38–39). The text is an invented language that contains a bewildering mix of French, English, German, Italian, Spanish and Russian:

> Der France is el beau pays, mit eine climax tempérofsky, baigné of the 3 mers, ein ocean, and chains del mountains … Dans la rue, el Frenchman rencontre the woman. Esta la occazione della ge-montren el galanteria frantcheze reputovitch on todo the el mondo.

In *Rubrique à brac* Gotlib also sent up various forms of Francophone popular culture, both ancient and modern, but he was progressing beyond *Gai-Luron's* imitative parody. Charles Perrault's folktale 'Le Petit Poucet' (1697), for example, provides the basis for Gotlib's gag 'Continuons sur la Lancée' (*Rubrique à brac*, II, pp. 60–61).[8] Like Perrault, Gotlib tells of a poor couple who, in time of famine, abandon their numerous children in the forest; Petit Poucet, the youngest child, finds his way back by marking the homeward route with stones. In Perrault's original story the wretched parents abandon their children again, but Petit Poucet marks the homeward route with breadcrumbs, which are eaten by birds. However, Perrault's story ends happily because, after numerous adventures, Petit Poucet wins the king's favour and returns home in triumph.

Gotlib turned Perrault's story upside down: the parents are the victims and Petit Poucet is a little tyrant. Petit Poucet's parents try seven times to abandon him, and their attempts grow increasingly desperate. They make their getaway on a motorbike and in a helicopter, but each time Petit Poucet finds his way back home. He leaves a trail of birds, a trail of bolts and a trail of anvils. The seventh time, his exasperated parents are waiting for him with a cannon. Gotlib's inappropriately happy end rounds the joke off with the French fairytale equivalent of 'they lived happily ever after': 'Mais comme la bonté et l'amour finissent toujours par triompher, ils furent heureux et eurent beaucoup d'enfants'.

Gotlib's 'Passeur malhonnête' is a much shorter, very tightly written medieval spoof, again based on Perrault (*Rubrique à brac*, II, p. 73; Perrault, pp. 47–59). This gag combines Perrault's 'Barbe bleue' with old-fashioned French and contemporary slang to give a punning punchline. 'Le Passeur malhonnête' begins in Bluebeard's castle, where Bluebeard's long-suffering wife waits for deliverance. She asks her sister, Anne, whether their brothers are coming to the rescue. Echoing Anne in Perrault's tale, Gotlib's Anne replies, 'Je vois bien la route qui poudroie, l'herbe qui verdoie'. Gotlib's Anne cannot see much because she is short-sighted, and so she adds, 'Mais c'est tout ce que je voyois, parce que j'ai la vue qui baissoit'. Here Gotlib imitates old-fashioned French spelling by changing the 'a' to 'o' in the imperfect verb ending.

Gotlib's Soeur Anne leaves Bluebeard's castle to seek help. She crosses a river, where a cheating ferryman makes her pay to dis-embark as well as to embark. The punchline is a moral: 'Soeur Anne aux deux berges raque'. 'Raquer' is a slang-word meaning to 'cough up'; phonetically, the moral also says 'Cyrano de Bergerac', in reference to Edmond Rostand's comedy (1897). When I interviewed Gotlib, he told me that he had based 'Le Passeur malhonnête', with its absurdly punning moral, on *fables express* by the French humorous writer Alphonse Allais (1854–1905).[9]

Gotlib also drew inspiration from more contemporary aspects of popular culture. He continued taking off comic strip artists, using an ever wider range of graphic styles. 'Ingratitude. La Double Vie de Clark Kent' knocks Superman off his pedestal: Superman triumphs yet again, only to be reprimanded for skipping work at *The Daily Planet* (*Rubrique à brac*, II, pp. 14–15). Gotlib also parodied his fellow artists at *Pilote*. 'Terra me voilà' lampoons Philippe Druillet's *Lone Sloane* by exaggerating Druillet's detailed, grandiose panels (*Rubrique à brac*, IV, pp. 78–80). In 'La Statue qui rend fou', Gotlib even parodied himself (*Rubrique à brac*, II, pp. 86–87). 'La Statue qui rend fou' starts off as a mysterious Indian legend about a statue that causes insanity. In the second line of panels, Gotlib's graphic style gradually becomes ever more disorganised, and words lose their meaning. On the next page, Superman crawls on all fours beneath a nonsensical text: 'Quand vient la mousson le tigre se met en chasse. On le surnomme mangeur de moteurs.' The breakdown in meaning is followed by a note that reads, 'A la suite d'un événement encore inexpliqué, Gotlib se trouve dans l'obligation de cesser toute activité'. The implication is that the statue has driven Gotlib mad too.

In *Rubrique à brac* Gotlib also made jokes about films, including more adult-oriented titles such as François Truffaut's *Enfant sauvage* (1969). Truffaut's film is based on a real event that occurred in Aveyron in 1800. A boy named Victor, who had never learned how to speak, was found living like a wild animal in the forest. Jean-Marie Gaspard Itard (1774–1858), a scholar, attempted to educate Victor and to bring him into normal human society.[10] In Gotlib's gag 'Rééducation', Itard tries to assess Victor's ability to laugh by putting on a false nose and pulling silly faces (*Rubrique à brac*, III, pp. 20–23). Victor is not amused, and yet he bursts out laughing when he sees Itard quietly reading in an armchair. 'Rééducation' ends on a wry note of irony: Victor, now totally gormless, 'a enfin repris sa place dans les rangs des hommes. Je lui ai trouvé un emploi intéressant comme clerc, chez un notaire de mes amis.'

The detective story is another popular, adult-oriented form parodied in *Rubrique à brac*. The series contains several gags about Inspecteur Bougret, whose name combines two fictitious policemen, Bourrel and Maigret. The French Inspecteur Bourrel appeared in the long-running TV whodunnit *Les Cinq Dernières Minutes* (first screened in January 1958); the detective Maigret was invented by the

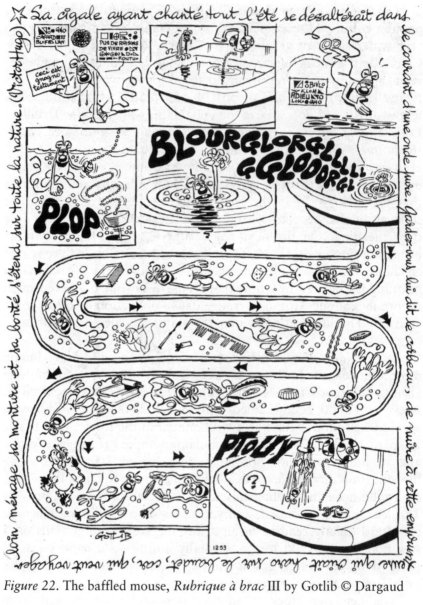

Figure 22. The baffled mouse, *Rubrique à brac* III by Gotlib © Dargaud

Belgian author Georges Simenon (1932). Bougret uses a phrase popularised by Bourrel, 'bon sang, mais c'est bien sûr!', as well as Sherlock Holmes' famous expression 'élémentaire'.

Bougret's stories always repeat the same pattern: a dead body is discovered, and so he investigates. The murderer's identity is obvious, but Bougret solves the case in a ridiculously irrelevant way. Sometimes, Gotlib mixed Bougret's detective stories with parodies of other forms. His title 'Le Commissaire est bon enfant' echoes the nursery rhyme 'Cadet-Rousselle est bon enfant' (*Rubrique à brac*, III, pp. 40–42; *Comptines, chansons et chansonnettes*, p. 52).

As well as parodying popular culture, Gotlib made fun of the French literary classics. 'Entr'acte' works in Victor Hugo, Jean Racine and La Fontaine, as well as a proverb (*Rubrique à brac*, III, p. 48). The accompanying pictures show a cartoon mouse who goes down a plughole, through a plumbing system and out of a tap (Figure 22). The text, which circles round the outside of the page, begins thus: 'La cigale ayant chanté tout l'été se désaltérait dans le courant d'une onde pure'. The first seven words of this sentence quote La Fontaine's fable 'La Cigale et la fourmi' (lines 1–2, p. 50); the rest quotes 'Le Loup et l'agneau' (lines 3–4, p. 59). Put together these quotations mean nothing. La Fontaine's wise words lack significance once they are denied a context; they are robbed of their exemplary status, becoming preposterous.

As the text continues its way round the page, Gotlib's absurdity scales greater heights. His caption 'cette emprunteuse qui criait haro sur le baudet' combines La Fontaine's 'Cigale et la fourmi' ('dit-elle à cette emprunteuse', line 18, p. 50) with 'Les Animaux malades de la peste' ('A ces mots on cria haro sur le baudet', line 55, p. 181). Gotlib's caption breaks off with the words 'qui veut voyager loin ménage sa monture et sa bonté s'étend sur toute la nature (Victor Hugo)'. The first half of this sentence quotes a popular French proverb; the second half is not actually a quotation from Hugo at all, but from Jean Racine's play *Athalie* (1690).[11] The original text is a speech by Joas (Act II scene VII), which reads

> Aux petits des oiseaux il donne leur pâture,
> Et sa bonté s'étend sur toute la nature.

The inevitable question arises: why did Gotlib do it? Either he misattributed the quotation deliberately in order to make his readers laugh, on the assumption that they knew the source, or he made a

genuine error. When I asked Gotlib whether his mistake was deliber-
ate, he replied,

> Pas du tout. C'est un pur hasard. Ce n'est même pas que je l'ai fait
> exprès, je m'en foutais! Le mélange de ces deux vers, le proverbe et
> l'autre que je viens d'apprendre est de Racine, ces deux choses-là,
> rimaient et n'avaient aucun rapport. Voilà pourquoi j'ai mis ça. Puis
> il me restait un petit blanc à remplir et j'ai mis 'Victor Hugo'. J'ai
> mis n'importe quoi. C'est absurde. Il ne faut pas essayer de com-
> prendre ça!

Gotlib wrote Hugo's name simply to use up space, but his humour is
no less effective for all that: after such a barrage of nonsense readers
are completely baffled and disoriented, just like the mouse going
down the plughole.

'Souvenirs verdâtres' is another literary joke, which combines the
fifteenth-century French poet François Villon with a subtle comment
about racism (*Rubrique à brac*, III, pp. 38–39). 'Souvenirs verdâtres'
is ostensibly a lament for the idyllic public spaces of yore, and it has
the recurring refrain 'où sont les squares d'antan?' Gotlib is
paraphrasing Villon's 'Ballade des dames du temps jadis', an elegy for
the beautiful women of yesteryear, which has the refrain 'où sont les
neiges d'anten? [sic]'.[12] In 'Souvenirs verdâtres', Gotlib's pictures
contradict the elegiac tone. A French boy plays with an African boy
in the square; the French boy's mother then tells him to wash his
hands and come and get something to eat. While she is preparing her
son's snack he plays with a dog, but she does not make him wash his
hands again, so he eats it with dirty hands. The mother's actions
suggest that she sees the African as being dirtier than the dog.

As Gotlib matured, some of his gags reflected wistfully upon the
ageing process and upon childhood's lost innocence. In 'Chanson
rose chanson mauve', for instance, Gotlib takes readers into his
confidence, telling them about his own past and his private life. As a
boy, he thought the world was a place full of poetry and wonder;
growing up and acquiring knowledge robbed the world of its magic
because he learnt, for example, that 'les gros nuages blancs ne sont
plus rien, sinon de la vulgaire eau en suspension dans l'air' (*Rubrique
à brac*, I, pp. 16–17).

Occasionally, *Rubrique à brac* draws upon international problems. 'Désamorçage' opens with a picture of a starving African child,
which is accompanied by a statement taking up a whole panel:
'Chaque jour, des centaines d'enfants meurent de faim'. Newsreaders

then present the famine on TV, experts analyse it, pop stars organise a charity concert, jokes even circulate about the famine. The original text about starving children is repeated eight times, getting smaller and smaller until it is almost invisible. Gotlib is implying that the dreadful truth about children starving is trivialised by media person-alities who are pushing self-seeking agendas, and that the public cares little anyway (*Rubrique à brac*, IV, pp. 64–65).

Gotlib left *Pilote* in 1972. After working at *L'Echo des savanes* with Bretécher and others, he founded his own humorous magazine, *Fluide glaciale,* in 1975. By now, Gotlib's humour was becoming more sexual and scatological; among much else, *Fluide glaciale* carried an eroticised version of *Gai-Luron*.[13] 'God's Club' is a good example of Gotlib's work from the mid-1970s.[14] Here Gotlib ridicules Jehovah, Christ, Buddha, Allah, Krishna and Wotan by showing them getting drunk, squabbling, telling smutty jokes and reading pornography. Portraying Gods as men behaving badly blasphemously inverts the Judeo-Christian tradition, which claims that man was made in God's image: 'So God created man in his own image; in the image of God he created them' (Gen. 1.27).

Gotlib's use of sex as a weapon against religion and established morality places him within a long-standing French-speaking tradition that goes back to the Marquis de Sade (1740–1814). Dalia Judowitz's comment on Sade fits 'God's Club': 'Through his exhaustive exposi-tion of sexuality Sade succeeds in expanding its meaning ... to challenge all moral referents'.[15] Mme Delbène's speech from de Sade's *Histoire de Juliette* (1797) recalls 'God's Club': Delbène ridicules God, calling him an anthropomorphic 'polisson' (or 'smutty old devil'), who was created by men, being 'un pur effet de l'embrasement de leur cerveau'.[16]

In the United States too, Underground artists such as Robert Crumb were using sexuality to attack established religion and morality during the late 1960s and the 1970s.[17] As noted in Chapter 4, the Underground scathingly caricatured American society and its problems. Gotlib, however, drew inspiration chiefly, though not exclusively, from his native, French-speaking cultural tradition. Gotlib's later jokes about Francophone culture are in a scabrous vein. His 'J'ai le feu' lampoons the Belgian Symbolist poet Emile Verhaeren (1855–1916) by using the short, free-rhyming lines of irregular length that characterised some of Verhaeren's work:

J'ai le feu
Au cul
Quand je pète
Ca sent le brûlé
Au feu
Les pompiers (*Rhââ lovely*, II, p. 16).

Fluide glaciale also published *Superdupont,* which Gotlib drew in collaboration with Jacques Lob, Jean Solé and Alexis (Dominique Vallet). Superdupont, the *bande dessinée*'s only superhero, is the scourge of anyone who would presume to challenge French culture: Superdupont stops a teenager listening to English punk rock, and converts him to traditional French folk songs; he also saves the nation's camembert.[18] *Superdupont* makes light of French fears about loss of identity to the dreaded 'Anglo-Saxons', as well as parodying America's superheroes: Superdupont always saves the day, but his victories are vain and trivial. Although Gotlib drew fewer BDs in the 1980s and 1990s, he is still widely read, and he was awarded the Grand Prix at Angoulême in 1991.

Gotlib sends up everything that shaped his educational background and identity as a Frenchman. Sadoul commented,

> Gotlib se moque des choses qu'il aime et qui l'ont formé. Dans le contexte d'une tentative d'accéder à son autonomie, il devait en premier lieu rompre avec les bribes d'enfance accrochées à ses basques, donc les démolir. Si l'on y regarde bien, cette histoire est d'ailleurs bâtie en l'exorcisme de l'enfance.[19]

As Sadoul says, Gotlib humorously charts the progress from childhood to adulthood. Two further points could be added: first, Gotlib laughs at the process of growing up in a specifically Francophone culture; and secondly, he always does so in complicity with his French-speaking readers. Thus, Gotlib gives humorous *bandes dessinées* an identity of their own, distinct from that of American comics.

Gai-Luron was playful, protected and innocent. Humour mostly revolved around simple in-jokes about schooldays, nursery rhymes, and comic strips that were easily recognised by French-speaking children. In *Rubrique à brac,* experience of the wider world beyond school and childhood is needed: humour is aimed at older readers, and it relies less on simple mimicking. Numerous references to French history, film and literature are made, which little children could not necessarily be expected to recognise. Beneath Gotlib's indefatigable spoofing there lurks a sense that youth is slipping away, nostalgia for lost innocence, and growing concern about national and international problems.

Gotlib's work with *Fluide glaciale* combines cynical, abrasive humour with sexually explicit drawings and almost unremitting scatology. Some readers will find it offensive, and it is suitable for adults only.

Claire Bretécher: A Human Comedy

Claire Bretécher (b.1940) is the *bande dessinée*'s best-known female artist, and she was awarded the Grand Prix at Angoulême in 1984. Bretécher is French but, during the 1960s, she occasionally published in the Belgian magazines *Le Journal de Tintin* and *Le Journal de Spirou*.[20] In the late 1960s Bretécher rose to prominence at *Pilote* with *Céllulite*, which was drawn in a style similar to Brant Parker's *Wizard of Id*.[21] Both strips had a mock-medieval setting with castles, forests and knights drawn in simple, casual-looking lines. Like Parker, Bretécher undermined fairytale romanticism: Céllulite is a bad-tempered, unmarriable harridan, not a beautiful princess. Also like Parker, Bretécher employed humorous anachronisms by bringing topics such as feminism and social exclusion into the medieval setting.

Bretécher left *Pilote* in 1973 to start *Les Frustrés*, which had a style reminiscent of the American artist Jules Feiffer. There is little movement and virtually no action; humour is almost entirely verbal; the drawings are very concise and settings are deliberately vague; physically, there is not much difference between the shapeless men and women.[22] Despite those general similarities, Bretécher's terms of reference are different from Feiffer's. Feiffer makes humorous allusions to American current affairs, and his characters are particularly worried about America's problems: Vietnam, race riots, Cuban missiles etc. Bretécher's characters, on the other hand, are not overly concerned by the United States.

Very occasionally, Bretécher focuses specifically upon international issues. Her 'Bethleem' uses the birth of Christ to make a barbed comment on the problems in the Middle East (p. 16). In the stable, the Virgin Mary gives birth to twins: one wears an Arab headdress like the Palestinian leader Yasser Arafat; the other wears an Israeli army uniform and an eyepatch like the Israeli commander Moshe

Dayan. Bretécher is pointing up the religious source of the Israeli-Palestinian conflict. She also implies that there are more similarities between Israel and Palestine than either side might care to admit: the Israelis and the Palestinians are bedfellows; as they live in such close proximity, one people's problems inevitably rebound on the other.

More frequently, however, *Les Frustrés* deals with events specific to France. One example is the May '68 revolt, which had flared up just five years before she began *Les Frustrés*. Bretécher frequently expressed frustration and disillusionment with that aborted left-wing revolution. In 'Rêvons c'est l'Heure' May '68 is a fake rebellion, which merely gave rise to a new consumerism: a chair-maker complains that since May '68 his business has suffered because people no longer sit down properly any more; they lounge around on sofas instead (p. 29). Other gags suggest that a degree of pretence lay behind May '68's barricades. In 'Ancien Combattant', a *soixante-huitard embourgeoisé* attempts to convince his daughter that she can see him in old newsreel footage of a demonstration; she does not believe he was ever even present at the scene (p. 64).

As May '68 gave way to disillusionment in the 1970s, Bretécher mocked her generation's inability to live according to its ideals: she often suggested that ageing *soixante-huitards* forget their revolutionary fervour the moment they are tempted by material gain. In 'Ode à Tintin' she uses a Belgian comic strip, Hergé's *Aventures de Tintin,* to make that very point (p. 70). A sanctimonious left-winger scolds his daughter for reading Hergé's anti-Communist *Tintin au Pays des Soviets*, but he soon changes his tune on noticing that the album may be a valuable first edition.

In 'Un Homme simple', left-wing posturing is again exposed as a sham (p. 21). A man tells a woman about an interesting conversation he had with a gardener, adding, 'en lui parlant j'ai ressenti profondément que les barrières de classe sont en train de disparaître'. But the man's lofty rhetoric is not backed up by his actions: the woman he addresses is a maid, who is kneeling down in front of him cleaning his shoes.

In 'Le Droit à l'erreur', a man declares that he once collaborated with the Nazis during World War II, then he became a Stalinist, then he got involved in May '68, and now he likes the New Romantics (p. 256). May '68, Bretécher suggests, was just another passing fad, devoid of any serious, political content.

Faddishness among the fashion-conscious Parisians is another favourite target of Bretécher's. 'Les Intellectuels', for example, pokes fun at the vogue for structuralism (p. 24). Structuralism was a philosophical, linguistic and literary movement that made headlines in 1960s and 1970s France. Structuralism was committed to revealing the structures that underlie social and cultural phenomena. As we saw in the Introduction, Fresnault-Deruelle's and Groensteen's academic studies into *bandes dessinées* applied structuralist approaches to the ninth art. In 'Les Intellectuels', on the other hand, structuralism is merely a way of gaining social status. A woman says, 'On peut très bien vivre aussi sans rien piger au structuralisme', to which her friend replies 'oui mais on brille moins dans les salons!'

Whether portraying ex-*soixante-huitards* or Parisian socialites, Bretécher derides hypocrites: her characters make themselves laughable by pretending to have beliefs and feelings that they do not actually have. As Dina Sherzer demonstrated, laughing at hypocrisy links Bretécher with a French comic tradition that dates back at least as far as Molière's play *Tartuffe* (1664).[23] Bretécher's 'Famille chrétienne', like Molière's *Tartuffe,* mocks religious hypocrisy, although Bretécher's treatment of Molière's ancient theme is very much of her own epoch (p. 141). 'Famille chrétienne' alludes to the crisis in French Roman Catholicism during the mid/late twentieth century: after World War II the Church began losing touch with lay society, and religious practice declined. The crisis deepened after May '68 as young people, in particular, rejected Roman Catholicism's moral authority.[24] A rising secularism was apparent across Europe, including in Belgium.[25]

In 'Famille chrétienne', a priest seems out of touch because he can only speak in Latin. He rebukes a young man for reading an *Astérix* comic about pagans and druids. The young man angrily answers him back, causing his mother to protest 'Comment oses-tu parler ainsi de ton père?' Her innocuous little word 'ton' lets slip that, against every tenet of Christian morality, the youth is the priest's illegitimate son. The priest is indulging in Tartuffery: he is imposing moral standards on others to which his own behaviour does not conform. A young woman (the priest's daughter perhaps?) appears, announcing that she wants to become ordained. Women priests are, of course, anathema to Roman Catholicism. The priest then faints, saying 'In Galliae ecclesia magna est crisis'.

As well as ridiculing various forms of hypocrisy, Bretécher, more than any cartoonist before her, focuses upon women's social condition.

Les Frustrés, which ran from 1973 to 1980, covers a period of French history in which the status of women was changing rapidly. After May '68, French women gained greater equality and more financial independence. In 1972 equal pay and equal opportunity legislation was introduced to France, in 1974 the law on abortion was relaxed, and in 1975 divorce by mutual consent was permitted.[26] In other countries too, great changes were afoot. The USA legalised abortion in 1973. In Belgium, divorce laws were reformed in 1976 and equal pay legislation was introduced in 1978, although abortion was not legalised until 1990.[27] In France and Belgium, as in other countries throughout the developed world, more and more women were entering the labour market, couples cohabited instead of getting married, and single parents became more common. Bretécher's humour sometimes results from men and women grappling with those radical social changes.

'Le Prix d'une larme' jokes about women's growing economic independence: a woman demands money when her partner drinks whisky at home, because she was the one who bought it (p. 123). In 'L'Addition', a financially independent woman settles the restaurant bill, even though her male dining companion admits, 'j'ai un vieux fantasme: me faire inviter à déjeuner par une femme libérée' (p. 195). 'L'Addition' suggests that, despite the supposed sexual equality, the female submits to male fantasies.

Bretécher often touches upon problems specific to women: balancing work with having children, unplanned pregnancy, domestic violence. 'Clair Foyer' is about choosing between a job and having a child: after hearing a female friend boast about her glittering career, a young mother puts the baby in the rubbish bin (p. 47). 'Les Battus' deals with the ugly reality of domestic violence beneath the facade of social respectability: a wife says that her politician husband beats her up every time he loses an election; she accepts it all passively and she does not divorce him, because 'les campagnes électorales sont si fatigantes pour lui' (p. 206).

Although she is obviously sensitive to the problems faced by women, Bretécher always resisted the feminist label: 'Dans mes histoires, les femmes ne sont pas plus gâtées que les hommes, la connerie est bien répartie, non?'[28] Her refusal to take sides in the war of the sexes shows up throughout *Les Frustrés*, in which she treats women no more leniently than men. 'Belle-Maman' deals with divorce in this way: a mother's homily is shallow and insincere; she admonishes her daughter for leaving her partner, but she looks smugly pleased to learn that her daughter's new boyfriend has a well-paid job at an embassy (p. 234).

'Le Père indigne' deals with single parenthood, again without being partisan (p. 129). A model single father tells two women that he is bringing up his son alone; he makes sacrifices and does all he can, but when he goes out he hires 'une baby sitter'. When he leaves the room, someone snidely comments that he said *'une* baby-sitter' (Figure 23). As in 'Famille chrétienne', one little word gives all of the characters away. In 'Le Père indigne', the feminine form 'une' is particularly revealing: the man still assumes that a woman will have the poorly paid job of looking after his child whenever he wants to go out; the woman gives the man no credit at all for bringing up his child alone. Neither man nor woman is shown in an especially flattering light.

In 'Le Père indigne', as in Bretécher's other gags discussed above, the characters barely move; they are just sitting or standing around and talking, amid almost non-existent décor. Lack of background and of physical action focuses attention on the dialogues. An unusual absence of speech-balloons accentuates the dialogues still further:

Figure 23. The single dad, *Les Frustrés* by Claire Bretécher © 2001 Hyphen

according to comic strip convention, speech-balloons firmly enclose words within bold, solid-looking contours; in so doing, the balloons make characters' statements look reliable and authoritative. The balloon's tail, meanwhile, clearly indicates who says what. In *Les Frustrés,* a lack of speech-balloons achieves precisely the opposite effect. When they speak, Bretécher's men and women frequently claim solidarity with social, political, ethical and religious ideals, yet their claims are only dubiously genuine, often betraying a latent hypocrisy. In Bretécher's world, what people say is neither reliable nor authoritative, so, quite appropriately, their words are not firmly encased by balloons. Words are literally up in the air; looking uncertain and indecisive they float queasily around, somewhere between people's heads and the ceiling.

At times, the lack of a balloon with a tail creates uncertainty about who is saying what. This effect robs speakers of their individuality, making them virtually indistinguishable from the rest of their social group. As Irène Pennacchioni wrote,

> Ici, l'absence de bulle empêche de désigner nettement celui qui parle. Peu importe, puisque 'ce' qui parle est toujours la voix du groupe, et non une personne. Le groupe s'adresse à lui-même la parole, et se répond à travers les membre identiques ou équivalents qui le constituent.[29]

Although Bretécher usually references Franco-Belgian culture and current affairs, she has found a readership in the USA.[30] Bretécher travels unusually well, because she extracts humour from shared experiences so successfully. Hers is a universal, very human comedy. Most of Bretécher's settings, unlike those of Gotlib, are not country-specific; moreover, the society she depicts is recognisable the developed world over. It is affluent and undergoing rapid change, but it cannot shake off its long-standing prejudices and stupidities. Bretécher's characters are immediately recognisable too, as they are universal types: disillusioned idealists, working mothers, single parents, divorcees. We laugh at Bretécher's men and women, but we also sympathise with them because we see ourselves, our families and our friends in *Les Frustrés.*

Bretécher has raised the ninth art's international profile and strengthened its identity especially in the USA, which is usually so impervious to *bandes dessinées.* Bretécher helps define the ninth art's image to the American audience; as such she is something of a cultural ambassador.

Figure 24. Picture of Régis Franc taken by the author in Paris, 5 September 2001

Régis Franc's Animal Comics

Regis Franc (b. 1948) is best known for his gags and stories about humanised animals (Figure 24). Anthropomorphic animals predate *bandes dessinées* by several centuries; they form part of an ancient European tradition that stretches back to Aesop's allegorical Greek fables in the sixth century BC. In twelfth/thirteenth-century France *Le Roman de Renart*, a story about a sly fox, continued the tradition of giving animals human characteristics, which was subsequently rediscovered by La Fontaine. The USA also has a very strong tradition of humanising animals, apparent from the earliest days of comics. The best-known stories are, of course, Disney's, which depict anthropomorphic animals in a humorous/adventure context. Other notable animal strips exist also: Walt Kelly's *Pogo* used talking animals in a satirical allegory about current events in America; more recently, Art Spiegelman's *Maus* depicted Hitler's holocaust, with the Nazis as cats and the Jews as mice.[31]

Anthropomorphic animals have been well represented in *bandes dessinées* too. Gotlib's *Gai-Luron* was popular from the 1960s. In the early 1970s, F'Murr (Richard Peyzaret) drew *Génie des Alpages* in a style that recalls Franquin.[32] *Le Génie des Alpages* is about a dreamy shepherd who has philosophical discussions with his sheep, sometimes making punning references to French literature which readers are expected to recognise. For instance, in an allusion to Balzac's novel *Eugénie Grandet* (1833), one animal says: 'Ici Eugénie Grandet ... C'est moi, l'Eugénie des Alpages' (p. 34).

Franc's early album *Histoires immobiles et récits inachevés*, like *Le Génie des Alpages*, used humanised animals to make references to Francophone culture, but Franc took the idea further. In 'Le Marin grec', he incorporated the words to Georges Moustaki's famous love-song 'Milord' into a coherent bar-room conversation between a male rabbit and a female bird: 'Allez venez m'sieur milaur ... vous asseoir à ma table ... Fait pas chaud, dehors! Oui, ici c'est confortable' (pp. 13–17).[33] Transposing Moustaki onto an animal comic looks very amusing to those who know the original.

Franc's full-length masterpiece, *Le Café de la plage*, is black and white; it has a greater economy of line than *Histoires immobiles*, and a rather more angular graphic style.[34] *Le Café de la plage*'s hero is a snub-nosed dog, who writes a novel in a beachside café. Franc removed the distinction between what the dog-writer imagines and the world outside his mind. The dog sits writing; in the same panel, fictional characters from his book chat at a nearby table (p. 26; Figure 25). Then a group of children walk up the beach, past the writer's fictional characters and on past the writer himself (p. 35). Readers are left to wonder whether the children are part of the beach scene, or whether they are passing figments of the dog's imagination. As the children look neither more nor less real than the dog, there is no way of telling.

Franc blurred the boundary between the real and the imagined still further by making the dog-writer's creations immerse themselves in their own ephemeral thoughts. One of his characters, Anne Irène, sits on the beach; in the next panel, she has a brief flashback to a day she spent at a swimming pool; only after that, do we see the dog writing about her (pp. 17–19). There is a comical effect of surprise once we realise that Anne Irène exists only in the dog's mind. In this gag we catch a glimpse into the mind of a fictional character who is imagined by a dog; but the dog himself is, of course, a fictional character who is imagined by Franc. In truth, the dog is no more real than anybody else in the café or on the beach. Towards the end, the dog becomes aware that he is only make-believe, just like all of the

Figure 25. The dog-writer and his characters, extract from *Le Café de la Plage* by Franc © Casterman SA

other characters. He says, 'Hélas je suis dans cette bande comme personnage et je veux vivre encore' (p. 349).

The dog also grows uncertain as to whether his own characters are real or imagined. He fears losing control of them, saying 'les personages m'échappent' (p. 21). By the end he is wondering whether Rita, a character invented by him, exists in reality: 'Je ne suis pas certain qu'elle ait existé mais aujourd'hui, j'ai choisi de le croire car elle donne un sens à tout cela … Je la vois rangée dans un petit appartement, sereine et déjà vieillissante' (p. 349). An absurd climax is reached when, at the very end, Rita appears as a child, and throws the dog's manuscript away. How can a fictional character destroy her own creator's script?

In *Le Café de la plage*, Franc playfully asks us to untangle what is supposedly real from what is not; his jokes about where reality begins and where the imaginary ends humorously complement *nouveau réalisme* and 'la question du réel'. Franc told me that he knew about 'Cauchemar blanc' and *nouveau réalisme*; he even called Moebius 'le plus grand dessineur … un virtuose du dessin'. However, Franc was not consciously working in tandem with the *nouveaux réalistes*. His original intention in *La Café de la plage* had been to break with convention, by basing the story around a place (the café), rather than around a hero; gradually, the café became a place where the real meets the imagined. Franc told me,

> En faisant *Le Café de la plage,* je n'ai pensé à personne en ce qui concerne la BD. Dans la BD il faut toujours trouver un personnage, un héros, et moi je trouvais que tout le monde avait fait ça. Il fallait trouver une autre idée, et l'autre idée était un endroit. Cette espèce de baraque au bord de la mer. Il y avait des gens qui entraient et qui sortaient. Ce que vous dites sur le réel et l'imaginaire s'est mis en place à cause de cette structure.

Franc went on to elaborate about his influences, citing the Impressionist painters:

> J'ai toujours pensé que la BD est un médium inachevé. A partir du moment où vous commencez à faire la bande dessinée on s'attend à ce que vous fassiez la tête d'Astérix ou la tête de Tintin. Il se trouve qu'un siècle plus tôt, lorsque les Impressionnistes sont arrivés, ils ont utilisé de nouveaux codes et ces codes, à chaque instant, ils les ont remis en jeu en se disant: 'comment faire pour les détruire ou pour faire mieux'? Et mon propos, dans la bande dessinée, n'a été que ça.

Franc's comparison with Impressionism may be surprising, though it is far from out of place. Like Impressionists such as Claude Monet (1840–1926), Franc deliberately defied existing conventions; also like Monet, Franc drew (sometimes colourful) landscapes and seascapes that captured the subject's fleeting, insignificant thoughts. Belinda Thomson's comment on Impressionism applies to *Le Café de la plage*:

> Impressionist painting entailed a rejection of previously accepted themes … Instead, it focused on the much more immediate and restricted goal of conveying the artist's passing, fragmentary perceptions … One finds a comparable questioning of existing forms and an emphasis upon the subtle, sensory sensations of the creative subject.[35]

Franc and the *nouveaux réalistes* are marked by different traditions: Impressionism on the one hand, Modernism, the avant-garde and May '68 on the other. Franc told me that he had not been involved at all in May '68. Franc and the *nouveaux réalistes* arrived at 'la question du réel' independently and by following quite different paths. Even so, both paths lead back to the same origin: French-speaking culture.

Drawing inspiration from his native, Francophone culture, Franc was blurring the boundary between the real and the imaginary at precisely the same time as Moebius, Tardi and the other *nouveaux réalistes*. That fact is remarkable. By the mid-1970s 'la question du réel' was becoming a unique, distinct aspect of both humorous and non-humorous *bandes dessinées*, with no direct equivalent in American comics.

Franc's next album, *Nouvelles Histoires*, continued his characteristic blend of humanised animals and literary gags.[36] 'Les Madeleines du petit Marcel' (pp. 3–7) depicts a rabbit-like novelist called Marcel Proust, who is writing his autobiography. Franc's Proust says 'je ne deviendrai jamais écrivain', and the accompanying caption reads, 'il le sentait bien, sa vie n'intéresserait personne'. In 'Les Madeleines du petit Marcel', as in Chapter 1 of Proust's *Du Côté de chez Swann* (1913), the author revisits his past, recalling people and places that he once knew.[37] Finally, in a direct reference to *Du Côté de chez Swann*, the writer eats a madeleine, which reawakens his childhood memories; as in Proust's novel, past and present are united by the taste of the madeleine. The gag's gentle irony contrasts what Proust believes (his writing is of no interest), with what Franc's readers presumably all know: Proust is one of the greatest twentieth-century French-language novelists.

Franc's following album, *Souvenirs d'un menteur*, used anthropomorphic animals to still more unorthodox result.[38] 'Le Bordel de Madame Antoine' is set in a high-class brothel, which is full of smartly dressed pigs and dogs; Mme Antoine herself is a bird (pp. 16–20). Long panels divide each page from top to bottom, and alternate panels are cut in half by a picture of a balcony. A rabbit stands on the balcony, recounting anecdotes about Mme Antoine's clients; below him, on the brothel's ground floor, the stories he tells unfold. The narrating rabbit and his stories coexist both within the same panel; but although they are united by the brothel setting, they are cut off at the balcony.

Figure 26. 'La Nuit du lézard', extract from *Souvenirs d'un menteur* ©
Régis Franc

Readers are uncertain how to react. Should they follow their conditioned reflexes, and read from top left to bottom right? That approach, although conventional, is nonsensical given the context: it entails reading the rabbit's version of events before they actually happened. Should one, then, break with convention and begin with the part beneath the balcony? This second way seems to be more sensible, as one would read what happened first, before going on to the rabbit's version. Alternatively, should one read each panel from top to bottom (or from bottom to top), thereby coming and going between the rabbit and his stories? We must make up our own minds as there is no single, 'correct' way to read. Franc is playing games with us. As he said,

> C'est vous qui choisissez. C'est au lecteur de choisir comment lire. Ca fait absolument parti du jeu. C'est l'histoire du magicien. Si le public connaît le tour, ça n'a aucun intérêt. Il faut toujours être en avance par rapport au public. Si j'entraîne le public dans un sens il me paraît intéressant, au moment où le sens va être dévoilé, de retrouver un autre sens.

Other strips in *Souvenirs d'un menteur* disrupt normal reading practices to produce equally unconventional effects. In 'La Nuit du lézard', for example, large, vertical panels again divide the page from top to bottom (pp. 56–60). In the foreground, elegant animals at a garden party make aimless small talk against the backdrop of a towering volcano. The mountainous scenery flows on uninterruptedly from one panel to the next, establishing a degree of continuity between each panel, and encouraging conventional left-to-right reading. Speech-balloons overlap the white spaces between the panels, further encouraging reading from left to right (Figure 26). Yet, once again, there is no 'correct' way to read: in order to make sense of the animals' gossip, one must read each panel from the top downwards. Moreover, defying comic strip tradition, the most significant event is taking place in the background: the volcano is erupting. Because of that, starting at the top and following the dialogues downwards produces an unexpected anticlimax: one starts off with what is important, and works one's way down to what is unimportant. The hero of 'La Nuit du lézard' has a trivial conversation and then, tipsy, drives away with the volcano erupting behind him, summing up the strip with the words 'Rien, il ne se passe rien … (justement)'.

The volcanic setting, as well as the boozy hero, invite comparisons with Malcolm Lowry's novel *Under the Volcano* (1947), which Franc called 'une espèce de prétexte pour "La Nuit du lézard"'. Yet Franc's narrative technique, previously unknown in comic strips, recalls Flaubert's rather than Lowry's. Luc Dellisse has already pointed out that much of Franc's work recalls 'le cas de Flaubert, chez qui l'ossature du récit finit toujours par s'enliser et se perdre dans l'ampleur des éléments secondaires'.[39] Certainly, a parallel exists between Franc's detailed panels and Flaubert's detailed descriptive passages. 'La Nuit du lézard', like Flaubert's prose, 'appears to fritter itself away, as it runs down towards the minute and trivial'.[40] In both cases, irony is involved. Readers reasonably expect what they read to be meaningful, but Flaubert's sentences and Franc's panels ironically deflate that expectation. Flaubert and Franc steer readers away from what is significant and towards what is not, tempting and teasing us as we look for meaning but find none. Flaubert and Franc are both 'undermining the conventions of reading, [and] hampering the operations which readers are accustomed to perform on texts so as "to make sense" of them'.[41]

I asked Franc whether he had read Flaubert, to which he replied 'bien sûr'. However, Franc was playfully focusing his readers' minds on trivialities without thinking consciously of Flaubertian irony:

> Je n'ai pas du tout pensé à Flaubert en faisant cette bande, et ce que vous me dites sur Flaubert est quelque chose que je ne savais pas. Lorsque le décor est en place, le romanesque surgit malgré moi. Si vous regardez *La Joconde,* vous ne voyez que le visage de *La Joconde.* Or, il y a dans *La Joconde* des paysages à l'arrière qui ne sont pas révélés au même titre que le sourire. Et ce qui m'intéressait, c'était mon jeu, il n'y a rien de sérieux là-dedans, c'était de prendre chaque élément du tableau, et de les faire revivre.

'Les Plus Belles Histoires d'Onc' Ducon', again from *Souvenirs d'un menteur*, combines literary references with more overt parody (pp. 11–15). Antoine de Saint Exupéry, author of *Le Petit Prince* (1945), appears in the guise of a talking pig called Saint Texte; the name Saint Texte refers to the Holy Bible. As the title suggests, 'Les Plus Belles Histoires d'Onc' Ducon' also sends up the Belgian strip *Les Belles Histoires de l'Oncle Paul*. During our interview, Franc called Oncle Paul 'la quintessence de la pensée occidentale chrétienne'.

Making a direct reference to *Le Petit Prince*, Onc' Ducon, who is another pig, tells his admiring nephews how Saint Texte's aeroplane crash-landed in the desert. As in *Le Petit Prince* Saint Texte then meets the Little Prince, who asks him for a drawing; but Saint Texte draws yet another pig, whereas Saint Exupéry drew a sheep. Franc's Little Prince immediately takes fright and runs away. Saint Texte explains, in illiterate French, that the Little Prince ran off because 'j'y ai dessiné un cochon. Les musulmans y supportent pas ça!' Thus, Western Christian thought puts Islam to flight, and Onc' Ducon provides the triumphalist, pseudo-edifying moral conclusion: 'Et voila comment Saint Texte s'en sortit mes enfants. Grace a cet esprit, (virgule) ... Cet a-propos qui mille fois plus qu'ailleurs est notre propriété à nous en FRANCE!'

With *Le Marchand d'opium* Franc returned to 'la question du réel'.[42] In one strip, 'Le Sommeil', a dreamlike, exaggeratedly poetic caption suggests that the hero may be asleep (pp. 55–58): 'Il suffit alors de fermer les paupières et le blé sous le vent récite une poésie. Dans le rêve, la maison est si loin ... Un seul désire obsède le dormeur: s'approcher.' This text is accompanied by a picture of a wheatfield and a distant house. Although the scene does not look especially dreamlike, it may (or may not) be part of the hero's dreamscape.

In the second panel the hero slowly awakes to a different landscape, which now contains green fields, pylons and a hunter. Again, the caption is exaggeratedly poetic: 'Tourné du côté droit, le Coeur dégagé invite le sommeil. La célèbre fée électricite déchire les larges étendues ... Un coup de feu signale un chasseur. Surpris encore une fois le dormeur s'éveille, déçu. Il reconnaît son lit.' Once the hero is awake, reality turns dreamlike: for no apparent reason he is sitting in a tree, wearing a Nazi helmet (p. 56). He then goes straight back to sleep again ('ça y est, le dormeur dort'), but the accompanying picture shows an accurately drawn, visually realistic picture of a café terrace with chairs, tables and an empty dancefloor. Why? We do not know. On the last page a small, round picture of the hero lying in long grass is set into a larger picture of him lying in bed. The caption reads: 'Il sourit. Couché dans l'herbe. Le Sommeil.'

The hero's comings and goings between his realistic dream and his dreamlike reality are utterly mystifying. He experiences his dreams as though they were real, and vice-versa. Readers cannot tell whether he is asleep or awake; they are not even sure where he is. Is the hero in bed, in a field, in a tree, in a house or in a café? 'Le

Sommeil' explores a state of mind similar to that of a somnambulist, suspended between sleep and wakefulness. Franc himself compared the sleepwalking hero to an artist, absorbing his influences unawares:

> Quand j'ai dessiné 'Le Sommeil' je voulais parler du moment de l'endormissement. Je dirais que la somnolence, cet état entre le sommeil et l'éveil, est l'une des marques de mon travail. Le travail d'un créateur est un travail de somnambule. On commence par faire quelque chose sans savoir en quel sens ça va, et on s'aperçoit qu'on a été nourri de différentes influences, qu'au fond on n'a pas vu passer.

In the early 1980s, Franc's humour turned darker with the album *Nuits de Chine*.[43] The title strip parodies Hergéen realism (pp. 13–15). A character with a Tintinesque quiff, called Toutin, rides in a rickshaw down a street with signs written in Chinese characters. Unlike Hergé's exemplary hero, Toutin swears and has a walkman. He also treats a Chinaman with racist contempt, calling him a 'chink'. Finally, Toutin is thrown out of a party after a fracas.

'Intérieurs', from the same album, is very unorthodox black humour (pp. 3–6). Imitating a movie camera, the panels pan slowly round a banal-looking room. No character is visible, but a voice off says, 'J'ai traversé le salon comme si cela avait été la première fois, chaque objet, chaque meuble m'apparaissait étrangement nouveau'. We see a mirror, a radiator, a bookshelf and various other utterly unexceptional objects. Then, in the last three panels, there is an effect of surprise: the narrating character has been stabbed in the back. He falls to the ground, and the final caption reads, 'Il me reste un peu de conscience. Un regret: Comment se termine ce bouquin de Jack London?' His anticlimactic statement is ludicrous in the mouth of a dying man.

Following Francois Mitterrand's Socialist party's victory in the French presidential elections of 1981, Franc took up more conventional political cartooning. He created Tonton Marcel, a rat-like character whose name was inspired by Marcel Dassault, an industrialist opposed to Mitterrand.[44] Tonton Marcel is a paranoid millionaire and an anti-communist bigot; he sits behind a desk, pontificating about the evils of socialism and the horrors of trade unionism; he is surrounded by flatterers and sycophants. Among other things, Tonton Marcel sticks pins into a voodoo doll of Mitterrand and sends the president an anonymous letter. Marcel is also self-righteous and cynical. In a reference to the Falklands War he sells arms to both Margaret Thatcher and the Argentinian dictatorship because 'Dans n'importe quelle guerre c'est moi qui gagne' (p. 52).

Although Franc's anthropomorphic animals link him to a venerable tradition, his humour is very distinctive. Franc introduced 'la question du réel' to humorous *bandes dessinées* with *Le Café de la plage*. He then went on to discover new literary effects by experimenting with panels, décor and speech-balloons; he never lost his taste for acerbic parodies of songs, novels, other BDs, public figures and current affairs. As we shall see, Franc's characteristic blend of animals, humour and innovation resurfaced in the work of Lewis Trondheim during the 1990s.

Bandes dessinées by Gotlib, Bretécher and Franc range from light-hearted spoofing through biting social satire to cerebral experimenting. Yet a common thread connects them all: by generating laughter, each artist fosters an agreeable sense of belonging to a shared French-speaking culture. Complicity between the Francophone artist and his public is essential to understanding Gotlib's joking; Bretécher humorously references French current events and Franco-Belgian BDs; Franc plays with ideas thrown up by France and Belgium, from Impressionism, Proust, Flaubert and Mitterrand to Tintin and Oncle Paul.

Gotlib, Bretécher and Franc all operate the typically folkloric process of reworking the old into the new. What is more, all three artists assume prior knowledge of their native, Francophone cultural background; readers need to recognise the cultural references made or else they cannot share in the jokes. Inevitably therefore, English speakers miss the point and feel left out; that explains why, except for Bretécher's universally human comedy, very little of this *bande dessinée* humour has ever crossed the Atlantic or even the English Channel.

Gotlib, Bretécher and Franc hit both French and Belgian readers on the funny-bone. Our three artists show how the ninth art's ability to produce folklore reinforced Franco-Belgian identity up to the 1980s, all the while giving millions of people shared pleasures.

CHAPTER SEVEN

Reconstructing the Narrative and After

Le Retour au récit I: Moebius and Jodorowsky: *L'Incal* and *Edena*

So far in Part II of this book, the masters of the ninth art were all working during an era of rapid modernisation. Let us briefly review developments. After World War II in France and Belgium, imperial pretensions had given way to American-led consumerism, European integration and rising prosperity. The upheavals of the late 1960s/ early 1970s then questioned traditional aesthetics, authorities and conventions, while emphasising personal freedoms. Censorship was relaxed, there was increasing secularism and women won greater independence. The above developments all impacted strongly on the ninth art, as we have seen.

By the late 1970s/early 1980s France and Belgium were changing once more, again with major repercussions for the ninth art. This period is characterised by a new shift in the public mood, widely dubbed 'le repli sur soi', which provoked much debate, especially in France. John Ardagh's *France in the 1980s* summarises 'le repli sur soi': thirty years of uninterrupted post-war economic expansion were giving way to a growing malaise; unemployment was rising, bringing with it greater insecurity and anxieties about the future; post-May '68 radicalism and politics were out of fashion. A widespread desire existed to withdraw from the uncertainties of the present, which was expressed in various ways. Rather than trying to alter society, many people now turned back to a common past; they sought re-establish links with their traditional, historical and cultural roots. Significantly, Ardagh associates 'le repli sur soi' with a popular desire to rediscover an identity, following the era of modernisation:

> It all added up to quite a striking change of mood. These new tendencies began to emerge even before the 1973 energy crisis, and

they seemed to mark a desire of the French to regain their balance and rediscover their identity, after the era of hectic modernization.[1]

By the turn of the 1980s, the ninth art was a firmly established Franco-Belgian tradition with an accompanying mythology and folklore. Not only that: the ninth art had become a defining feature of Franco-Belgian mass culture. To many French-speakers, the ninth art even formed an inextricable part of their notion of who they were. In short, the ninth art had established a strong, Franco-Belgian identity. So, quite logically, *bandes dessinées* played their part in satisfying the popular desire to rediscover an identity. At the level of popular culture, 'le repli sur soi' coincided with a striking return to more traditional *bande dessinée* narratives, which was widely known among critics as *le retour au récit*. *Le retour au récit* was particularly prevalent in genres that let readers withdraw from contemporary reality entirely: science fiction and historical drama. In this chapter I shall consider both science fiction and historical *récits*, beginning with SF.

Historical and science fiction stories of the late 1970s and the 1980s re-established links with the narrative conventions of 'classic' strips as well as with traditional folktales; they thus showed the ninth art's increasing awareness of its own traditions. Unlike most *nouveaux réalistes*, *le retour au récit* told adventure stories centred around heroes and heroines, with plots structured by coherent sequences of events; despite that, these new heroes and heroines are marked by the malaise underpinning 'le repli sur soi', as their victories over evil are uncertain and very much open to question. *Le retour au récit* did not merely hark back to tradition, it accelerated the long-standing, Franco-Belgian trend away from superheroes.

Le retour au récit was started by some of the artists who had been at the forefront of *nouveau réalisme* and experimental science fiction in the 1970s. In the domain of science fiction, Moebius' and Alejandro Jodorowsky's *Incal*, also called *Les Aventures de Jean Difool*, provides an excellent example.[2] Moebius drew the pictures and Jodorowsky wrote the story. Jodorowsky, Moebius' friend since the mid-1970s, was an enthusiastic scholar of the Kabbala, the tarot, numerology and other things esoteric.

L'Incal is more orthodox than Moebius' 1970s experiments such as *Arzach* or *Le Garage hermétique*. It is an SF blockbuster in the style of Steven Spielberg's *Star Wars* (1977), bristling with the trappings of space operas: robots, zap guns, bug-eyed monsters and intergalactic battles. Moreover, unlike *Arzach* and *Le Garage hermétique*, *L'Incal* is based around a traditional hero who rights a wrong. *L'Incal* is also the story of an initiation: the hero John Difool rises from seedy private detective to cosmic messiah. Jodorowsky said, 'John Difool c'est le Fool ... le fou du tarot. Il représente toute l'énergie, toutes les possibilités de l'univers.'[3]

L'Incal has a conventional narrative structure. It opens with a widely used device borrowed from adventure films: there is hard-hitting action, which later developments clarify. Difool is beaten and thrown down a huge shaft running through the Cité Puits where he lives; he is picked up at the last minute by Roboflics, who want to question him. As is so often the case in *L'Incal*, this opening scene is symbolic: Difool starts by plummeting downwards; the rest of the story turns his fall into an ascent. The arresting opening establishes Difool as a weak member of a sick society that cries out for a saviour: passers-by shoot at him for fun as he falls. The opening allowed Moebius to draw a dizzying, highly detailed picture of Difool plunging headlong down an apparently endless shaft.

L'Incal's plot is far too long to be recounted in full. Put briefly, Difool gains possession of the Incal lumière, an object with religious attributes: it guides and protects those who believe in it. The Incal lumière commands Difool to find its twin, the Incal noir, and Difool tracks it down in the technologically nightmarish Cité Techno. Difool's enemy is the Technopape, who wants to obliterate light by creating photon-devouring 'oeufs d'ombre'. Cité Puits is attacked by hostile monsters called Bergs. Difool and six companions leave the city, travelling through strange places like the Forêt de Cristal and Détritus Vallée. The Incals are united by the androgynous Solune, who turns into a 'Vaisseau étoile', a living spaceship. The Incal tests Difool's faith by commanding him to fertilise the Bergs' Queen, which he unwillingly does. To defeat the Technopape, Difool and friends must pass through a Cercle de Cauchemar, where everyone's worst fears come true. Difool helps his companions through the nightmare by making them recognise the goodness in themselves. Darkness is overcome, and Difool is brought before Orh, the Incal's God-like father (Figure 27). Orh tells Difool he must remember what he has witnessed. Difool falls away from Orh, and suddenly finds himself where he was at the beginning, plummeting down the shaft.

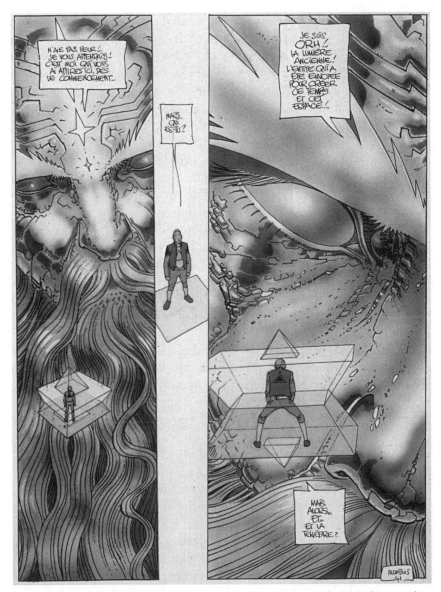

Figure 27. John Difool and Orh, *La Cinquième Essence* by Moebius and Jodorowsky © 2000 Les Humanoïdes Associés SA, Geneva

L'Incal's plot comes full circle, immediately distancing it from America's SF superhero comics with their linear narratives. *L'Incal*'s circularity creates an impression of order, which also distances it from Moebius' *Arzach* and *Le Garage hermétique*. In *L'Incal* a circular plot, rather than a deliberately fragmented plot, raises questions about the hero's actions. *L'Incal*'s circularity blocks the unambiguous moral message: Difool, unlike Grubert and Arzach, does appear to triumph as a conventional hero should; but despite this, readers are left wondering. Was Difool's titanic struggle in vain? Was it just a thought flashing through his mind as he fell? Is Difool condemned to repeat the same struggle for all eternity, like a latter-day Sisyphus?

Whatever the answer may be, *L'Incal*'s circularity undoubtedly produced a new mythological hero for the ninth art. *L'Incal*'s circular plot affords Difool mythological status: he has what Eco termed 'an emblematic and fixed nature which renders him easily recognizable'. Difool is effectively removed from 'the law that leads from life to death through time'.[4] Yet circularity simultaneously robs Difool's triumph of any clear significance.

L'Incal has a vast network of symbols built into its story, which come from various cultural traditions: the opposition between light (positive) and dark (negative) is common to Christianity, Zoroastrianism, Taoism, Islam, Buddhism and the Kabbala. Light and darkness are but two of the symbolic oppositions in *L'Incal*. Solune's name, for example, combines 'soleil' and 'lune', traditional symbols of male and female. Androgynous Solune also recalls the tarot pack: the sun card has a picture of twins, who are 'an expression of ... primeval parthenogenesis and hermaphroditism'; in the tarot pack, the positive sun is opposed to the negative moon, and the moon symbolises 'the sullying of the spiritual by the material'.[5] Solune harmoniously unites positive and negative, darkness and light, male and female, sun and moon, spirit and matter.

Other symbolic elements range from Antiquity to twentieth-century psychology. Difool and his six companions are opposed by seven enemies. Among the ancient Egyptians, seven symbolised 'the dynamic perfection of a complete cycle'.[6] How fitting for a story with a circular plot. Difool's female companion, Animah, has a name that recalls Carl Jung, who called the Anima 'the female archetype which plays an especially important part in the male unconscious'.[7] Further examples could be added almost *ad infinitum*.

Sometimes humour arises from allusions to religion and occultism. The Incal's command that Difool fertilise the Bergs' Queen recalls Jesus' words: 'What I tell you is this: love your enemies' (Matt. 5.44). The result of their union is seventy-eight billion Difools. Jodorowsky said, 'Ce nombre n'est pas sans rapport avec les 78 cartes du tarot'.[8] Humour is also generated by Difool, whose human failings clash amusingly with his messianic status. Difool grows wiser but he remains a grumbling, reluctant messiah, who would rather go to the bar or run off with Animah than save the world.

Jodorowsky gave Moebius a powerful story. The plot demands numerous scene-changes and the fragmentation of Moebius' graphic style, already apparent in *Le Garage hermétique*, goes to extremes in *L'Incal*: the detailed architecture of Cité Puits and the complex, metallic spacecraft contrast with naive-looking pastoral scenes. The Forêt de Cristal is beautiful, but the almost formless, light-devouring shapes created by the Technopape are disturbingly hideous when one turns a page and comes upon them unexpectedly. Swirling, harmonious bands of colour and geometric shapes produce indescribable effects as Difool rises up to Orh. Narrow, vertical pictures divide the page from top to bottom in an unconventional layout. Difool's fall is depicted in a vertical panel bordered by multi-coloured light that emphasises his headlong plunge.

Moebius' artwork and Jodorowsky's prodigious imagination put *L'Incal* in a class of its own among comic strips, although certain parallels do exist with other art forms. The grandiose story reinterprets ancient myths and legends to create ingenious symbolic patterns in the manner of English poet and artist William Blake (1757–1827), whose work Giraud told me he had seen. Despite obvious differences in the form, Blake's poetry, like *L'Incal*, is made up of symbolic elements that suggest meanings by their mutual relationships; much of the pleasure of reading Blake and *L'Incal* comes from deciphering the symbolism. Orh, a bearded patriarch, looks like Blake's *Ancient of Days*, whose creation is a 'mighty circle turning'. Blake and Jodorowsky both invent names, which 'become related to intelligible ideas ... This unusual universe is peopled by beings who are radiant quintesessences of the dancing energies of mankind'.[9]

L'Incal is Moebius' most commercially successful work; it sold over one million copies in French alone, and it was translated into more than ten languages.[10] Such strong sales figures show the impact of *le retour au récit* on 1980s science fiction *bandes dessinées*. By the middle of the decade Giraud, now almost universally known as Moebius, was the dominant influence over science fiction BDs. His example encouraged other artists to draw long SF *récits*, some of which also sold very well. Two such SF artists, Arno (Arnaud Dombre) and Silvio Cadelo, collaborated with Jodorowsky to draw adventures based, like *L'Incal*, on mystico-initiatory fantasies and structured by the exploits of heroes.[11]

* * *

Moebius continued to draw science fiction adventure stories for the rest of the twentieth century, many of which are marked by his ever-growing personal mysticism. Over the course of the 1980s he became particularly interested both in Buddhism and in the dietician Guy-Claude Burger, whose work he read with enthusiasm.[12] In his book *Instinctothérapie*, Burger advised eating only food untouched by industrial processing and to 'se nourrir seulement d'aliments crus, sans autre règle que l'instinct du plaisir'.[13]

Given Moebius' preoccupations, it is perhaps surprising that his as yet unfinished adventure series, *Edena*, began as an advertisement for Citroën cars.[14] At the end of the first volume a pyramid goes up into the air and turns into the Citroën logo, a double chevron. Nonetheless, *Edena* soon became a story in its own right.

Stel and Atan, *Edena*'s two main characters, are conditioned by a future society that has lost all contact with nature and where food is synthetic. They are androgynous, and they think the natural world is disgusting. Following a space accident, Stel and Atan are marooned on a planet of great natural beauty. There they eat a raw apple for the first time, and their sexuality is aroused. This is a clear reference to Adam and Eve (Gen. 2–4), and to instinctotherapy. Burger wrote, 'La nutrition concerne l'ensemble de l'organisme. Pourquoi pas la fonction sexuelle[?]'.[15] He also noted that 'En supprimant l'intoxication culinaire, on observe des changements dans toutes les fonctions psychiques et instinctives'.[16]

After eating the apple, Stel and Atan change and develop. They struggle to lose their conditioning and to reinvent themselves; they try to comprehend what they have never seen or known before. They experience complex, conflicting emotions (fear, enthusiasm, denial), as they come to realise that they are a man and a woman.

Edena's emphasis on character development is very unusual in science fiction comics. In the 1980s and 1990s, the vast majority of

SF comics (particularly in America) still followed the conventions of the genre defined by Umberto Eco, offering stories in which super-heroes triumphed; this reiterative narrative structure ruled out the complexities of character development. Moebius' interest in charac-terisation is more common in nineteenth-century novels than in SF comics. *Edena* recalls *La Faute de l'Abbé Mouret* by Emile Zola, a similarity particularly unexpected as Moebius told me during our interview 'je n'ai jamais lu une ligne de Zola'.[17] Nonetheless Zola's novel, like *Edena*, explores conflicting states of mind that accompany release from conditioning and sexual awakening in Edenic surround-ings. Like Zola, Moebius inverted the biblical story:

> The act of love (corresponding to the eating of the apple) performed by his new Eve and Adam beneath a tree which is less the 'arbre du mal' than the Tree of Life, is surely not meant to be regarded by the reader as a transgression. Serge and Albine [like Stel and Atan] are complying with the natural law.[18]

Despite these similarities, Zola and Moebius used very different narrative techniques. Zola wrote psychological analyses of Serge and Albine, describing their idyll in detail. Moebius represented Stel's and Atan's thought with balloons, drawing pictures of their surround-ings. His graphic style is mostly simple and calm, while colours are soft and gentle.

Moebius criticised what he called 'la surenchère dans le bom-bardement d'informations, donc le blocage du rêve du lecteur'.[19] Moebius was drawing pure, clear, harmonious lines, and he was developing a 'dessin purement objectif … totalement dénué de traces de l'ego … Le seul véritable dessin sans ego est le dessin sacré … qui va de pair avec une démarche spirituelle approfondie'.[20] Moebius' pronouncements suggest Zen influence. Artist and Zen practitioner Frederick Franck, who used drawing as a meditation technique, also associates his art with absence of over-stimulation and with self-transcendence:

> A 'non-creative' environment is one that constantly bombards us … with noise, with agitation and visual stimuli … [Seeing and drawing] establishes an island of silence, an oasis of undivided attention … I forget this Me, am liberated from it and dive into the reality of what confronts me.[21]

Moebius continues to publish *bandes dessinées*. Among many other things he has drawn another initiatory tale with Jodorowsky, an anti-slavery Western with Charlier called *Jim Cutlass*, and a collection of abstract paintings, which Pierre Sterckx called 'des condensateurs devenus émeraudes ... des lapis-lazulis se faisant fusibles ... [des] fossiles d'histoires encore à venir'.[22]

Jean Giraud's huge, varied body of work finds unity in its creator's drive to experiment. His role in raising comics to the level of an art form is second only to that of Hergé. After opening up new possibilities for *bande dessinée* Westerns, realism and science fiction in the 1960s and 1970s, Giraud spearheaded *le retour au récit* in 1980s SF. Whatever genre Giraud adopts, he persistently displays a strong interest in ideas. Giraud's full-length Western and science fiction narratives encourage metaphysical speculation; in so doing they connect with ancient, religious and cultural traditions. He thus reworks the old into the new in the finest folkloric fashion. *Lieutenant Blueberry* takes up the Biblical theme of revelation in the wilderness; *Le Garage hermétique* renews the ancient story of the tower of Babel; *L'Incal* has abundant mystical symbolism; Stel and Atan are a latter-day Adam and Eve; *Edena*'s artwork suggests Zen influence.

The name Moebius suits Jean Giraud remarkably well. He fuses contrasting, even opposing ideas, registers and styles with the ease of the Möbius strip: a circle that joins one side of a sheet of paper to its opposite. As Giraud once said, the Möbius strip risks becoming 'un cercle dont on est prisonnier à jamais'.[23] Hence his need to push back the boundaries, and to seek new horizons.

Le Retour au récit II: François Bourgeon: *Les Passagers du vent*

Science fiction was not alone in witnessing *le retour au récit*. The trend was even more apparent in the vogue for adventures with historical settings. One early indication of the revived interest in history was Tardi's popular series *Les Aventures extraordinaires d'Adèle Blanc-Sec*.

Le retour au récit in historical *bandes dessinées* is well illustrated by Francois Bourgeon's very successful five-album series, *Les Passagers du vent*.[24] Bourgeon (b. 1945) was a maker of stained glass who studied at l'Ecole des Métiers (Paris). He shot to prominence with *Les Passagers du vent*, a seafaring adventure set in the mid/late eighteenth century. During that time slave-ships were plying their lucrative trade between Africa and the New World, and France was supporting American attempts to win independence from Britain. Unusually for an adventure story, *Les Passagers du vent* does not tell the story of a hero who opposes villainy; rather, its complicated plot tells of changing inter-personal relationships, struggles for power and shifting alliances. Here is a brief summary.

The heroine, a strong-willed, aristocratic young woman called Isabeau, is swindled out of her inheritance. She puts to sea and falls in love with Hoel, a Breton sailor. Hoel is imprisoned after a sea battle against the British. Isabeau helps him to escape, and the lovers sail away to Fort Saint Louis de Juda, a French slave-trading colony in Africa. Here Hoel is poisoned by a slave-trader who covets Isabeau, and so she must find an antidote. Once Isabeau has cured Hoel the pair sail on to Haiti, but the slaves revolt during the voyage. Their stricken ship eventually reaches Haiti, where Hoel is persuaded by his friends to leave Isabeau and go treasure-hunting. Isabeau and Hoel come from such different social strata that their parting seems natural enough. Isabeau gravitates towards gentlemen of her own rank: captains, doctors, colonial officials; Hoel is a poor sailor, who feels more at ease among his own kind.

Isabeau is a very original character. Although she is, arguably, too independent and liberated to be an eighteenth-century lady, she is far more complex than most adventure strip heroines. To be sure, Isabeau has some of the traits of conventional heroes and heroines: she is beautiful, clever, strong, brave, resourceful and magnanimous; she is also an excellent shot. Yet Isabeau is capable of errors of judgement, and her femininity gives her a certain vulnerability. Hoel does not conform to the traditional, adventure comic stereotypes any more than Isabeau. Although Hoel is brave, strong and handsome, he is unusually passive. He is easily led and weak-minded. More than once, Isabeau intervenes to get him out of trouble. In general, Hoel seems less intelligent than Isabeau and, unlike her, he rarely questions what is happening around him. Hoel completely fails to grasp Isabeau's opposition to slavery; he even defends the slave trade with spurious, rationalising arguments such as 'Ce n'est tout de même pas si terrible. Les nègres seront bien gardés, tu sais' (*Le Ponton*, p. 47).

Throughout *Les Passagers du vent*, relatively complex characterisation prevents the distinction between 'good' and 'bad' from becoming oversimplified. Rather than just putting forward an anti-slavery message, for example, the narrative explores Isabeau's moral dilemmas. As Isabeau comes to realise, the world is not divided up neatly into right and wrong. Isabeau abhors slavery; however, when the slaves revolt she is forced to fight them off in order to save her own life.

Numerous secondary characters come and go during the story. Like Isabeau and Hoel they have an unusual depth of characterisation, which is enhanced by their very expressive faces. Each secondary character speaks differently, their conversations ranging from coarse sailor's banter to philosophical discussions. Mary, Isabeau's English friend, is amusing because she speaks anglicised French, and she confuses genders of nouns.

Secondary characters must also face moral dilemmas. Abbé Chaplan, Fort Saint Louis de Juda's chaplain, is something of a hypocrite: as Isabeau says, he represents 'une église qui, tout en prêchant l'amour du prochain, n'hésite pas à se faire complice et alliée des marchands d'esclaves' (*Le Comptoir de Juda*, p. 38). Yet Chaplan genuinely believes that he is doing what is right and wishes to evangelise the slaves, whom he considers to be poor savages. Chaplan comes to Isabeau's aid when Hoel has been poisoned, further attenuating *Les Passagers du vent*'s anti-clerical undertones.

Interaction between Isabeau, Hoel and the other characters is especially powerful because the ships and the fort are both cramped places, where everyone lives in uncomfortably close proximity to everyone else. There is little privacy, and Isabeau's presence in the tough, exclusively male preserve of eighteenth-century shipping causes the inevitable disciplinary problems. In order to move around unmolested, Isabeau sometimes dresses up as a man. According to Louis-Antoine de Bougainville's seafaring journal (1771), Isabeau's ruse was not unknown in the eighteenth century.[25]

Taking his cue from Hergé, Bourgeon documented the setting carefully. He did a vast amount of background reading, including Bougainville; he consulted academic specialists in the field, and visited the Maritime Museum in Nantes.[26] Indeed, Bourgeon's ships and fort are microcosms of the eighteenth century with its politics, its prejudices and its injustices. The aristocrats enjoy certain privileges, but the sailors work terribly long hours and live in squalid conditions.

Les Passagers du vent's historical setting is painstakingly reconstructed, and Bourgeon combined social realism with mimetic realism. He drew authentic-looking depictions of the various places Isabeau and Hoel visit (France, Africa, the Caribbean), with detailed tall ships, period costumes and colonial architecture. *La Marie Caroline*, one of the ships on which Isabeau and Hoel sail, was based on a genuinely existing vessel called *La Marie Séraphique*; Fort Saint Louis de Juda really existed, and Bourgeon copied it from a map in France's Royal Archives, which he reproduced in the albums. Bourgeon even made scale models of *La Marie Caroline* and of the Fort Saint Louis de Juda. His models helped him to ensure that the dimensions and the interior layouts were correct; they also enabled him to draw the ship and the fort from different angles with shadows cast accurately, according to the position of the sun.

Les Passagers du vent is a masterpiece of narrative pacing as it evokes the boredom, excitement, friendships, enmities and petty jealousies of life aboard ship and in isolated colonial outposts. Sea battles are shown in all their gory detail, as are the filthy prison hulks and the appalling treatment meted out to the slaves; violent, action-packed sequences alternate with tenderness and humour.

Bourgeon uses various narrative techniques to draw readers into the story. Often, readers learn about new developments at the same time as Isabeau, encouraging identification with her. When Hoel is seduced by the manipulative Mme de Morgane, readers do not know what is happening until Isabeau enters the room unexpectedly (*Le Bois d'ébène*, p. 48). At other times, information about new developments comes from Isabeau's diary, further encouraging identification with her (*Le Bois d'ébène*, p. 16).

Colour makes an important contribution to the narrative rhythm. Outside the ship, the sea constantly changes colour depending on the hour and the weather; inside, candle-light and shadow-play produce impressive results. Colour is enhanced by a variety of differently shaped panels. Panoramic seascapes are depicted in long, horizontal panels. When Hoel falls off the mast, the panel has the opposite shape: it is thin and vertical, emphasising his vertiginous plunge; readers look down him from above, making him seem helpless and vulnerable (*La Fille sous la dunette*, p. 45).

Sometimes Bourgeon inserts several small panels inside a large one; the small panels are in close-up, showing characters speaking; the large panel shows the surrounding decor. One particularly effective use of that technique is in *La Fille sous la dunette* (p. 31). A sequence of small vignettes shows the sailors receiving orders; a large panel shows the ship on which they are sailing. The effect of contrast between these different sized panels is comparable to the contrast between two French past tenses: the imperfect and the passé simple. The large descriptive panel, like the imperfect tense, depicts an ongoing situation whose precise beginning and end is not specified. The small vignettes, like the passé simple, evoke shorter, completed actions in the past.

Les Passagers du vent had everything needed for massive sales: top-quality drawing, rip-roaring drama, historical authenticity, a sexy heroine and sophisticated characterisation. The strip won Bourgeon the Angoulême festival prize in 1980, and it achieved 'des chiffres de vente que l'on croyait réservés aux grands classiques'.[27]

Les Passagers du vent paved the way for numerous strips about French history. Among many others, *Aigles décapités* takes place in thirteenth-century France, and it depicts courtly intrigues surrounding Saint Louis; *Arno*, strongly influenced by 'clear line', has a Napoleonic setting; *Chemins de Malefosse* is about France's sixteenth-century religious wars.[28]

The popularity of *Les Passagers du vent* and others fits with 'le repli sur soi', which was particularly visible in late 1970s/early 1980s France. John Ardagh observed 'the very strong trend in recent years towards a renewal of links with the past, with tradition. Local folklore and handicrafts are being revived; history books are best-sellers.'[29] The boom in historical *bandes dessinées* is very much in keeping with the popular desire to rediscover identity by reconnecting with a common past, noted by Ardagh. Other critics have already associated *le retour au récit* with the fashion for historical novels in early 1980s France. Groensteen saw the dramatic return to such traditional types of fiction as reaction against the experimental *nouveau roman*:

> Le succès du roman historique est l'un des faits marquants de l'édition littéraire contemporaine. Beaucoup l'interprètent comme un symptôme du 'retour au récit' après les expériences du nouveau roman. Un phénomène analogue a pu être observé dans la bande dessinée, où la réhabilitation du héros et de l'aventure qui s'est accomplie au début des années 80 a entraîné l'éclosion, en France, de nombreuses séries historiques.[30]

Jacques Chabond observed, 'au moment où la bande dessinée retrouve ses cases et ses histoires avec un petit "h", les Français ... redécouvrent le roman historique'.[31]

French cinema had its equivalent of *le retour au récit*. Hayward writes, 'The 1980s cinema adopted a form of cultural nostalgia [which] manifested itself in films harking back to earlier cinema genres and traditions'.[32] Hayward adds that this trend was especially strong in neo *films noirs*, literary adaptations (especially Pagnol), and comedies in the style of Fernandel (1903–1971). Surprisingly, however, the trend was far less marked with regard to historical settings. Quoting the critic S. Brisset, Hayward suggests that this 'lack of representation of history in the 1980s cinema reflects the general apoliticised mood prevailing in France'.[33]

What else explains *le retour au récit*? Commercial considerations no doubt contributed: *nouveau réaliste bandes dessinées*, for all their originality, never sold as well as the 'classics', nor as well as *L'Incal* and *Les Passagers du vent*. Looming economic austerity coupled with rising unemployment gave artists and publishers financial jitters; almost everybody embraced a return to tested formulas whose commercial success had already been proven. Disillusionment with ideology fuelled the demand for apolitical escapism; hence the abundant historical and futuristic settings.

With *le retour au récit*, Moebius and Bourgeon retreated from *nouveau realiste* experimenting; yet instead of merely recycling 'classical' BD folktales, they reconstructed the narrative and produced new heroes and heroines for the age of uncertainty. *L'Incal*'s circular plot casts doubt on Difool's victory. *Edena* and *Les Passagers du Vent* are open-ended: neither Stel, Atan nor Isabeau are sure to emerge victorious. *Le retour au récit* also differs from the 'classical' *bandes dessinées* because women play far more active roles, and because artists use colours and panels in new ways. In addition, *L'Incal*, *Edena* and *Les Passagers du vent* have graphic scenes of sex and violence that the censor would have deemed unacceptable in *bandes dessinées* before *nouveau réalisme*.

In the USA, as in Europe, comic strip experimentalism faded after the mid-1970s; even so, there was nothing that corresponded directly to *le retour au récit*. In Ronald Reagan's America superheroes still held sway, with minimal character development and no historicism. Superheroes were allowed to be more violent in their pursuit of villainy, and many stories were distinctly revisionist: Frank Miller's *Dark Knight* depicts an ageing Batman who struggles to keep control of events; in Alan Moore's and Dave Gibbons' *Watchmen*, superheroes question their roles as dispensers of justice in a world where caped crusaders are outlawed.[34]

Nonetheless Batman and the Watchmen, like Spiderman, the X Men and the Hulk before them, retained their exceptional physical strength; moreover, *The Dark Knight* and *The Watchmen* both refer specifically to Cold War nuclear tensions between the USA and Soviet Russia. *The Dark Knight* and *The Watchmen* regenerated the superhero genre rather than reconstructing it or altering it radically; these strips were, after all, produced for companies that had a large vested interest in various superhero franchises.

Experimentalism and Humour post-1980

Although *le retour au récit* predominated for much of the 1980s, a number of *bande dessinée* artists continued to experiment. Following the trail blazed in the 1970s by Moebius, *Bazooka* and others, some such artists dispensed with the devices that had generally been considered essential to BDs. *Carpets bazaar*, by Martine Van and François Mutterer, tells an adventure story without once showing the characters' faces: the opening scene shows a party with drinks, a record player, a ceiling light and people's feet; the phone rings, but all we can see is the receiver (pp. 1–5); readers must imagine what everyone looks like.[35] In Edmond Baudouin's *Un Flip coca!*, which is drawn in a style similar to 'Cauchemar blanc', readers do not see the heroine's face until the last three pages.[36]

Other artists broke with convention in different ways. In Avril's and Petit Roulet's *Soirs de Paris*, readers must imagine all of the words: there are no dialogues at all, just pictures inside speech-balloons.[37] A man invites a woman to dance with a balloon that contains a pair of dancing figures; she turns him down with a picture that contains the figures crossed out; later, somebody comments on how crowded the room is with an image of a sardine tin (pp. 2–3 and 8).

In the mid-1980s a new Belgian humorist emerged, Philippe Geluck, whose humorous strip *Le Chat* is now a bestseller in France. The eponymous Chat is drawn in an unadorned graphic style, reminiscent of Schulz. Le Chat wears a suit and tie; he offers pithy, deadpan aphorisms, whose unimitigated absurdity is emphasised by Geluck's sensible-looking drawings. For example, Le Chat informs us that 'Ce n'est pas parce qu'un coureur bat son propre record … qu'il est forcément en avance sur son temps'.[38]

Le Chat plays with the punning possibilities of the French language, often inviting readers to participate in constructing the joke. Le Chat wears a toga and stands by some Grecian pillars, saying 'Homère d'alors' (p. 58); readers must think twice if they are to discover the vulgar ejaculation, 'ô merde alors', beneath the wrong spelling, the classical reference and the Greco-Roman props. Elsewhere, following a tradition in French punning, we are obliged to rearrange Le Chat's words. His sentence 'Monsieur et Madame Bricot ont un fils … il l'appellent "Judas"', only gives the punchline 'jus d'abricot' if we put Judas's Christian name before his surname (p. 30).

Sometimes Le Chat makes jokes about the French literary classics. When Le Chat says, 'Longtemps avant Balzac, Homère avait raconté … l'histoire d'Ulysse dans la vallée', he is alluding to Balzac's novel *Le Lys dans la vallée* (1835).[39] Le Chat's statement, 'Je téléphone à un avocat … Allô? Maître Renard? C'est ici Maître Corbeau', combines 'Maître', the formal term of address given to lawyers, with La Fontaine's fable 'Le Corbeau et le renard'.[40]

By the 1990s a new generation of artists was appearing, many of whom combined innovation with humour. The most surprising experiment of the early 1990s was *Après tout, tant pis*, by Anne Baraou and Corinne Chalmeau.[41] The strip, if one can call it that, consists of three dice. Each side of each die contains a picture and an accompanying text in a balloon. One die has six main clauses (e.g. 'je mange les tomates'), the second has six adverbial phrases of time (e.g. 'certains nuits'), the third has six subordinate clauses or adverbs (e.g. 'parce que tu fais la gueule', and 'bêtement'). As the texts can be put together in any order, each dice-throw spontaneously produces a three-panelled strip; when readers throw the dice, they construct their own story.

Marc-Antoine Mathieu is a better-known recent artist. In his album *L'Origine* the hero, Julius Corentin Acquefacques, is a 'prisonnier des rêves' who works at the Orwellian 'Ministère de l'Humour'.[42] Julius lives in a small, box-like apartment; his job at the ministry is deciding which jokes are suitable for publication in *bandes dessinées*.

Like Gaston Lagaffe, Achille Talon and early Tintin, Julius works in *bande dessinée* publishing; but Julius's profession, unlike the others', does not even pretend to authenticate fiction. The reverse is true: Mathieu constantly reminds us that Julius is pure make-believe. For example, Julius opens a copy of *L'Origine* and discovers a picture of himself inside it (p. 27).

Sometimes Mathieu jokingly asks readers to believe that Julius exists, with exceptionally unorthodox methods. One of Julius's colleagues says, 'Nous n'existons pas par nous-mêmes! La raison de notre existence nous dépasse! Nous faisons partie d'un projet dont l'explication se trouve dans le monde tri-dimensionnel' (p. 40). These words clearly separate our real, three-dimensional world from Julius's imaginary, two-dimensional paper world. But at that very point, a panel is cut out; the empty space left by the missing panel enables readers to see right through to a picture of Julius on the next page. Julius's world is now three-dimensional, just like the real world.

Mathieu's second album about Julius, *La Qu ...*, is similarly tongue in cheek.[43] The album opens with a huge explosion, which throws Julius up into the air. A caption reads 'Si la plupart des histoires se terminent par une chute ... n'était-il pas logique qu'un nouvel épisode commençat par une attraction vers le haut?' (p. 4). Mathieu is playing upon the double meaning of 'chute': a gag's punchline and a fall. He is overturning convention by opening the album with an inverted 'chute'.

After that, by combining hand-drawn pictures with a photograph, Mathieu fragments the graphic style. Julius falls back to earth and lands in a photographed cup of coffee. Julius then awakes to his Orwellian unreality, where he is arrested for not closing his drawer. At his trial, the lawyers sing in rhyme. Julius is 'condamné à rejoindre la gare', a building that resembles the Gare de Lyon in Paris (pp. 18–22).

Julius sets out for the station but, as in a dream, it recedes from him, remaining at a constant distance away. Julius goes to sleep, and when he awakes the station has moved closer to him, apparently of its own accord. After reaching the station and boarding a train Julius arrives at a lighthouse, and black-and-white artwork gives way to colour. In the final dialogue, characters ask once more where reality ends and where dreams begin:

> – Croyez-vous que nous rêvons en noir et blanc?
> – Quelle drôle de question voisin! Bien sûr!! La preuve: regardez autour de vous.
> – Alors la couleur existe peut-être réellement?
> – On peut rêver! (p. 48).

Mathieu's stories, like some strips by Régis Franc, make jokes that blur the distinction between the real and the imaginary.

However, Mathieu's graphic style is closer to Tardi's than to Franc's *Café de la plage* and 'Sommeil'. Mathieu's tall, sinister buildings with staring windows resemble those in 'La Bascule à Charlot'; Julius's dreamlike reality, in which everything keeps changing inexplicably, recalls Tardi's *Véritable Histoire du soldat inconnu.*

Other young artists, both humorous and non-humorous, appeared during the 1990s, centred around a new French publisher, L'Association. The most prolific among the humorists is Lewis Trondheim. Trondheim's *Lapinot et les Carottes de Patagonie* begins as a Disneyesque tale about a humanised rabbit's love of magical carrots; but the plot is exaggeratedly complex and labyrinthine, lasting a staggering 500 pages.[44] *Lapinot et les Carottes* is perhaps the longest (and certainly one of the most deliberately anti-commercial) comic strips ever published. One wonders how many children read it right through.

Trondheim's and Jean-Christophe Menu's *Moins d'un Quart de seconde pour vivre* is also noteworthy, as it is a conscious attempt to limit the form.[45] This comic, which is 100 pages long, comprises different combinations of the same eight panels. The accompanying dialogues, which do vary, are comical, bogusly philosophical discussions. One repeated image shows a man talking to a frog; the frog only says 'kroa', which the man understands as 'croire', leading him to believe that the frog is God. Trondheim's album *Le Dormeur* limits the form still further: the same picture of a man in bed is repeated from the first page to the last. The immobile man has humorous bed-time conversations with a woman, whom the reader never sees.[46]

In Trondheim's album *Les Aventures de l'Univers*, some of the gags are rather more orthodox. A bird-like character in a French-speaking suburban home humorously comments on politics, current affairs and football. The nascent single currency gives rise to a salty phonetic pun: 'En 1999, la monnaie unique en Europe sera l'euro … en France l'euro reste désagréablement proche de "le rot"'.[47] However, there are also more unusual effects in *Aventures de l'Univers*. In the captions to 'Les Aventures de la chanson', adjectives echo the final syllable of their respective nouns. The result is an ingenious piece of poetic wordplay, which conjures up a picture: 'Le kangourou roux, sous l'érable bleu … cherche son verre vert et boit la blonde onde' (p. 28).

The humorous innovations of the early/mid-1990s happened at a time when *bande dessinée* sales were falling. The drop in sales may be explained by the deliberately anti-commercial aspects of some new artists, as well as by the prolonged recession; cut-throat competition from video and computer games also held sales down. According to Benoît Peeters, only 51 new albums were published in 1991 and 32 in 1992.[48] However, 'classical' strips still sold well, and new *bandes dessinées* outnumbered new novels.

By the end of the decade the European economies were recovering, and *bande dessinée* sales rose again. In 1999 Groensteen said that, according to a survey by *Livre Hebdo*, 'on a atteint le chiffre record de 1055 albums parus en langue française, dont 75% environ de créations originales'.[49] Such healthy figures bode well for the future. The ninth art's cultural contribution is now officially recognised in France just as much as it is in Belgium: to mark the new millennium, *bandes dessinées* gained their full *lettres de noblesse* with a prestigious exhibition, 'Maîtres de la bande dessinée européenne', at the Bibliothèque nationale in Paris (October 2000–January 2001).

In the USA comic strips have also prospered, although official recognition has come more slowly. Experimentalism, having all but disappeared with the Underground, returned in Chris Ware's still-continuing *Acme Novelty Library* series. Ware's eclectic graphic style is inspired by Franco-Belgian 'clear line' as well as by 'classic' American strips like *Superman*. Some panels take up almost a whole page; others measure barely half a centimetre across. Ware tells the life-story of 'Jimmy Corrigan, the smartest kid on earth'; the panels jump between various stages of Jimmy's life (childhood, youth, old age) without explanations; as in *Le Garage hermétique*, readers have to piece the narrative together.[50] The story focuses on Jimmy's relationships with his parents and with a God-like Superman figure, whose inexplicable appearances and disappearances punctuate the story.

Superhero comics still flourish in America. In *Superman. Peace on Earth*, Superman finally reached his limits.[51] Not before time, Superman decides to alleviate world hunger; unfortunately, his efforts at food redistribution lead to instability, rioting and an act of war. Superman causes as many problems as he solves. However, the moral message remains intact, for he abandons his quest with the words,

> I now see that taking on this responsibility was too ambitious for one man, even a Superman. The welfare of Earth and all its people

will always be my primary concern. But if there is a solution to the problem of hunger, it must be one that comes from the compassionate heart of man and extends outward toward to his fellow man (n.pag).

In *Superman. Peace on Earth*, Superman no longer rights a wrong. Arguably, Superman does the opposite: he makes an already bad situation worse, while fuelling false expectations. How America's superheroes react to unfolding events in the twenty-first century will be a continuing point of interest.

Conclusion

Between the late colonial period and the turn of the twenty-first century, attitudes towards *bandes dessinées* changed out of all recognition in France and in Belgium. When Hergé's Tintin first appeared, *bandes dessinées* were under America's shadow and were frequently viewed with suspicion. Nowadays, the ninth art is an integral part of Franco-Belgian culture that is consumed by almost everybody, from the Presidents downwards. The ninth art's cultural contribution is officially recognised; *bande dessinée* museums and festivals exist in Brussels and in Angoulême, partly funded by the Belgian and French governments. In the USA, the picture is different. The American artist Will Eisner, who drew *The Spirit*, commented that comic strips command far less respect in America than they do in France:

> Ce que j'apprécie surtout, c'est le climat intellectuel qui règne en France. C'est le seul pays où les auteurs de bande dessinée sont à ce point intégrés dans la communauté artistique traditionnelle. C'est très important à mes yeux, parce que cette reconnaissance officielle entraîne les auteurs à se montrer plus exigeants envers eux-mêmes, pour être dignes de ce qu'on attend d'eux. Ici, on ne me considère pas comme un pauvre type quand je dis que je fais de la bande dessinée.[1]

If *bandes dessinées* are now a serious art form, then each artist that we have studied must take some credit. Hergé is the leading figure because, with *Les Aventures de Tintin*, *bandes dessinées* first established their own, peculiarly Franco-Belgian identity. Many critics have commented on Hergé's work: Tisseron read *Les Aventures de Tintin* as Hergé's subconscious search for a personal identity; however, cultural identity is what primarily concerns us in this book.

Hergé's influence on Franco-Belgian popular culture was immense. *Les Aventures de Tintin* reiterated a commonly used folktale structure, although Hergé's scepticism about America immediately distanced his work from US comics; rather than being another mythological superhero Tintin was a model boy scout, with whom young French-speakers could sympathise far more readily. Tintin gradually became less perfect and more human; this development encouraged readers to imagine him sharing their everyday reality. By the 1950s, Hergé had convinced most people that Tintin was living both in France and Belgium; Moulinsart was a space in which the two countries merged.

Hergé also invented a very influential graphic style: 'clear line'. 'Clear line', combined with well-documented depictions of real places, formed Hergéen realism's central planks. Hergéen realism, which had no direct American equivalent, remained the uncontested model for depicting reality in BDs until *nouveau réalisme* in the 1970s. It was later rediscovered by French artists such as François Bourgeon, during *le retour au récit*. Hergé's commercial arrangements set the pattern for almost all later artists. He started the characteristically Franco-Belgian process of turning *bandes dessinées* into art: his impeccable graphic techniques and his beautiful hardback albums transformed comic strips into long-lasting aesthetic objects.

André Franquin, another Belgian, also made a significant impact in France. After drawing stories that were obviously influenced by Hergé and Disney, Franquin achieved different results in *Les Aventures de Spirou*: anti-militarism, irony at the hero's expense, and moral ambiguity. Like Hergé, Franquin brought in a cast of original, secondary characters, while perfecting his distinctive graphic style: the quintessentially post-war Franco-Belgian 'style atome'. With *Gaston Lagaffe* Franquin reinvented gags to great comic effect, and he developed another immediately recognisable graphic style, which combined detailed, exaggeratedly caricatural chaos with tight graphic control. In *Idées noires* Franquin adopted a harsher, uglier style, taking black humour to extremes not seen in *bandes dessinées* before.

Our masters of the ninth art are not only worth studying because of their originality, but also because their work is a revealing page of popular history; sometimes *bandes dessinées* tell decidedly unpalatable truths about the societies in which they operate. Early Hergé and Franquin were strongly influenced by European assumptions of racial and cultural superiority but, as the colonial era receded, both artists ceased to reinforce such values. While Hergé was bringing 'clear line' to perfection, Franquin glorified the prevailing technological optimism and American-led consumerism. Spirou's later adventures, like *Les Aventures de Tintin*, evinced a disenchantment with consumerism long before May '68, the Underground and *nouveau réalisme.* Gaston Lagaffe, who first appeared in 1957, foreshadowed the questioning of previously hallowed attitudes (such as militarism and the work ethic) that became widespread during the late 1960s; Gaston also prefigured the rise of environmentalism in the 1980s and 1990s. With *Idées noires*, Franquin took anguish about loss of innocence to extremes. His unremittingly black humour even surpassed the defiant despair of 1970s punk.

Les Aventures d'Astérix is by far the bestselling *bande dessinée*; to many people across the world, Astérix is the ninth art. He is a cultural asset, and his high profile greatly reinforces the ninth art's identity at the international level. Astérix is a hero with whom almost anyone anywhere can identify, as he can represent whatever readers like. And yet Astérix is also a distinctly Franco-Belgian European: the French and Belgians are both descended from the Gauls, and the two countries' histories are closely entwined. Moreover, Goscinny and Uderzo exploit the resources of the shared French language fully; they make innumerable jokes about European Francophone history, culture and current events; they also reinvigorate a French-speaking tradition of anachronistic humour, which dates back at least as far as Touchatout.

Since the 1960s and *Pilote*, the centre of *bande dessinée* activity has moved to France, although Belgium is still an important player. Belgian artists Hergé and Franquin won the prestigious Grand Prix at the French Angoulême BD festival in the 1970s; to this day *Les Aventures de Tintin*, *Gaston Lagaffe* and *Le Chat* are bestsellers in France. The ninth art has given France and Belgium a common folk-lore, as well as a plethora of shared mythological heroes and heroines: Tintin, Gaston, Astérix, Blueberry, Brindavoine, Adèle, Difool and more. France and Belgium form part of the same market, cultural barriers are down, and exchanges between the two countries flourish as never before. Belgian publishers Casterman, Dupuis and Pepper-land publish leading French artists such as Giraud, Tardi, Montellier and Franc; in Paris, Rombaldi and Audie publish Franquin; Belgian publishers bring out studies on French artists, and vice versa.

The Frenchman Jean Giraud (aka Gir and Moebius) was the most influential *bande dessinée* artist of his generation. In *Lieutenant Blueberry* Gir's experiments with panels, colours and balloons freed Western comics, an American genre *par excellence*, from Holly-wood's influence. Western BDs continue to this day thanks chiefly to Gir's influence and example.

Moebius' 'Cauchemar blanc' is a violent *fait divers* whose cold, straight lines marked a new departure by introducing 'la question du réel' to *bandes dessinées*. 'La question du réel' links *bandes dessinées* to European Modernism and the avant-garde, which first appeared in late nineteenth/early twentieth-century Paris. 'La question du réel' resurfaces particularly strongly in French-speaking culture: Dada, Surrealism, Absurdism, Céline and May '68, as well as humorous and realist *bandes dessinées*. *Nouveau réalisme*, like the US Underground, coincided with an era of unrest and social change; however, Underground artists caricatured American culture and society.

Moebius and his friend Philippe Druillet continued the tradition of experimenting with science fiction strips, which dated back to Pellos in pre-war France. Even more than Pellos and Druillet, Moebius challenged American SF comics' most basic assumptions. *Arzach* had no written text. *Le Garage hermétique* was not a series of panels arranged in a logical sequence. In *L'Incal*, Moebius' artwork and Jodorowsky's story-telling introduced a fragmented graphic style, an esoteric symbolism and a circular plot, which were previously unknown in SF comics. *Edena* drew upon Moebius' personal preoccupations of religion and instinctotherapy. Along with Moebius, Pellos and Druillet, other artists gave science fiction *bandes dessinées* an identity distinct from that of American SF comics: neither *Valérian* nor *Les Pionniers de l'Espérance* had superheroes; both criticised capitalism.

Continuing the Franco-Belgian trend set by Hergé, Giraud bridged the gap between *bandes dessinées* and what Eisner called 'la communauté artistique traditionnelle'. Giraud's comics consistently point to 'high art', by which I mean painting, sculpture, poetry and novels. 'Cauchemar blanc' asks the 'la question du réel' in ways that are comparable to Modernist sculpture and painting. *Arzach* has the suggestive power and the mysterious symbolism of poetry. *Le Garage hermétique* exchanges old forms for new by disrupting the narrative's linear flow; it involves readers in generating meaning in ways comparable to Robbe-Grillet's *nouveau roman*. *L'Incal* is built on grandiose, Blakean symbolism. *Edena* recalls a Zola novel.

Jacques Tardi is another major talent. His experiments with 'la question du réel' played a crucial role in giving *bande dessinée* realism new directions from the 1970s. Tardi, like Hergé, Moebius and others, bridged the gap separating *bandes dessinées* from 'la communauté artistique traditionnelle': Tardi gave BDs a literary dimension that makes them comparable to nineteenth/early twentieth-century French novels. *Le Démon des glaces* is influenced by Jules Verne, albeit with added irony. 'La Bascule à Charlot' questions the hero's reliability, achieving results that are comparable to Flaubert. 'La Fleur au fusil' and *C'était la Guerre des tranchées* have a level of characterisation that is worthy of the Great War novelists. *Les Aventures extraordinaires d'Adèle Blanc-Sec* humorously rework clichés from *romans feuilletons*. Tardi further strengthened the *bande dessinée*'s Franco-Belgian identity by approaching war in Europe from a specifically Franco-Belgian standpoint: he drew upon the painful, shared recollections of neighbouring countries that had been fought over and occupied during the twentieth century. Tardi's non-humorous war strips, like Astérix's burlesque comedies, thus helped the French and the Belgians engage with their collective past.

After Franquin's success, many other *bande dessinée* artists drew humorous gags. By making people laugh, our three French humorists all fostered a sense of belonging to Franco-Belgian culture. Marcel Gotlib sent up French and Belgian historical figures, BDs, films, songs, popular novels and literary classics; his cultural in-joking is often all but impenetrable to English-speakers. Claire Bretécher's human comedy is more accessible to people outside France and Belgium, yet, unlike satirists in the USA, Bretécher took European Francophone culture and society as her principal frame of reference. Régis Franc's *Café de la plage* plunges readers into a comically *nouveau réaliste* world, where the real is indistinguishable from the imaginary; some of Franc's jokes play with ideas coming from Francophone comic strips; others make fun of French-speaking writers and painters, singers and politicians.

The late 1970s and the 1980s witnessed *le retour au récit*, with its profusion of historical and futuristic settings. The trend reveals a popular desire to turn away from contemporary reality, to establish links with the past, and to find new uses for pre-existing forms. Since *le retour au récit* the next generation has already emerged.

At a time when English-speaking popular culture dominates, the *bande dessinée*'s contribution to a strong identity should not be underestimated. In the age of mass communication, *bandes dessinées* give French and Belgian culture a clear, distinctive voice that reaches vast numbers of people. Whether consciously or not, *bande dessinée* artists are influenced by their joint historical and cultural heritage; by bringing those influences to bear on BDs artists rework the old into the new, thus constructing contemporary Franco-Belgian folklore.

Bandes dessinées perform another key function: they make a shared sense of Franco-Belgian identity pleasurable. BDs offer a multitude of cultural references, both playful and serious, which the French-speaking public evidently enjoys recognising. I have picked many of those references out, but there is no shortage of others.

Since the very beginning, *bandes dessinées* have been overturning the rules of American comics. Most remarkably the ninth art binds France and Belgium together with a common mythology, which is quite unlike that of the American mega-power: French and Belgian readers never identify collectively with superheroes, who unambiguously embody victorious strength. In the USA superheroes triumphed almost to the end, even though violence sometimes overshadowed their moral high ground. The ninth art produced very different artistic and literary effects, with triumphant might giving way to character development, moral ambivalence, irony and 'la question du réel'. In the *bande dessinée* 'classics' studied in Part I, Hergéen realism slowly makes Tintin fallible, Spirou is undermined, Gaston is morally ambiguous, while Astérix means anything and nothing. The trend away from superheroes gathers pace among the artists studied in Part II: Blueberry, Tío José, Arzach, Grubert, Brindavoine, Choumacher, Adèle, Difool, Stel, Atan, Isabeau and Hoel are all vulnerable, contradictory, mistake-prone and struggling to keep up with events; their victories over evil are by no means certain.

During the twentieth century, French-speakers often expressed fears about losing the qualities which make them unique by becoming over-Americanised; today, as Ardagh states, it is quite plain that those fears have not materialised. Despite the widespread misgivings, 'the worst has not happened'.[2] Belgium and France have not been entirely submerged by outside influences. The opposite is true: France and Belgium have managed to retain a distinctive identity. That achievement has been possible thanks to the two countries' cultural vibrancy just as much as to their politics, economics and military.

Bandes dessinées play an active, high-profile role in sustaining Franco-Belgian culture's vibrancy; the ninth art has even become one of Franco-Belgian culture's distinguishing characteristics; thus, it satisfies the deep-rooted need for a unique, distinct cultural identity. Given the ninth art's importance we can only assume that, despite stiff competition from TV, computers and video games, *bandes dessinées* will be consumed in large numbers well into the twenty-first century.

Notes

Introduction

1 *Grand Dictionnaire Hachette*, 2nd edn (Paris: Hachette, 1996), p. 96.

2 Richard Reynolds, *Superheroes, a Modern Mythology* (Jackson, MI: University of Mississippi Press, 1992), p. 7.

3 Matthew Screech, 'André Franquin, Master of the Ninth Art', *Journal of Popular Culture*, 33.3 (1999), pp. 95–133. Matthew Screech, 'Jean Giraud/Moebius: Nouveau Réalisme and Science Fiction', in *Francophone Bandes dessinées*, ed. Laurence Grove and Charles Forsdick (Rodopi: Amsterdam, forthcoming). *Francophone Bandes dessinées* is a collection of articles based on papers given at the *bande dessinée* conference held at Glasgow University in 1999. Matthew Screech, 'Gotlib's Progress', in the online journal *Belphegor* (forthcoming). This edition of *Belphegor* is a collection of articles based on papers given at the *bande dessinée* conference held at Leicester University in 2003.

4 For a helpful summary see Susan Hayward, who traces the European concept of 'nation-ness' back to the French Enlightenment, in *French National Cinema* (London: Routledge, 1993), pp. 1–5.

5 Anne-Marie Thiesse, *La Création des identités nationales* (Paris: Seuil, 1999), p. 14.

6 Henri Pirenne, *Histoire de Belgique*, 7 vols (Brussels: Lamertin, 1908–1932), VII, pp. 388–89.

7 Frank Huggett, *Modern Belgium* (London: Pall Mall, 1969), p. 89.

8 David Gordon, *The French Language and National Identity* (The Hague: Mouton, 1978), pp. 4 and 102.

9 Ernest Renan, 'Qu'est-ce qu'une Nation?', in *Oeuvres complètes d'Ernest Renan*, ed. Henriette Psichari, 10 vols (Paris: Calmann Lévy, 1947), I, pp. 887–906 (903–04).

10 Vladimir Propp, *Theory and History of Folklore*, trans. Ariadna and Richard Martin (Manchester: Manchester University Press, 1984), p. 13

11 Scott McCloud, *Understanding Comics* (New York: Harper Perennial, 1994), p. 144.

12 Rodolphe Töpffer, *M. Jabot et M. Vieux Bois* (Paris: Seuil, 1996). For more on Töpffer's publishing history see Thierry Groensteen's introduction to that edition. See also Thierry Groensteen and Benoît Peeters, *Töpffer: L'Invention de la bande dessinée* (Paris: Hermann, 1994).

13 Many *bandes dessinées* have publishing histories complex enough to merit a

separate study in themselves. To keep notes reasonably simple, I shall give author, title, and first year and place of publication. Georges Colomb, *La Famille Fénouillard,* first published by *Petit Français illustré* (Paris, 1889). Maurice Languereau and Joseph-Porphyre Pinchon, *Bécassine,* first published by *Semaine de Suzette* (Paris, 1905). Louis Forton, *La Bande des Pieds Nickelés,* first published by *L'Epatant* (Paris, 1908). For further information on the history of those strips and others discussed below, see Henri Filippini, *Dictionnaire de la bande dessinée* (Paris: Bordas, 1989), pp. 184–85, 51 and 408.

14 Alain Saint Ogan, *Zig et Puce,* first published by *Dimanche illustré* (Paris, 1925). See Filippini, pp. 572–73.

15 Rodolph Dirks, *The Katzenjammer Kids,* first published by *New York Journal* (New York, 1897). Published in France under the title *Pim Pam Poum* (Paris: Hachette, 1934). *Pim Pam Poum* also appeared in Walt Disney's *Journal de Mickey* (Paris, 1934). See Filippini, p. 411.

16 Walt Disney's Mickey Mouse first appeared in the movie *Plane Crazy* (1927). His first comic was published in 1930. Elzle Segar, *Popeye,* first published under the title *The Thimble Theatre* by King Features Syndicate (New York, 1929). George McManus, *Bringing up Father,* first published by *New York American* (New York, 1913). Alex Raymond, *Flash Gordon,* first published by King Features Syndicate (New York, 1934). Harold Foster, *Tarzan,* based on the character invented by Edgar Rice Burroughs, first published by Metropolitan Newspaper Service (New York, 1929). Jerry Siegel and Joe Shuster, *Superman,* first published by *Action Comics* (New York, 1938). For more on the above strips' publishing histories see Filippini, pp. 351, 418, 186, 196, 513 and 505.

17 Filippini, p. xiv.

18 David Manning White and Robert Abel, *The Funnies* (London: Collier Macmillan, 1963), p. 95.

19 Filippini, p. xvi.

20 For more on this subject, see André Franquin and Joseph Gillain, *Comment on devient Créateur de bandes dessinées* (Verviers, Belgium: Marabout, 1969), p. 45.

21 René Henoumont, *Au Bonheur des Belges. Histoire d'une identité* (Monaco: Rocher, 1992), p. 134; italics in original.

22 For example, Frédéric Gaussen, 'La Génération du regard', *Monde Campus* [Paris], 20 November 1986, p. 8.

23 Umberto Eco, 'The Myth of Superman', in *The Role of the Reader* (Bloomington, IN: Indiana University Press, 1979), pp. 107–24.

24 Evelyne Sullerot, quoted on flyleaf of Pierre Fresnault-Deruelle, *La Bande dessinée. Essai d'analyse sémiotique* (Paris: Hachette, 1972).

25 Pierre Couperie et al., *History of the Comic Strip,* trans. Eileen Hennessy (New York: Crown, 1968). Patrick Gaumer and Claude Moliterni, *Dictionnaire mondial de la bande dessinée* (Paris: Larousse, 1994).

26 Thierry Groensteen, *Système de la bande dessinée* (Paris: Presses Universitaires de France, 1999). For Fresnault-Deruelle see note 24 above.

27 Jean-Bruno Renard, *Clefs pour la bande dessinée* (Paris: Seghers, 1978), pp. 227–28.

28 Bruno Lecigne and Jean-Pierre Tamine, *Fac-Similé* (Paris: Futuropolis, 1983).

29 Serge Tisseron, *Psychanalyse de la bande dessinée* (Paris: Presses Universitaires de France, 1987), p. 15.

30 François Schuiten and Benoît Peeters, *L'Aventure des images: de la bande dessinée au multi-média* (Paris: Autrement, 1996).

31 Roger Sabin, *Adult Comics* (London and New York: Routledge, 1993); *Comics, Comix and Graphic Novels* (London: Phaidon, 1996).

32 Jerry Robinson, *Comics. An Illustrated History* (New York: G.P. Putnam and Sons, 1974). Maurice Horn, *The World Encyclopedia of Comics* (New York: Chelsea House, 1976). Denis Gifford, *The International Book of Comics* (London: Deans International, 1984). Steve Duin and Mike Richardson, *Comics. Between the Panels* (Milwaukee: Dark Horse, 1998).

33 Libbie McQuillan, 'Between the Sheets at *Pilote*, 1968–1973', *International Journal of Comic Art*, 2.1 (2000), pp. 159–77. K.A. Laity, 'Construction of a "Female Hero": Iconography in *Les Aventures extraordinaires d'Adèle Blanc-Sec*', *International Journal of Comic Art*, 4.1 (2002), pp. 163–69.

1 Constructing the Franco-Belgian Hero: Hergé's *Aventures de Tintin*

1 For more on Hergé's early life and work see Harry Thompson, *Tintin, Hergé and his Creation* (London: Hodder and Stoughton, 1991).

2 After serialisation in *Le Petit Vingtième*, Tintin's first adventure was republished in the album *Tintin au Pays des Soviets* (Brussels: Editions du Petit Vingtième, 1930). Tintin's publishing history is extremely long and complex. Put briefly, his adventures were serialised in the Brussels-based magazines *Le Petit Vingtième* (1929–1940), *Le Soir jeunesse* (1940–1945) and *Le Journal de Tintin* (1945–1976). Following serialisation, each Tintin adventure was republished in hardback album form by Casterman (Tournai, Belgium). All following references to *Les Aventures de Tintin* give dates and page numbers from the albums. For a full account of Hergé's publishing history, see Thompson, pp. 217–18.

3 Hergé is quoted as saying he read *Bringing up Father*, *Krazy Kat* and *Zig et Puce* in Numa Sadoul, *Entretiens avec Hergé* (Tournai: Casterman, 1989), pp. 26, 29, 37 and 123. All following references to Sadoul in this chapter come from this book. George Herriman, *Krazy Kat*, first published by King Features Syndicate (New York, 1911). First published in France by *Charlie mensuel* (Paris, 1970). See Filippini, p. 299

4 Hector Malot, *Sans Famille*, 2 vols (Paris: Dentu, 1879).

5 Benjamin Rabier and Fred Isly, *Tintin Lutin* (Paris: Juven, 1898).

6 Gaston Leroux, *Les Chefs d'œuvre de Gaston Leroux*, ed. Gilbert Sigaux, 4 vols (Paris: Laffont, 1969), I, p. 11. Hergé read Rouletabille according to H. Van Opstal in *Tracé RG.* (Brussels: Lefrancq, 1998), p. 164.

7 Quoted in Sadoul, p. 40.

8 Dominique Labesse, 'Le Comique chez Hergé', *Cahiers de la bande dessinée, spécial Hergé* [Grenoble], 14/15 (1971), pp. 52–54 (p. 54). Labesse is paraphrasing Molière's *Premier Placet présenté au Roi sur la comédie de Tartuffe* (1682): 'Le

devoir de la comédie étant de corriger les hommes en les divertissant', François Molière, *Œuvres complètes,* ed. Georges Couton, 2 vols (Paris: Pleiade, 1971), I, p. 889.

9 Scott McCloud discusses the particular importance of the spaces between panels and reader participation at length in *Understanding Comics,* pp. 60–93.

10 Quoted in Sadoul, p. 56.

11 Thompson, p. 10.

12 See, for example, G.R., 'Tintin le «vertueux»', *Jeune Afrique* [Tunis], 3–9 January 1962, p. 25.

13 Quoted in Sadoul, p. 74.

14 Frédéric Soumois, *Dossier Tintin* (Brussels: Jacques Antoine, 1987), p. 30.

15 Thompson, p. 47.

16 Quoted in Sadoul, p. 61.

17 'War of 1812', *Frontline Combat* [New York], May/June 1952, n. pag [artist unknown]. 'War of 1812' is not thought to have been published in French.

18 Mark Estren, *A History of Underground Comics,* 3rd edn (Berkeley, CA: Ronin Publishing, 1993), pp. 198–99.

19 Jon Tuska, *The Filming of the West* (London: Robert Hale, 1978), p. 533. Tuska's italics.

20 René Gonnard, *La Légende du bon sauvage* (Paris: Medicis, 1946), pp. 10–11.

21 Thompson, p. 55.

22 Pierre Sterckx, *Tintin et les Médias* (Brussels: Bibliothèque d'Alice, 1997), pp. 50–51.

23 Quoted in Sadoul, p. 66.

24 Vladimir Propp, *Morphology of the Folktale,* trans. Laurence Scott, 2nd edn (Austin and London: University of Texas Press, 1968). The hero's 'absentation', testing and triumphant return summarised in my next three paragraphs are described in Propp, pp. 25–60. For a critical appraisal of Propp see Martin Barker, *Comics, Ideology, Power and the Critics* (Manchester and New York: Manchester University Press, 1989), pp. 160–84.

25 Propp, *Morphology of the Folktale,* p. 92.

26 Propp, *Morphology of the Folktale,* p. 50.

27 Walt Disney, *Mickey Mouse in Color: 1930s Comic Strip Classics* (New York: Pantheon Books, 1988). For an in-depth discussion of foreign countries in Disney see Barker, pp. 279–99. For more on Superman see Les Daniels, *Superman: The Complete History* (San Francisco: Chronicle, 1998).

28 Reynolds, p. 74.

29 Claude Levi-Strauss, quoted in Serge Tisseron, *Tintin et le Secret d'Hergé* (Paris: Editions Hors Collection, 1993), p. 8. For more on Hergé's realism see Michael Farr, *Tintin. Le Rêve et la réalité* (Brussels: Moulinsart, 2001).

30 Benoît Peeters, *Tintin and the World of Hergé,* trans. Michael Farr, 2nd edn (London: Methuen Children's Books, 1995), p. 48.

31 Peeters, *Tintin and the World of Hergé,* p. 52.

32 Peeters, *Tintin and the World of Hergé,* p. 53

33 Soumois, p. 138.

34 Reynolds, p. 19.

35 Jacques Tardi was interviewed by me in Paris on 2 September 2001. All following quotations from Tardi come from this interview unless otherwise stated.

36 For more on *Tarzan*'s settings, see Francis Lacassin, *Tarzan ou le Chevalier crispé*, 2nd edn (Paris: Henri Veyrier, 1982).

37 Milton Caniff, *Terry and the Pirates*, first published by News Syndicate (Chicago and New York, 1934). First published in France by *L'As* magazine (Paris). Date not known. See Filippini, pp. 517–18. For more on Caniff's realism, see Lawrence E. Mintz, 'Fantasy, Formula, Realism and Propaganda in Milton Caniff's Comic Strips', *Journal of Popular Culture* [Bowling Green, Ohio], 12.4 (1979), pp. 653–80.

38 Thompson, p. 92.

39 Peeters, *Tintin and the World of Hergé*, p. 67.

40 Peeters, *Tintin and the World of Hergé*, p. 71.

41 Quoted in Sadoul, p. 165.

42 Peeters, *Tintin and the World of Hergé*, p. 76.

43 Diane Hennebert, 'Bruxelles, la Ville de Tintin, n'apparaît qu'en filigraine', *Géo hors série* [Paris], November 2000, pp. 166–71 (p. 171).

44 Jean-Marie Apostolides, *Les Métamorphoses de Tintin* (Paris: Seghers, 1984), p. 42.

45 Quoted in Sadoul, p. 165.

46 Serge Tisseron, *Tintin chez le Psychanalyste* (Paris: Aubier, 1985); *Hergé* (Paris: Seghers, 1987); *Tintin et le Secret d'Hergé*. See note 29 above.

47 Tisseron, *Tintin et le Secret d'Hergé*, p. 41.

48 Tisseron, *Tintin et le Secret d'Hergé*, p. 43.

49 Tisseron, *Tintin et le Secret d'Hergé*, p. 43.

50 Tisseron, *Tintin et le Secret d'Hergé*, p. 47.

51 Tisseron, *Tintin et le Secret d'Hergé*, p. 100.

52 Quoted in Sadoul, p. 149.

53 Tisseron, *Tintin et le Secret d'Hergé*, p. 69.

54 Tisseron, *Tintin et le Secret d'Hergé*, p. 48.

55 Tisseron, *Tintin et le Secret d'Hergé*, p. 43.

56 Quoted in Sadoul, pp. 68–69.

57 Apostolides, p. 158.

58 Pierre-Louis Augereau, *Hergé au Pays des Tarots* (Paris: Cheminements, 1999). Jean-Paul Tomasi and Michel Deligne, *Tintin chez Jules Verne* (Brussels: Lefrancq, 1998).

59 Quoted in Sadoul, p. 97.

60 Peeters, *Tintin and the World of Hergé*, p. 90.

61 Quoted in Sadoul, p. 170.

62 Quoted in Sadoul, p. 171.

63 Hergé, 'Heure par heure', *Paris Match* [Paris], 29 November 1969, pp. 30–33. Jean Cau, 'La Victoire d'Apollo XII', *Paris Match*, 29 November 1969, pp. 34–35 (p. 34). 'Maison de la radio', *France soir* [Paris], 22 July 1969, p. 6.

64 Quoted in Sadoul, pp. 172–74.

65 Quoted in Sadoul, p. 70. Sadoul's italics.

66 Tisseron, *Tintin et le Secret d'Hergé*, p. 54.

67 Tisseron, *Tintin et le Secret d'Hergé*, p. 68.

68 Tisseron, *Tintin et le Secret d'Hergé*, p. 68. Tisseron's italics.

69 Alain Chante, *99 Réponses sur la bande dessinée* (Montpellier: Reseau CRDP, 1996), p. 81.

70 Quoted in Sadoul, p. 62.

71 Satish Kumar, *The CIA and the Third World*, 2nd edn (London: Zed Books, 1981), pp. 58–62. Gabriel García Márquez, *One Hundred Years of Solitude*, trans. Gregory Rabassa (London: Picador, 1970).

72 Alan Moore and Bill Sienkiewicz, *Brought to Light* (London: Titan, 1989).

73 Stan Lee and Steve Ditko, *Spiderman*, first published by Marvel Comics (New York, 1962). First published in French by *Superstrange* magazine (Paris, 1968). Stan Lee and Jack Kirby, *X Men*, first published by Marvel Comics (New York, 1963). First published in French by *Strange* magazine (Paris, 1970). Stan Lee and Jack Kirby, *The Incredible Hulk*, first published by Marvel Comics (New York, 1962). First published in French by *Fantask* magazine (Paris, 1969). See Filippini, pp. 495, 563 and 248.

74 White and Abel, p. 13.

75 Régis Franc was interviewed by me in Paris on 5 September 2001. All following quotations from Franc come from this interview.

76 'Tintin au Pays du commerce', *Libération* [Paris], 5–6 March 1983, p. 26.

77 The international *bande dessinée* festival, held at Angoulême (France) every January since 1974, awards an annual Grand Prix to one outstanding artist.

78 Tim Judah, 'Tintin in the Dock', *Guardian Weekend Supplement* [London], 30 January 1999, pp. 8–18 (p. 8).

79 Henri Amouroux, 'Tintin, le Capitaine Haddock et les Bachi-Bouzouks', *Loire Matin* [Saint Etienne], 4 December 1981, pp. 1 and 6 (p. 1). Jean-Michel Helvig, 'Tintin-Chirac et les Picaroses', *Libération* [Paris], 5–6 March 1983, p. 6.

80 General Charles de Gaulle, quoted in André Malraux, *Les Chênes qu'on abat* (Paris: Gallimard, 1971), p. 52.

81 Judah, p. 18

82 Jacqueline Dana, 'Rencontre avec Tintin', *Marie-France* [Paris], January 1976, pp. 78–79 (p. 78). Jean-Pierre Allaux, 'Milou raconte Tintin', *Vie catholique* [Paris], 4 June 1975, pp. 24–26. Ariane Valadié, *Ma Vie de chien. Entretiens avec Milou* (Paris: J.C. Lattès, 1993). 'Tintin est mort', *Libération* [Paris], 5–6 March 1983.

83 Michel Serres, 'C'est l'Auteur qui a le plus marqué la culture contemporaine', *Libération* [Paris], 5–6 March 1983, p. 25.

84 Willy Vandersteen, *Bob et Bobette. Le Fantôme espagnol* (Brussels: Lombard, 1953). Maurice Tilleux, *Félix* (Brussels: Heroic Albums, 1949). Jacques Martin, *Lefranc et la Grande Menace* (Brussels: Lombard, 1954). Georges Chaulet and François Craenhals, *Les Quatre As et le serpent de la mer* (Tournai: Casterman, 1964).

85 Edgar Jacobs, *Blake et Mortimer. La Marque jaune* (Brussels: Lombard, 1956). Jacques Martin, *Alix l'intrépide* (Brussels: Lombard, 1956). Jacques Laudy, *Hassan et Kaddour. Les Mameluks de Bonaparte* (Brussels: Editions RTP, 1975). Bob de Moor, *Cori le Moussaillon* (Brussels: Distri BD, 1976). François Rivière and Jean-Claude Floc'h, *Le Rendez-vous de Sevenoaks* (Paris: Dargaud, 1977). Johan de Moor and Stephen Desberg, *Gaspard de la Nuit. De l'autre côté du masque* (Tournai: Casterman, 1987). Ted Benoît, *Ray Banana. La Berceuse électrique* (Tournai: Casterman, 1982).

86 Herr Seele and Kamagurka, *Maurice le Cowboy* (Paris: Albin Michel, 1986). Yves Chaland, *Freddy Lombard. Le Testament de Godefroid le Bouillon* (Geneva: Humanoïdes Associés, 1996).

87 Françoise Sagan, *La Femme fardée* (Paris: J.-J. Pauvert, 1981), pp. 38–39.

88 Chris Donald, quoted in Tim Adams, 'Vizionary at Work', *Observer* [London], 14 November 1999, p. 3. For Di Caprio, see 'Great Blistering Barnacles!', *Economist* [London], 31 January 1999, p. 95.

89 Geoff Klock, *How to read Superhero Comics and why* (New York and London: Continuum, 2002), p. 144. Klock adds that Image Comics was set up in direct competition to DC comics and Marvel.

90 For more differences in commercial practices between France, Belgium and the USA, see Sabin, *Adult Comics*, p. 238.

2 Creating Ambiguity: André Franquin's Humorous Strips

1 André Franquin, quoted in Numa Sadoul, *Et Franquin créa Lagaffe* (Brussels: Distri B.D./Schlirf Book, 1986), p. 13. All following references to Sadoul in this chapter come from this book unless otherwise stated.

2 'Le Fureteur vous dira', *Journal de Spirou* [Charleroi], 16 January 1947, p. 4.

3 After serialisation in *Le Journal de Spirou*, each *Spirou et Fantasio* adventure was published in hardback album form by Editions Dupuis (Charleroi). *Spirou et la Maison préfabriquée* was published much later as a hardback album by Dupuis (Charleroi, 1977). Franquin's other early strips discussed below, *Le Tank*, *Radar le Robot* and *L'Héritage de Spirou* were first published in the hardback album *Spirou et Fantasio* (Charleroi: Dupuis, 1948). Unless otherwise stated, all following references give titles and dates from Franquin's albums, with page numbers from the definitive edition of his complete works: *L'Intégrale Franquin* (Paris: Rombaldi, 1985). The volumes in this edition are not numbered, but page numbers run on uninterruptedly from one volume to the next. For that reason, Franquin's strips are identified by page numbers alone. For a full account of Franquin's extremely complex publishing history see Philippe Queveau, *Presque tout Franquin* (Paris: Comset, 1991).

4 Quoted in Franquin and Gillain, p. 17.

5 Quoted in Sadoul, p. 121.

6 Quoted in Sadoul, p. 99.

7 Henri Monnier, *Grandeur et décadence de M. Joseph Prudhomme* (Paris: Michel Lévy, 1852), p. 15. Captain Haddock quotes Monnier in Hergé's *Temple du Soleil* when he says 'ce pisco c'est le plus beau jour de ma vie' (p. 2).

8 Sadoul, p. 102.

9 Rudolph Dirks, 'Pim Pam Poum', *Journal de Mickey* [Paris], 3 November 1935, p. 5. Elzie Segar, 'Popeye/Mathurin', *Robinson* [Paris], 30 January 1938, p. 15. Propp mentions the recurrence in folktales of magical creatures like the Marsupilami with 'extraordinary attributes', who 'offer their services and are accepted as helpers' (pp. 45–46).

10 Sadoul, p. 113.

11 For more on 'style atome' see Anton Makassar, *Le Style Atome* (Brussels: Magic Strip, 1983).

12 Led Tvonvina, 'Les Augures ont prononcé Franquin', *Falatoff* [Paris], November/December 1972, pp. 29–60 (p. 46).

13 See, for example, the reprint of Crumb's 'Modern America', in *Robert Crumb's America* (San Francisco: Last Gasp, 1995), p. 8. Originally published in *Arcade* (San Francisco, 1975).

14 Les Daniels, *Comix. A History of Comic Books in America* (London: Wildwood House, 1973), p. 68.

15 André Franquin, quoted in Pierre Sibille, 'André Franquin, l'Invité du mois', *Libre Belgique* [Brussels], 9 April 1981, pp. 14–15 (p. 14).

16 See Filippini, p. xvi.

17 Ramon Monzon, *Ch'apa et Group Group*, first published in *Vaillant* magazine (Paris, 1956). See Filippini, p. 105.

18 Annie Cordy, 'Houba Houba Hop! La Chanson du Marsupilami', Columbia ESRF 1284M, 1960.

19 Yves-Marie Labé, 'André Franquin, le Père de Gaston s'est arrêté à 950 gags', *Monde* [Paris], 7 January 1997, p. 29.

20 André Franquin, *Modeste et Pompon*, first published by *Journal de Tintin* (Tournai, 1955). Republished as hardback albums by Lombard (Brussels). See Filippini, p. 355.

21 André Franquin, quoted in Carine Van Zuylen, 'Gaston Lagaffe, Anti-héros de la bande dessinée' (unpublished dissertation, Université Libre de Bruxelles, 1982), p. 8.

22 George McManus, *La Famille Illico* (Grenoble: Glénat, 1980), p. 5. First published under the title *Bringing up Father* by King Features Syndicate (New York, 1945). André Franquin, *60 Aventures de Modeste et Pompon* (Brussels: Lombard, 1958), p. 42.

23 André Franquin, *Bonjour Modeste* (Brussels: Lombard, 1959), p. 93. The zapper was first marketed in Europe by Grundig (1969).

24 Franquin's sales figures are given in 'Des Chiffres et des dates', *Soir* [Brussels], 7 January 1997, p. 7. The restaurant 'Chez Gaston Lagaffe', 4–6 rue de l'Epée, Brussels, opened in 1981 but has since closed. Gaston is translated into Dutch, German, Norwegian, Swedish, Finnish, Portuguese, Spanish, Greek, Italian and Indonesian. My thanks to Christan Jasmes, archivist and librarian at Charleroi for this information, and for making available to me various articles about Franquin in the Belgian press to which I refer during this chapter.

25 Quoted in Sadoul, p. 157.

26 After publication in *Le Journal de Spirou*, *Gaston Lagaffe* was republished in hardback album form by Dupuis (Charleroi). Gaston's early appearances are collected in Rombald, pp. 11–32. All following references to *Gaston Lagaffe* give titles and dates of albums, with page numbers from Rombaldi.

27 André Franquin, *Gala de gaffes* (1963), p. 167.

28 André Franquin, *Les Premiers Gags* (1960), p. 40.

29 André Franquin, *Lagaffe mérite des Baffes* (1979), p. 986.

30 André Franquin, *Des Gaffes et des dégats* (1968), p. 424; *Un Gaffeur sachant gaffer* (1969), p. 519.

31 André Franquin, *Gare aux gaffes* (1966), p. 276; *Le Cas Lagaffe* (1971), p. 732.

32 André Franquin, quoted in Jean-Luc Cambier, 'Franquin l'Interview', *Télémoustique* [Charleroi], 20 November 1996, pp. 24–30 (p. 29).

33 See Gaumer and Moliterni, p. 273 and Van Zuylen.

34 Frank Margerin, *Bananes métalliques* (Paris: Humanoïdes Associés, 1982);

'Franquin' [cartoon], *Télérama* [Paris], January 1997, p. 10. Moebius and Druillet also paid tribute to Franquin here.

35 Charles Schulz, *Peanuts*, first published in various magazines (1950), then by United Feature Syndicate (New York). First published in French by Dupuis (Charleroi, 1965). See Filippini, pp. 393–94.

36 Gifford, p. 79

37 Sadoul, p. 163; André Franquin, *Le Bureau des gaffes* (1964), p. 185.

38 Franquin appeared in *Gare aux gaffes*, p. 282, and in *Gaffes bévues et boulettes* (1973), p. 841. M. Dupuis appeared in *Le Bureau des gaffes*, p. 199.

39 For example, Albert Feldstein, 'Cosmic Ray Bomb Explosion', *Weird Fantasy* [New York], July/August 1950, n. pag. Joe Orlando, 'The Ad.', *Weird Fantasy* [New York], July/August 1952, n. pag.

40 Richard Marschall, *America's Great Comic Strip Artists* (New York: Abbeville Press, 1989), p. 276. Later comics influenced by Schulz include Johnny Hart's *B.C.* (Field Newspaper Syndicate, 1958) and Garry Trudeau's *Doonesbury* (Universal Press Syndicate, 1968).

41 For more on that subject see Charles Forsdick's forthcoming article, provisionally titled 'Bécassine: Exorcising the Domestique', in the previously cited *Francophone Bandes Dessinées*.

42 André Franquin, *Lagaffe nous gâte* (1970), p. 645.

43 Quoted in Tvonvina, p. 42.

44 Sadoul, p. 26.

45 André Franquin, *La Saga des gaffes* (1982), p. 1055.

46 Maurice Tilleux and Francis Bertrand, *Allegro en Ford T* (Paris: Dargaud, 1968). Christan Godard and Mittei, *Un Cabriolet pour Désiré* (Brussels: Lombard, 1969).

47 Albert Desprechins and Pierre Seron, *Les Petits Hommes. L'Exode* (Charleroi: Dupuis, 1974).

48 Greg [Michel Regnier], *Achille Talon. Mon Fils et moi* (Paris: Dargaud, 1970).

49 Christian Darasse, *Le Gang Mazda fait de la BD* (Charleroi: Dupuis, 1988).

50 Quoted in Sadoul, p. 46.

51 André Franquin, *Idées noires*, first published in *Trombone illustré*, a supplement to *Journal de Spirou* (Charleroi, 1977). Republished in 2 vols (Paris: Editions Audie, 1981–1984). All following references to *Idées noires* give volume and page numbers from Audie.

52 André Franquin, quoted in Michel Pierre, 'Franquin le Virtuouse', *Magazine littéraire* [Paris], January 1980, pp. 62–63 (p. 62).

53 Quoted in Cambier, p. 29; 'No future' was popularised by the Sex Pistols' hit 'God Save the Queen' (1977).

54 Numa Sadoul, quoted in Oliver Vaerenbergh, 'Attention les Yeux, les doodles arrivent', *Soir* [Brussels], 11/12 January 1997, p. 10.

55 Philippe Douste-Blazy, 'Hommage à Franquin', *Figaro* [Paris], 7 January 1997, p. 20. For Margerin, Giraud and Druillet see note 34.

3 A Hero for Everyone: René Goscinny's and Albert Uderzo's Astérix the Gaul

1 Astérix's adventures were first published in *Pilote*, 1 [Paris], 29 October 1959, p. 20. After serialisation in *Pilote*, each Astérix adventure was republished in hardback album form by Dargaud (Paris). All following references to Astérix's adventures give dates and page numbers from the albums.

2 René Goscinny, quoted in Marie-Ange Guillaume and José-Louis Bocquet, *René Goscinny* (Arles: Actes Sud, 1997), p. 87.

3 Guillaume and Bocquet, p. 87.

4 François Clauteaux, 'Pourquoi Pilote?', *Pilote*, 1 [Paris], 29 October, 1959, p. 1.

5 René Goscinny and Albert Uderzo, *Oumpah-Pah*, first published in *Journal de Tintin* (Tournai, 1958). See Filippini, p. 380.

6 Goscinny, quoted in Guillaume and Bocquet, p. 115.

7 René Goscinny, quoted in Guy Vidal, Anne Goscinny and Patrick Gaumer, *René Goscinny: Profession humoriste* (Paris: Dargaud, 1997), p. 12. Uderzo, quoted in *Uderzo: de Flamberge à Astérix* (Paris: Philippsen, 1985), p. 19.

8 André Stoll, *Astérix: L'Epopée burlesque de la France* (Brussels: Editions Complexe, 1978), p. 24.

9 Stoll, pp. 24–26.

10 Quoted in Guillaume and Bocquet, p. 167.

11 Ernest Lavisse, *Histoire de France: moyen âge. Cours de 1ere année* (Paris: Armand Colin, 1890), p. 10. The original reads 'Nous ancêtres les Gaulois étaient de *véritables barbares*', Lavisse's italics.

12 William Hanna's and Joseph Barbera's *Flintstones* began as a TV series in 1960 and became a comic the following year. See Gifford, p. 234.

13 Stoll, p. 126; Touchatout [Léon Bienvenu], *Histoire de France tintamarresque* (Paris: Eclipse, 1872).

14 Touchatout, p. 16, Touchatout's italics

15 Stoll, pp. 141–42.

16 Joseph Jigourel and Yanna Fournier, *Costumes de Bretagne* (Brest: Télégramme, 2000), p. 84. Obélix sings a version of this song in *Astérix chez les Bretons* (p. 26).

17 Quoted in Vidal et al., p. 21.

18 See Gabriel Oliver, *L'Affaire du courrier de Lyon* (Paris: Arthaud, 1966).

19 Quoted in Stoll, p. 111.

20 René Goscinny and Albert Uderzo, 'Conférence de presse', *Pilote*, 260 [Paris], 15 October 1964, p. 48.

21 Touchatout, p. 336.

22 Vidal et al., p. 75.

23 Jean-Noel Gurgand, 'Le Phénomène Astérix', *Express* [Paris], 19–25 September 1966, pp. 24–26 (pp. 24 and 26).

24 Alain Peyrefitte, quoted in Pierre Lebedel, 'Astérix et Obélix Orphelins', *Figaro* [Paris], 7 November 1977, p. 32.

25 Guillaume and Bocquet, p. 166.

26 Irène Dervize, 'Les Triomphes d'Astérix', *Paris Match* [Paris], 30 April 1966, pp. 104–05 (p. 105).

27 Pierre Lindé, 'Astérix presque Milliardaire!', *Entreprise* [Paris], 4 May 1968, pp. 61–69 (p. 61).

28 Uderzo, p. 158.

29 For more on the upheavals at *Pilote,* see McQuillan's article cited above in note 33 of the Introduction.

30 Stoll, p. 147.

31 Vidal et al., p. 108.

32 Quoted in Huggett, p. 50.

33 Nelly Feuerhahn, 'Astérix, Obélix, nous et les autres', in Michel Colardelle et al., *Ils sont fous d'Astérix! Un Mythe contemporain* (Paris: Albert René, 1996), pp. 51–76 (p. 59).

34 Uderzo, p. 243.

35 John Ardagh, *France in the New Century* (London: Viking, 1999), p. 627.

36 Leo Lewis, 'What Gaul! Asterix Plans Invasion of Europe's Theme Parks', *Independent on Sunday Business Supplement* [London], 20 April 2001, p. 1. J.A. Rodriguez Tous, 'Y hora qué ?', *Mundo* [Barcelona], 1 May 2000, p. 4.

37 Jean Lartéguy, 'Ne touchez pas à Astérix!', *Figaro littéraire* [Paris], 2 June 1966, p. 8.

38 Thiesse, p. 17.

39 René Goscinny, quoted in Hervé Barraud and S. de Sède, 'La Mythologie d'Astérix', *Nouvelle Critique* [Paris], September 1969, pp. 35–40 (p. 39).

40 Bruno Frappat, 'Le Gaulois universel', *Monde*, 10 July 1974, p. 8.

41 René Goscinny, quoted in Jacques Glénat and Numa Sadoul, 'Entretien avec René Goscinny', *Cahiers de la bande dessinée* [Grenoble], 22 (1973), pp. 5–18 (p. 16).

42 Henri Bordillon, 'L' Ecume des jours et son public', *Obliques* [Paris], 8–9 (1976), pp. 77–84 (p. 83).

43 Frappat, p. 8.

44 Stoll, pp. 158–59.

45 Stoll, p. 18.

46 Quoted in Guillaume et Bocquet, p. 165.

47 Uderzo, p. 128.

48 See the following newpaper articles, all of which were published in Paris: Jean-Pierre Mogui, 'Tintin Orphelin', *Figaro*, 5–6 March 1983, p. 34; N.S., 'Le Père de Gaston à Drouot', *Figaro*, 7 January 1997, p. 20; Michel Daubert, 'Franquin', *Télérama*, 18–25 January, 1997, pp. 6–9 (p. 9); Bruno Frappat, 'René Goscinny, le Père d'Astérix', *Monde*, 8 November 1977, p. 29; Lebedel, 'Astérix et Obélix Orphelins'.

49 Eco, pp. 108–09.

50 Eco, pp. 109–10, Eco's italics.

51 Eco, p. 114.

4 A Challenge to Convention: Jean Giraud/Gir/Moebius

1 Marijac [Jacques Dumas], *Jim Boum*, first published by *Coeurs vaillants* (Paris, 1931). Fred Harman, *Red Ryder* first published by Newspaper Enterprises Association (New York, 1938); first published in French by *Journal de Spirou* (Charleroi, 1938). See Filippini, pp. 273 and 444.

2 Jean Giraud collaborated on the Jerry Spring story *La Route de Coronado* (Charleroi: Dupuis, 1962).

3 Jijé [Joseph Gillain], *Le Maître de la sierra* (Charleroi: Dupuis, 1960, repr. 1983), p. 6. The term 'subjective' for this use of colour was coined by McCloud (p. 190); McCloud notes that Giraud was among the first to use 'a subjective palette', and that the device began in Europe, spreading to the USA in the 1970s.

4 Gir [Jean Giraud] and Jean-Michel Charlier, 'Lieutenant Blueberry', first episode published in *Pilote*, 210 [Paris], 31 October 1963, pp. 16–17. After serialisation in *Pilote*, each Blueberry adventure was republished in hardback album form by Dargaud (Paris). The albums in the first *Lieutenant Blueberry* cycle are as follows: *Fort Navajo* (1965), *Tonnerre à l'ouest* (1966), *L'Aigle solitaire* (1967), *Le Cavalier perdu* (1968), *La Piste des Navajos* (1969). All following references to *Lieutenant Blueberry* give dates and page numbers from the albums.

5 The albums in the second cycle are as follows: *L'Homme à l'étoile d'argent* (1969), *Le Cheval de fer* (1970), *L'Homme au poing d'acier* (1970), *La Piste des Sioux* (1971), *Général Tête Jaune* (1971).

6 James Curwood, *The Treasure Hunters* (London and New York: Cassel, 1917). According to Numa Sadoul, Gir read the French translation. See *Moebius: Entretiens avec Numa Sadoul* (Tournai: Casterman, 1991), p. 161. All following references to Sadoul in this chapter come from this book. The French edition of *The Treasure Hunters* is *Les Chasseurs d'or*, trans. P. Gruyer and L. Postif (Paris: Hachette, 1954). The albums in Blueberry's third cycle are as follows: *La Mine de l'Allemand perdu* (1972) and *Le Spectre aux balles d'or* (1972).

7 The albums in the fourth cycle are as follows: *Chihuahua Pearl* (1973), *L'Homme qui valait $500,000* (1973), *Ballade pour un cercueil* (1974), *Le Hors-la-loi* (1974), *Angel Face* (1975), *Nez cassé* (1979), *La Longue Marche* (1980), *La Tribu fantôme* (1982), *La Dernière Carte* (1983), *Le Bout de la piste* (1986).

8 Quoted in Sadoul, p. 39.

9 Carlos Castaneda, *Tales of Power* (London: Arkana, 1975), p. 272.

10 Jean Giraud was interviewed by me in Paris on 15 December 1998. *Geronimo l'Apache* (Paris: Dargaud, 1999).

11 Gaumer and Moliterni, p. 77.

12 Jean Giraud and Jean-Michel Charlier, *La Jeunesse de Blueberry* (Paris: Dargaud, 1975). Jean Giraud and William Vance, *Martial Blueberry. Sur l'Ordre de Washington* (Paris: Dargaud, 1991). Laurence Harlé and Michel Blanc-Dumont, *Jonathan Cartland* (Paris: Dargaud, 1975). Roger Lécurieux and Norma [Norbert Morandière], *Capitaine Apache. L'Enfance d'un guerrier* (Paris: Rouge et or, 1980). Gérard Lauzier and Alexis [Dominique Vallet], *Al Crane* (Paris: Dargaud, 1976).

13 Sadoul, p. 174.

14 Moebius, *Hara-Kiri* [Paris], 28–40 (May 1963–June 1964). Republished in *Oeuvres complètes*, 6 vols (Paris: Humanoïdes Associés, 1980–1986), I, pp. 5–31.

All following references to Moebius give page numbers from *Oeuvres complètes* unless otherwise stated.

15 Moebius, 'Cauchemar blanc', first published in *Echo des savanes* [Paris], 8 (1974), pp. 39–50. Republished in *Oeuvres complètes*, I, pp. 97–108.

16 Quoted in Sadoul, p. 176.

17 Lecigne and Tamine, p. 47. Guido Crepax, *Valentina*, first published in Italy by *Linus* magazine (1965); first published in French by Losfeld (Paris, 1969). See Filippini, p. 547.

18 Georges Auclair, *Le Mana quotidien. Structures et fonctions de la chronique des faits divers* (Paris: Anthropos, 1970), pp. 122–23, 98 and 160.

19 Lecigne and Tamine, p. 11.

20 Golo and Frank, 'Sphinx de verre', *Charlie mensuel* [Paris], June 1980, pp. 79–93.

21 Chantal Montellier, 'Oscar Brown n'est pas un Espion', *Métal hurlant* [Paris], 56 (1980), pp. 36–45. This strip is based on a true story according to Lecigne and Tamine, p. 123.

22 Jean Teulé, 'Banlieue sud', *Copy rêves* (Grenoble: Glénat, 1984), pp. 47–89. Before 'Banlieue sud', Moebius had already broken with tradition by fragmenting the graphic style, but in the context of science fiction, not of *nouveau réalisme*, with *Le Garage hermétique* (1976).

23 Silvio Cadelo, *Envie de chien* (Tournai: Casterman, 1989), p. 46.

24 For more on *Bazooka* see Jean Seisser, *La Gloire des Bazooka* (Paris: Laffont, 1981).

25 José Perfección [Jean Rouzaud], 'Una Verdadera del Tío José', *Activité sexuelle normale* (Paris: Almonde Press, 1976), n. pag.

26 Jean Rouzaud was interviewed by me in Paris on 31 October 2001. All following quotations from Rouzaud come from this interview.

27 Jean-Michel Charlier and Eddy Paape, 'Les Belles Histoires de l'Oncle Paul', *Spirou* [Charleroi], 30 August 1951, n.pag.

28 Attempts have been made to explain the ninth art's predominantly male readership, with varying degrees of success. Alain Chante gives a summary, citing the lack of female characters, as well as the fact that 'les récits pour petites filles se démodent sous l'impact du féminisme'. Chante also suggests that 'la femme ne serait pas faite pour le message codé de la BD', adding 'par éducation, on les [filles] a poussées vers le joli … La bande dessinée a quelque chose d'agressif de brutal' (pp. 86–87).

29 Dominique Petitfaux, 'La Planète ensorcelée d'Hugo Pratt', *Géo hors série. Corto Maltese* [Paris], November 2001, p. 8. Hugo Pratt, *Corto Maltese. Ballade de la mer salée* (Tournai: Casterman, 1975).

30 Eugène Ionesco, *La Cantatrice chauve* in *Théâtre*, ed. Jacques Lemarchand, 5 vols (Paris: Gallimard, 1954), I, pp. 15–54 (p. 52).

31 Jean Baudrillard, *L'Echange symbolique et la mort* (Paris: Gallimard, 1976), p. 99.

32 The precise date at which Modernism emerged is an open question. Modernism has, for example, been traced to Flaubert in the mid-nineteenth century. For more on the subject see Malcolm Bradbury and James McFarlane, 'The Name and Nature of Modernism', in *Modernism 1890–1930* (London: Penguin, 1976), pp. 19–55.

33 René Bray, *Formation de la doctrine classique en France* (Paris: Nizet, 1926), p. 191.

34 Herbert Read, *Art Now* (London: Faber and Faber, 1936), p. 67.

35 Bradbury and McFarlane, p. 27.

36 Norbert Lynton, *The Story of Modern Art* (Oxford: Phaidon, 1980), pp. 61–62.

37 Lynton, p. 40.

38 Guillaume Apollinaire, 'La Peinture moderne', in *Œuvres complètes de Guillaume Apollinaire*, ed. Michel Decaudin, 4 vols (Paris: Gallimard, 1966), I, pp. 280–84 (p. 282).

39 Lynton, p. 146.

40 Matthew Gale, *Dada and Surrealism* (London: Phaidon, 1997), p. 128.

41 André Breton, *Manifestes du Surréalisme* (Paris: Gallimard, 1992), pp. 72–73. My italics.

42 Pierre Restany, *Le Nouveau Réalisme* (Paris: Union générale des Editions, 1978), p. 39; *Trente Ans de nouveau réalisme* (Paris: La Différence, 1990), p. 73. See also Catherine Francblin, *Les Nouveaux Réalistes* (Paris: Regard, 1997).

43 Harold Rosenberg, *The De-definition of Art* (New York: Horizon, 1972), p. 51. Bernard Brown, *Protest in Paris: Anatomy of a Revolt* (Morristown, NJ: General Learning Press, 1974), p. 215.

44 Examples of May '68 slogans include 'Rêve-olution', 'Prenez vos désirs pour les réalités', 'Sous les pavés, la plage', and 'Soyez réalistes, demandez l'impossible'. Moebius mentions May '68's 'verbiage' in his autobiography *Histoire de mon double* (Paris: Numéro 1, 1999), p. 188.

45 Richard Coe, *Ionesco: a Study of his Plays*, 2nd edn (London: Methuen, 1971), p. 66.

46 Brown, p. 35.

47 Serge Govaert, *Mai '68: C'était au Temps où Bruxelles contestait* (Brussels: Pol-His, 1990), pp. 9–10. Govaert's italics.

48 Klock, p. 113. Sally Stein, 'Good Fences make Good Neighbors. American Resistance to Photomontage between the Wars', in *Montage and Modern Life 1919–1942*, ed. Maude Lavin (Cambridge, MA: MIT Press, 1993), pp. 128–91. Alan Moore, *Rocks and Hard Places* (La Jolla, CA: Prometheus, 1999).

49 Moebius, 'Editorial', *Métal hurlant* [Paris], 4 (1975), p. 1. Republished in Moebius, *Oeuvres complètes*, II, p. 9.

50 For example, Greg [Michel Regnier] and Eddy Paape, *Luc Orient. Les Dragons de feu* (Brussels: Lombard, 1969), first published by *Journal de Tintin* (Brussels, 1967). Marijac and Auguste Liquois, *Guerre à la Terre*, 2 vols (Grenoble: Glénat, 1975–1976), first published by *Coq hardi* (Paris, 1946). Jean-Claude Forest and Paul Gillon, *Les Naufragés du temps. L'Etoile endormie* (Paris: Hachette, 1974), first published by *Chouchou* (Paris, 1964). See Filippini, pp. 323, 231–32 and 368–69.

51 Pellos [René Pellerin], *Futuropolis*, first published by *Junior* (Paris, 1937). See Filippini, p. 661.

52 Couperie et al., p. 77.

53 Roger Lécurieux and Raymond Poivet, 'Les Pionniers de l'Espérance', first published by *Vaillant* [Paris], 14 December 1945, n. pag.

54 Roger Lécurieux and Raymond Poivet, *Vers l'Ourang mystérieux*, in *Les*

Pionniers de l'Espérance 1945–1946, 3 vols (Paris: Futuropolis, 1989), I, n. pag.

55 Pierre Christin and Jean-Claude Mézières, *Bienvenue sur Alflolol* (Paris: Dargaud, 1972). *Valérian* was first published by *Pilote* (Paris, 1967). See Filippini, pp. 548.

56 Philippe Druillet, *Les Six Voyages de Lone Sloane* (Paris: Dargaud, 1972). First published by Losfeld (Paris, 1966), then by *Pilote* (Paris, 1970). See Filippini, p. 318.

57 Moebius, quoted in Pierre Couperie and Claude Moliterni, 'La SF en France', *Phénix* [Ivry], February 1973, pp. 2–15 (p. 13).

58 Moebius, *Arzach*, first episode published by *Métal hurlant* [Paris], 1 (1975), n.pag. Entire strip republished in *Oeuvres complètes*, II, pp. 17–62.

59 See, for example, Richard Corben, 'Ci-Dopey', *Métal hurlant* [Paris], 1 (1975), n. pag.

60 Moebius, *Le Garage hermétique*, first episode published by *Métal hurlant* [Paris], 6 (1976), pp. 16–17. Entire strip republished in *Oeuvres complètes*, III, pp. 46–144.

61 Moebius, *Oeuvres complètes*, III, p. 9.

62 Jerry Cornelius is a time-traveller invented by English SF writer Michael Moorcock.

63 Victor Moscosco, 'Untitled', *Zap Comics* [San Francisco], 2 (1968), pp. 6–7. Rick Griffin, 'Oxo 69', *Zap Comics* [San Francisco], 2 (1968), p. 4. My thanks to Dave Huxley for giving me photocopies of these strips.

64 Ben Stoltzfus, *Alain Robbe-Grillet and the New French Novel* (Carbondale, IL: Southern Illinois University Press, 1964), p. 12.

65 For more on Godard's cinematic techniques, see David Sterrit, *The Films of Jean-Luc Godard* (Cambridge: Cambridge University Press, 1999).

66 Quoted in Sadoul, p. 182.

67 Jacques Goimard, *Œuvres complètes*, III, p. 149.

68 Moebius, *Les Vacances du Major* (Paris: Humanoïdes Associés, 1990); *L'Homme du Ciguri* (Paris: Humanoïdes Associés, 1995); Moebius and Eric Shanower, *The Elsewhere Prince* (New York: Epic, 1990); Moebius and Jerry Bingham, *The Onyx Overlord* (New York: Epic, 1992).

5 New Visions of the Past: Jacques Tardi

1 Jacques Tardi, 'Un Cheval en hiver', first published by *Pilote*, 550 [Paris], 22 May 1970, pp. 18–23; republished in Tardi's anthology *Mouh Mouh* (Brussels: Pepperland, 1984), pp. 3–8. 'La Torpédo rouge sang', 'Knock Out' and 'La Bascule à Charlot' also appear in *Mouh Mouh*. All following references to the above strips give page numbers from *Mouh Mouh* unless otherwise stated.

2 Jacques Tardi, 'La Torpédo rouge sang', first published by *Pilote*, 567 [Paris], 11 September 1970, pp. 22–27.

3 Jacques Tardi, *Le Démon des glaces* (Paris: Dargaud, 1974).

4 Jacques Tardi, quoted in Alain Foulet, *Presque tout Tardi* (Dieppe: Sapristi, 1996), p. 98.

5 Jules Verne, *Le Sphinx des glaces* (Paris: Hetzel, 1897). Thierry Groensteen, *Tardi* (Paris: Magic Strip, 1980), p. 17.

6 Jacques Tardi, 'Knock Out', first published in *Pilote annuel* [Paris], 6 bis hors série, November 1974, pp. 25–30; Joe Kubert and Bon Kanigher, *Le Baron Rouge*, 2 vols, trans. Michèle Tingaud (Paris: Editions Fromage, 1978). According to a note in this translation, *Enemy Ace* was first published in *Our Army at War* (New York: DC Comics, 1965).

7 Jacques Tardi, 'La Fleur au fusil', first published by *Pilote*, 743 [Paris], 1 February 1974, pp. 38–47; republished as a hardback album under the title *Adieu Brindavoine suivi de la Fleur au fusil* by Casterman (Tournai, 1979). All following references to 'La Fleur au fusil' give page numbers from the album.

8 Jacques Tardi, *C'était la Guerre des tranchées*, first published by *A suivre* [Paris], March 1982, pp. 9–25; republished as a hardback album by Casterman (Tournai, 1993). All following references to *C'était la Guerre des tranchées* give page numbers from the album.

9 Robert Hoare, *World War I* (London: Macdonald, 1973), p. 46. Belgium, with its far smaller population, lost 46,000 men and had 50,000 seriously wounded; Belgium also sustained massive damage to its infrastructure and to its economy. See Vernon Mallinson, *Belgium* (London: Ernest Benn, 1969), p. 94.

10 Charles Genthe, *American War Narratives 1917–1918* (New York: David Lewis, 1969), p. 11.

11 Harvey Kurtzman, 'Old Soldiers Never Die!', *Two-Fisted Tales* [New York], January 1952, pp. 1–7.

12 John Severin and Will Elder, 'Zero Hour', *Frontline Combat* [New York], September/October 1951, n. pag.

13 Sabin, *Adult Comics*, p. 152.

14 Doug Murray and Michael Golden, *The Nam* (New York: Marvel, 1986).

15 See Estren, pp. 61, 178 and 267.

16 Marijac, *Les Trois Mousquetaires du Maquis*, first published by *Coq hardi* (Paris, 1944). See Filippini, pp. 540–41. For depictions of World War II in French cinema and the Resistance, see Hayward, p. 128.

17 Gérard Frydman and Touis, *Sergent Laterreur* (Brussels: Distri BD, 1976).

18 Georges Duhamel, *Vie des martyrs 1914–1916* (Paris: Mercure de France, 1917). Roland Dorgelès, *Les Croix de bois* (Paris: Albin Michel, 1919).

19 Quoted in Foulet, p. 103.

20 Louis-Ferdinand Céline, *Voyage au bout de la nuit*, illustrated by Tardi (Paris: Futuropolis, 1988).

21 Erika Ostrovsky, *Céline and his Vision* (London: University of London Press, 1967), p. 50.

22 Ernest Hemingway, *A Farewell to Arms* (London: Penguin, 1975), pp. 143–44.

23 Jacques Tardi, *La Véritable Histoire du soldat inconnu* (Paris: Futuropolis, 1974).

24 Joe Kubert, 'Bonhomme Richard', *Frontline Combat* [New York], September/October 1953, n. pag.

25 Lecigne and Tamine, p. 25; Reed Crandall, 'Carrion Death!', *Shock-Suspense* [New York], September 1953, pp. 1–7. My thanks to Dave Huxley for giving me a photocopy of this strip.

26 Jacques Tardi, 'La Bascule à Charlot', first published by *Charlie mensuel* [Paris], August 1976, pp. 73–96.

27 Lecigne and Tamine, p. 67.

28 Jonathan Culler, *Flaubert. The Uses of Uncertainty* (London: Paul Elek, 1974), p. 230.

29 Culler, p. 195.

30 See Luc Moullet, *Fritz Lang* (Paris: Seghers, 1963), p. 37. *Liliom* is based on a play by Ferenc Molnar (1901).

31 Ragna Stang, *Edvard Munch. The Man and the Artist* (London: Gordon Fraser, 1979), pp. 116–17.

32 Günter Busch et al., *Vallotton* (Lausanne: Bibliothèque des Arts, 1985), pp. 28–29.

33 Jacques Tardi, *Griffu* (Paris: Editions du Square, 1978).

34 Didier Comès, *L'Ombre du corbeau* (Brussels: Lombard, 1981).

35 Pierre Christin and Enki Bilal, *Phalanges de l'ordre noir* (Paris: Dargaud, 1979), p. 80.

36 Enki Bilal and Dominique Grange, 'La Mort permissionnaire', *A suivre hors série, BD polar* [Paris] (1981), pp. 70–71.

37 Michel Duveaux, 'Les Couperets de l'aube', *Echo des savanes* [Paris], 36 (1977), pp. 50–53.

38 Jacques Violeff, *Coup sur coup* (Tournai: Casterman, 1984).

39 Chantal Montellier, 'Recours en grâce', *A suivre hors série, BD polar* [Paris] (1981), pp. 82–83; 'So Fast in their Shiny Metal Cars', *1996* (Paris: Humanoïdes Associés, 1978), pp. 21–60.

40 Jacques Tardi, *Les Aventures extraordinaires d'Adèle Blanc-Sec* first published in *Sud ouest* [Bordeaux], 25 January 1975. See Claude Moliterni and Philippe Mellot, *Chronologie de la bande dessinée* (Paris: Flammarion, 1996), p. 197. Following serialisation, *Les Aventures extraordinaires d'Adèle Blanc-Sec* were republished in hardback album form by Casterman (Tournai). All following references to *Les Aventures extraordinaires d'Adèle Blanc-Sec* give dates and page numbers from the albums.

41 Georges Bourdin, 'Arsène Lupin', *France soir* (Paris, 1948); Jacques Blondeau, 'Arsène Lupin', *Parisien libéré* (Paris, 1957). See Filippini, p. 31.

42 Edgar Jacobs, *SOS Météores* (Brussels: Lombard, 1959).

43 Maurice Dubourg, 'Image de la bourgeoisie et idéologie bourgeoise', *Europe* [Paris], June 1974, pp. 75–86 (p. 83).

44 François Walthéry and Gos [Roland Goossens], *Natacha. Hôtesse de l'air* (Charleroi: Dupuis, 1970).

45 Groensteen, *Tardi*, p. 36.

46 Raymond Rudorff, *Belle Epoque* (London: Hamish Hamilton, 1972), p. 204.

47 Maurice Leblanc, *Arsène Lupin*, ed. Francis Lacassin, 4th edn, 5 vols (Paris: Laffont, 1992), I, pp. 182–95 (p. 195).

48 Quoted in Groensteen, *Tardi*, p. 73.

49 Fred [Othon Aristides], *Philémon. L'Ile des brigadiers* (Paris: Dargaud, 1975), p. 24.

50 Pierre Wininger, *La Pyramide oubliée* (Grenoble: Glénat, 1978). Annie Goetzinger, *Aurore* (Paris: Editions des Femmes, 1978). Chantal Montellier, *La Fosse aux*

serpents (Tournai: Casterman, 1990). Pierre Guilmard, *La Java des Gaspards. L'Egorgeoir* (Paris: Vents d'Ouest, 1990).

6 Laughing Together: Humour and Shared Identity

1 Marcel Gotlib, *Gai-Luron*, first episode published by *Vaillant* (Paris, 1964). See Filippini, p. 211. Republished after serialisation as two hardback albums by Rombaldi (Paris, 1987). All following references to *Gai-Luron* give page numbers from the first album.

2 Marcel Gotlib, quoted in Numa Sadoul, *Gotlib* (Paris: Albin Michel, 1974), p. 21. All following references to Sadoul in this chapter come from this book.

3 *Comptines chansons et chansonnettes* (Paris: Safrat, 1998), pp. 64–67.

4 Jean de La Fontaine, *Fables*, ed. Antoine Adam (Paris: Garnier Flammarion, 1966), p. 106. La Fontaine's *Fables* were originally published from 1668 to 1694.

5 Quoted in Sadoul, p. 30.

6 Marcel Gotlib, 'Le Clou à travers l'histoire', *Trucs en vrac*, 2 vols (Paris: Dargaud, 1977 and 1985), I, pp. 53–54. Originally published in *Pilote*, 286 [Paris], 15 April 1965, pp. 10–11.

7 Marcel Gotlib, *Rubrique à brac*, first published by *Pilote*, 447 [Paris], 16 May 1968, pp. 4–5. Republished as five hardback albums by Dargaud (Paris, 1970–1974). All following references to *Rubrique à brac* give page numbers from the albums.

8 Charles Perrault, *Le Petit Poucet*, in *Contes de ma mère l'oie* (Paris: Gallimard, 1988), pp. 101–21.

9 Marcel Gotlib was interviewed by me in Paris on 30 October 2001. All following quotations from Gotlib come from this interview unless otherwise stated.

10 See Thierry Gineste, *Victor de l'Aveyron* (Paris: Hachette, 1993).

11 Frédéric Delacourt, *Proverbes, dictons et citations* (Paris: De Vecchi, 1996), p. 69. Jean Racine, *Œuvres complètes*, ed. Georges Forestier (Paris: Gallimard, 1999), p. 1040. My thanks to Chris Powell for his help in tracking down the quotation from Racine.

12 François Villon, 'Ballade des dames du temps jadis', *Poèsies complètes*, ed. Claude Thiry (Paris: Livre de Poche, 1991), pp. 117–19.

13 See Filippini, p. 211.

14 Marcel Gotlib, 'God's Club', *Rhââ lovely*, 3 vols (Paris: Editions Audie, 1977), II, pp. 4–15.

15 Dalia Judovitz, 'Sex or the Misfortunes of Literature', in *Sade and the Narrative of Transgression,* ed. David Allison, Mark Roberts, Allen Weiss (Cambridge: Cambridge University Press, 1995), pp. 171–98 (p. 171).

16 Donatien, Marquis de Sade, *Histoire de Juliette*, ed. Gilbert Lely, 3 vols (Paris: Union Générale d'Editions, 1976–77), I, pp. 42 and 46.

17 See Estren, pp. 114–39.

18 Marcel Gotlib, Jacques Lob, Jean Solé, Alexis [Dominique Vallet], *Super-dupont* (Paris: Rombaldi, 1987). First published by *Pilote* (Paris, 1972), then by *Fluide glaciale* (Paris, 1975). See Filippini, p. 505.

19 Sadoul, p. 103.

20 See Filippini, p. 592.

21 Claire Bretécher, *Céllulite*, first published by *Pilote*, 502 [Paris], 17 June 1969, pp. 43–47. Brant Parker, *Wizard of Id*, first published by Hall Syndicate (New York, 1964). First published in France under the title *Le Magicien Pogo* (Paris, 1969). See Filippini, p. 560.

22 Claire Bretécher, *Les Frustrés*, first published by *Nouvel Observateur* (Paris, 1973). See Filippini, p. 209. Republished after serialisation in hardback (Paris: Hyphen SA, 1997). All following references to *Les Frustrés* give page numbers from the album. Jules Feiffer, *Jules Feiffer's America from Eisenhower to Reagan* (London: Penguin, 1982).

23 Dina Sherzer, 'Claire Bretécher: Queen of BD', *Journal of Popular Culture* [Bowling Green, Ohio], 13.2 (1980), pp. 394–404 (p. 395).

24 For more on the crisis in the Church, see Norman Rabitch, *The Catholic Church and the French Nation* (London: Routledge, 1990), pp. 155–65.

25 Huggett, p. 270.

26 See *The Condition of Women in France, 1945 to the Present*, ed. Claire Laubier (London: Routledge, 1990), pp. 70–167.

27 For developments in Belgium, see Marie Denis and Suzanne van Rokeghem, *Le Féminisme est dans la rue* (Brussels: Pol-His, 1992).

28 Claire Bretécher, quoted in Jacques Glénat and Numa Sadoul, 'A Bâtons rompus avec Claire Bretécher', *Cahiers de la bande dessinée* [Grenoble], 24 (1974), pp. 6–14 (p. 14).

29 Irène Pennacchioni, *La Nostalgie en images* (Paris: Méridiens, 1982), pp. 171–72.

30 Sherzer states that Bretécher was published in the USA by National Lampoon (New York, 1978). She also mentions an article introducing Bretécher to the American public by Susan Anderson in the magazine *Viva* (April, 1978), pp. 77–79. See Sherzer, p. 403, note 2.

31 Walt Kelly, *Pogo*, first published by *New York Star* (New York, 1948). First published in French by Dupuis (Charleroi, 1966). See Filippini, p. 416. Art Spiegelman, *Maus*, first published in the US magazine *Raw* (1980). First published in French by Flammarion (Paris, 1987). See Filippini, p. 343.

32 F'Murr [Richard Peyzaret], *Génie des Alpages* (Paris: Dargaud, 1976).

33 Régis Franc, *Histoires immobiles et récits inachevés* (Paris: Dargaud, 1977), pp. 13–17. Georges Moustaki's original reads

    Allez venez, Milord
    Vous asseoir à ma table
    Il fait si froid dehors
    Ici c'est confortable.

See Georges Moustaki, *Moustaki en Ballades*, 2 vols (Paris: Christian Pirot, 1996), I, p. 26.

34 Régis Franc, *Le Café de la plage*, first episode published by *Matin de Paris* [Paris], 18 February 1977, p. 21. Republished after serialisation in hardback album form by Casterman (Tournai, 1989). All following references give page numbers from the album.

35 Belinda Thomson, *Impressionism* (London: Thames and Hudson, 2000), pp. 11–12.

36 Régis Franc, *Nouvelles Histoires* (Paris: Dargaud, 1978).

37 Marcel Proust, *Du Côté de Chez Swann*, ed. Jean Milly (Paris: Flammarion, 1987), p. 142.

38 Régis Franc, *Souvenirs d'un menteur* (Paris: Dargaud, 1979).

39 Luc Dellisse, 'Une Duplicité stratégique', *Cahiers de la bande dessinée, dossier Régis Franc* [Grenoble], 57 (1984), pp. 11–13 (p. 13).

40 Culler, p. 76.

41 Culler, p. 80.

42 Régis Franc, *Le Marchand d'opium* (Paris: Dargaud, 1981).

43 Régis Franc, *Nuits de Chine* (Paris: Dargaud, 1982).

44 Régis Franc, *Tonton Marcel, Capitaine de l'Industrie* (Tournai: Casterman, 1983), p. 52.

7 Reconstructing the Narrative and After

1 John Ardagh, *France in the 1980s* (London: Penguin, 1982), p. 20.

2 Moebius and Alejandro Jodorowsky, *L'Incal*, first episode published by *Métal hurlant* [Paris], 58 (1980), pp. 5–14. After serialisation in *Métal hurlant*, each of Difool's adventures was republished as hardback albums by Humanoïdes Associés (Paris) as follows: *L'Incal noir* (1980), *L'Incal lumière* (1981), *Ce qui est en bas* (1983), *Ce qui est en haut* (1985), *La Cinquième Essence I* (1988), *La Cinquième Essence II* (1989).

3 Jodorowsky, quoted in J.L.F., 'L'Homme de l'année, Moebius et Jodorowsky', *Année de la bande dessinée* [Paris] (1981/2), pp. 197–203 (p. 202).

4 Eco, pp. 110 and 114.

5 Jean Chevalier and Alain Gheerbrant, *Dictionary of Symbols*, trans. John Buchanan Brown (London: Penguin, 1996), pp. 951 and 674.

6 Chevalier and Gheerbrant, p. 859.

7 Chevalier and Gheerbrant, p. 898.

8 Alejandro Jodorowsky, quoted in Moebius, Jodorowsky and Jean Annestay, *Les Mystères de l'Incal* (Paris: Humanoïdes Associés, 1989), p. 50.

9 John Beer, *Blake's Visionary Universe* (Manchester and New York: Manchester University Press, 1969), p. 8; *The Ancient of Days*, frontispiece to *Europe: a Prophecy* (1794), in *Blake's Poetry and Designs*, ed. Mary Johnson and John Grant (London and New York: W.W. Norton, 1979), colour plate 17. Blake was appreciated among Moebius' group of friends: Jean-Pierre Dionnet wrote a mock-heroic tribute to Blake in *Métal hurlant*, 3 (1975), p. 51.

10 My thanks to Anne Caisson at Humanoïdes Associés for *L'Incal*'s sales figures. Information about translations comes from *Les Mystères de l'Incal*, p. 8.

11 Alejandro Jodorowsky and Arno [Arnaud Dombre], *Alef Thau* (Paris: Humanoïdes Associés, 1982). Alejandro Jodorowsky and Silvio Cadelo, *Le Dieu jaloux* (Paris: Humanoïdes Associés, 1984).

12 Quoted in Sadoul, p. 79.

13 Guy-Claude Burger, *Instinctothérapie. Manger vrai* (Monaco: Rocher, 1990), quoted from back cover.

14 Moebius' *Edena* series is published in hardback as follows: *Sur l'Etoile* (Paris: Aedena, 1984), *Les Jardins d'Edena* (Tournai: Casterman, 1988), *La Déesse* (Tournai: Casterman, 1990), *Stel* (Tournai: Casterman, 1994).

15 Burger, p. 129.

16 Burger, p. 422.

17 Emile Zola, *La Faute de l'Abbé Mouret* (Paris: Charpentier, 1875).

18 F.W.J. Hemmings, *Emile Zola*, 2nd edn (Oxford: Oxford University Press, 1966), p. 107.

19 Quoted in Sadoul, p. 122.

20 Quoted in Sadoul, p. 196.

21 Frederick Franck, *The Zen of Seeing*, 3rd edn (London: Wildwood House, 1976), pp. xii and 6.

22 Moebius and Alejandro Jodorowsky, *Griffes d'ange* (Paris: Humanoïdes Associés, 1994). Moebius and Jean-Michel Charlier, *Jim Cutlass*, first published by *Pilote* (1976) in a special edition devoted to Westerns. See Gaumer and Moliterni, p. 420. Pierre Sterckx, quoted in Moebius, *Quatre-Vingt-Huit* (Paris: Humanoïdes Associés, 1990), p. 6.

23 Moebius, *Venise céleste* (Tournai: Casterman, 1984), p. 30.

24 François Bourgeon, *Les Passagers du vent*, first episode published by *Circus* [Paris], 18 (1979), pp. 11–18. After serialisation in *Circus*, each adventure was republished in hardback album form by Glénat (Grenoble) as follows: *La Fille sous la dunette* (1979), *Le Ponton* (1980), *Le Comptoir de Juda* (1981), *L'Heure du serpent* (1982), *Le Bois d'ébène* (1983). All following references to *Les Passagers du vent* give page numbers from the albums.

25 Louis-Antoine de Bougainville, *Voyage autour du Monde*, ed. Jacques Proust (Paris: Gallimard, 1982), p. 294.

26 François Bourgeon, quoted in Thierry Groensteen, 'Entretien avec François Bourgeon', *Cahiers de la bande dessinée* [Grenoble], 65 (1985), pp. 8–16.

27 Thierry Groensteen, *La Bande dessinée depuis 1975* (Paris: Albin Michel, 1985), p. 31.

28 Patrice Pellerin and Jean-Charles Kraehn, *Aigles décapités. La Nuit des jongleurs* (Grenoble: Glénat, 1985). Jacques Martin and André Juillard, *Arno. Le Pique rouge* (Grenoble: Glénat, 1984). Daniel Bardet and François Dermaut, *Chemins de Malefosse. Le Diable noir* (Grenoble: Glénat, 1983).

29 Ardagh, *France in the 1980s*, p. 27.

30 *La Bande dessinée depuis 1975*, p. 90.

31 Jacques Chabond, quoted in Association Clovis, *Bourgeon à la Hune* (Grenoble: Glénat, 1986), p. 16.

32 Hayward, p. 247.

33 Hayward, p. 285.

34 Frank Miller, *Batman. The Dark Knight Returns* (New York: DC Comics, 1986). Alan Moore and Dave Gibbons, *The Watchmen* (New York: DC Comics, 1986).

35 Martine Van and François Mutterer, *Carpets bazaar* (Paris: Futuropolis, 1983).

36 Edmond Baudoin, *Un Flip coca!* (Paris: Futuropolis, 1984).

37 Avril and Petit Roulet, *Soirs de Paris* (Paris: Humanoïdes Associés, 1989).

38 Philippe Geluck, *Le Chat* (Tournai: Casterman, 1986), p. 70.

39 Philippe Geluck, *Le Retour du Chat* (Tournai: Casterman, 1987), p. 4.

40 La Fontaine, p. 52; Philippe Geluck, *La Vengeance du Chat* (Tournai: Casterman, 1988), p. 24.

41 Anne Baraou and Corinne Chalmeau, *Après tout, tant pis* (Paris: Hors Gabarit, 1991).

42 Marc-Antoine Mathieu, *L'Origine* (Paris: Delcourt, 1991).

43 Marc-Antoine Mathieu, *La Qu* ... (Paris: Delcourt, 1991).

44 Lewis Trondheim, *Lapinot et les Carottes de Patagonie* (Paris: L'Association, 1992).

45 Lewis Trondheim and Jean-Christophe Menu, *Moins d'un Quart de seconde pour vivre* (Paris: L'Association, 1991).

46 Lewis Trondheim, *Le Dormeur* (Paris: Cornélius, 1993).

47 Lewis Trondheim, *Les Aventures de l'Univers* (Paris: Dargaud, 1997), p. 9.

48 Benoît Peeters, *La Bande dessinée* (Paris: Flammarion, 1993), p. 66.

49 Thierry Groensteen, quoted in Sylvie Lisiecki-Bouretz, 'Maîtres du neuvième art', *Chroniques de la Bibliothèque nationale de France* [Paris], September 2000, p. 8.

50 Jimmy Corrigan first appeared in Chris Ware, *Acme Novelty Library 6* (Seattle, WA: Fantagraphics, 1995).

51 Alex Ross and Paul Dini, *Superman. Peace on Earth* (New York: DC Comics, 1999).

Conclusion

1 Will Eisner, quoted in Thierry Groensteen and Thierry Smolderen, 'Entretien avec Will Eisner', *Cahiers de de la bande dessinée* [Grenoble], 61 (1985), pp. 86–89 (p. 88). *The Spirit*, a thriller, first appeared 'dans les pages d'un comic book offert avec l'édition dominicale de certains grands journaux américains' in 1940. See Filippini, p. 496.

2 Ardagh, *France in the New Century*, p. 731.

Bibliography

Adams, Tim, 'Vizionary at Work', *Observer* [London], 14 November 1999, p. 3

Allaux, Jean-Pierre, 'Milou raconte Tintin', *Vie catholique* [Paris], 4 June 1975, pp. 24–26

Amouroux, Henri, 'Tintin, le Capitaine Haddock et les Bachi-Bouzouks', *Loire Matin* [Saint Etienne], 4 December 1981, pp. 1 and 6

Apollinaire, Guillaume, 'La Peinture moderne', in *Œuvres complètes de Guillaume Apollinaire*, ed. Michel Decaudin, 4 vols (Paris: Gallimard, 1966), I, pp. 280–84

Apostolides, Jean-Marie, *Les Métamorphoses de Tintin* (Paris: Seghers, 1984)

Ardagh, John, *France in the 1980s* (London: Penguin, 1982)

  France in the New Century (London: Viking, 1999)

Aristides, Othon [Fred], *Philémon. L'Ile des brigadiers* (Paris: Dargaud, 1975)

Arrouye, Jean et al., *A la Rencontre de Tardi* (Brussels: Bédésup, 1982)

Association Clovis, *Bourgeon à la Hune* (Grenoble: Glénat, 1986)

Auclair, Georges, *Le Mana quotidien. Structures et fonctions de la chronique des faits divers* (Paris: Anthropos, 1970)

Augereau, Pierre-Louis, *Hergé au Pays des Tarots* (Paris: Cheminements, 1999)

Avril and Petit Roulet, *Soirs de Paris* (Paris: Humanoïdes Associés, 1989)

Baraou, Anne and Corinne Chalmeau, *Après tout, tant pis* (Paris: Hors Gabarit, 1991)

Bardet, Daniel and François Dermaut, *Chemins de Malefosse. Le Diable noir* (Grenoble: Glénat, 1983)

Barker, Martin, *Comics, Ideology, Power and the Critics* (Manchester and New York: Manchester University Press, 1989)

Barraud, Hervé and S. de Sède, 'La Mythologie d'Astérix', *Nouvelle Critique* [Paris], September 1969, pp. 35–40

Baudoin, Edmond, *Un Flip coca!* (Paris: Futuropolis, 1984)

Baudrillard, Jean, *L'Echange symbolique et la mort* (Paris: Gallimard, 1976)

Beer, John, *Blake's Visionary Universe* (Manchester and New York: Manchester University Press, 1969)

Benoît, Ted, *Ray Banana. La Berceuse électrique* (Tournai: Casterman, 1982)

'Best of Gaffes', *Canard enchaîné* [Paris], 8 January 1997, p. 5 [journalist unknown]

Bienvenu, Léon [Touchatout], *Histoire de France tintamarresque* (Paris: Eclipse, 1872)

Bilal, Enki and Jean-Pierre Dionnet, *Exterminateur 17* (Paris: Humanoïdes Associés, 1989)

Bilal, Enki and Dominique Grange, 'La Mort permissionnaire', *A auivre hors série, BD polar* [Paris] (1981), pp. 70–71

Blake, William, *Blake's Poetry and Designs*, ed. Mary Johnson and John Grant (London and New York: W.W. Norton, 1979)

Bordillon, Henri, 'L'Ecume des jours et son public', *Obliques* [Paris], 8–9 (1976), pp. 77–84

Bougainville, Louis-Antoine de, *Voyage autour du Monde*, ed. Jacques Proust (Paris: Gallimard, 1982)

Bourgeon, François, *Le Bois d'ébène* (Grenoble: Glénat, 1984)
    Le Comptoir de Juda (Grenoble: Glénat, 1981)
    La Fille sous la dunette (Grenoble: Glénat, 1979)
    L'Heure du serpent (Grenoble: Glénat, 1982)
    'Passagers du vent 1', *Circus* [Paris], 18 (1979), pp. 11–18
    Le Ponton (Grenoble: Glénat, 1980)

Bradbury, Malcolm and James McFarlane, *Modernism 1890–1930* (London: Penguin, 1976)

Bray, René, *Formation de la doctrine classique en France* (Paris: Nizet, 1926)

Bretécher, Claire, 'Céllulite', *Pilote*, 502 [Paris], 17 June 1969, pp. 43–47
    Les Etats d'âme de Céllulite (Paris: Dargaud, 1977)
    Les Frustrés (Paris: Hyphen SA, 1997)

Breton, André, *Manifestes du Surréalisme* (Paris: Gallimard, 1992)

Brown, Bernard, *Protest in Paris: Anatomy of a Revolt* (Morristown, NJ: General Learning Press, 1974)

Burger, Guy-Claude, *Instinctothérapie. Manger vrai* (Monaco: Rocher, 1990)

Busch, Günter et al., *Vallotton* (Lausanne: Bibliothèque des Arts, 1985)

Cadelo, Silvio, *Envie de chien* (Tournai: Casterman, 1989)

Calvocoressi, Richard, *Magritte,* 3rd edn (London: Phaidon, 1997)

Cambier, Jean-Luc, 'Franquin l'Interview', *Télémoustique* [Charleroi], 20 November 1996, pp. 24–30

Castaneda, Carlos, *Tales of Power* (London: Arkana, 1975)

Cau, Jean, 'La Victoire d' Apollo XII', *Paris Match* [Paris], 29 November 1969, pp. 34–35

Céline, Louis-Ferdinand, *Voyage au bout de la nuit* (Paris: Futuropolis, 1988) [illustrated by Tardi]

Chaland, Yves, *Freddy Lombard. Le Testament de Godefroid le Bouillon* (Geneva: Humanoïdes Associés, 1996)

Chante, Alain, *99 Réponses sur la bande dessinée* (Montpellier: Réseau CRDP, 1996)

Charlier, Jean-Michel and Eddy Paape, 'Les Belles Histoires de l'Oncle Paul', *Spirou* [Charleroi], 30 August 1951, n. pag.

Chaulet, Georges and François Craenhals, *Les Quatre As et le serpent de la mer* (Tournai: Casterman, 1964)

Chevalier, Jean and Alain Gheerbrant, *Dictionary of Symbols*, trans. John Buchanan Brown (London: Penguin, 1996)

Christin, Pierre and Enki Bilal, *Phalanges de l'ordre noir* (Paris: Dargaud, 1979)

Christin, Pierre and Jean-Claude Mézières, *Bienvenue sur Alflolol* (Paris: Dargaud, 1972)

Clark, Alan and Laurel, *Comics, an Illustrated History* (London: Greenwood, 1991)

Clauteaux, François, 'Pourquoi Pilote?', *Pilote*, 1 [Paris], 29 October 1959, p. 1

Coe, Richard, *Ionesco: a Study of his Plays*, 2nd edn (London: Methuen, 1971)

Combe, Jacques, *Jerome Bosch* (Paris: Rombaldi, 1946)

Comès, Didier, *L'Ombre du corbeau* (Brussels: Lombard, 1981)

Comptines, chansons et chansonnettes (Paris: Safrat, 1998)

Corben, Richard, 'Ci-Dopey', *Métal hurlant* [Paris], 1 (1975), n. pag

Corteggiani, F., *François Bourgeon, le Passager du temps* (Grenoble: Glénat, 1983)

Couperie, Pierre et al., *History of the Comic Strip*, trans. Eileen Hennessy (New York: Crown, 1968)

Couperie, Pierre and Claude Moliterni, 'La SF en France', *Phénix* [Ivry], 26 February 1973, pp. 2–15

Crandall, Reed, 'Carrion Death!', *Shock-Suspense* [New York], September 1953, pp. 1–7

Crumb, Robert, *Robert Crumb's America* (San Francisco: Last Gasp, 1995)

Culler, Jonathan, *Flaubert. The Uses of Uncertainty* (London: Paul Elek, 1974)

Curwood, James, *The Treasure Hunters* (London and New York: Cassel, 1917)
    Les Chasseurs d'or, trans. P. Gruyer and L. Postif (Paris: Hachette, 1954)

Dana, Jacqueline, 'Rencontre avec Tintin', *Marie-France* [Paris], January 1976, pp. 78–79

Daniels, Les, *Comix. A History of Comic Books in America* (London: Wildwood House, 1973)
    Superman: The Complete History (San Francisco: Chronicle, 1998)

Darasse, Christian, *Le Gang Mazda fait de la BD* (Charleroi: Dupuis, 1988)

Daubert, Michel, 'Franquin', *Télérama* [Paris], 18–25 January 1997, pp. 6–9

Delacourt, Frédéric, *Proverbes, dictons et citations* (Paris: De Vecchi, 1996)

Dellisse, Luc, 'Une Duplicité stratégique', *Cahiers de la bande dessinée, dossier Régis Franc* [Grenoble], 57 (1984), pp. 11–13

Denis, Marie and Suzanne Van Rokeghem, *Le Féminisme est dans la rue* (Brussels: Pol-His, 1992)

Dervize, Irène, 'Les Triomphes d'Astérix', *Paris Match* [Paris], 30 April 1966, pp. 104–05

'Des Chiffres et des dates', *Soir* [Brussels], 7 January 1997, p. 7

Desprechins, Albert and Pierre Seron, *Les Petits Hommes. L'Exode* (Charleroi: Dupuis, 1974)

Dionnet, Jean-Pierre, 'William Blake', *Métal hurlant* [Paris], 3 (1975), p. 51

Dirks, Rudolph, 'Pim Pam Poum', *Journal de Mickey* [Paris], 3 November 1935, p. 5 [trans. unknown]
    Pim Pam Poum (Paris: Hachette, 1934) [trans. unknown]

Disney, Walt, *Mickey Mouse in Color, 1930s Comic Strip Classics* (New York: Pantheon, 1980)

Dorgelès, Roland, *Les Croix de bois* (Paris: Albin Michel, 1919)

Douste-Blazy, Philippe, 'Hommage à Franquin', *Figaro* [Paris], 7 January 1997, p. 20

Druillet, Philippe, *Les Six Voyages de Lone Sloane* (Paris: Dargaud, 1972)

Dubourg, Maurice, 'Image de la bourgeoisie et idéologie bourgeoise', *Europe* [Paris], June 1974, pp. 75–86

Duhamel, Georges, *Vie des martyrs, 1914–1916* (Paris: Mercure de France, 1917)

Duin, Steve and Mike Richardson, *Comics. Between the Panels* (Milwaukee: Dark Horse, 1998)

Dumas, Jacques [Marijac) and Auguste Liquois, *Guerre à la Terre*, 2 vols (Grenoble: Glénat, 1975–76)

Duveaux, Michel, 'Les Couperets de l'aube', *Echo des savanes* [Paris], 36 (1977), pp. 50–53

Eco, Umberto, 'The Myth of Superman', in *The Role of the Reader* (Bloomington, IN: Indiana University Press, 1979), pp. 107–24

Estren, Mark, *A History of Underground Comics*, 3rd edn (Berkeley, CA: Ronin Publishing, 1993)

Farr, Michael, *Tintin. Le Rêve et la réalité* (Brussels: Moulinsart, 2001)

Feiffer, Jules, *Jules Feiffer's America from Eisenhower to Reagan* (London: Penguin, 1982)

Feldstein, Albert, 'Cosmic Ray Bomb Explosion', *Weird Fantasy* [New York], July/August 1950, n. pag.

Feuerhahn, Nelly, 'Astérix, Obélix, nous et les autres', in Michel Colardelle et al., *Ils sont fous d'Astérix! Un Mythe contemporain* (Paris: Albert René, 1996), pp. 51–76

Filippini, Henri, *Dictionnaire de la bande dessinée* (Paris: Bordas, 1989)

Flaubert, Gustave, *Œuvres*, ed. A. Thibaudet and R. Dumesnil, 2 vols (Paris: Gallimard, 1952)

Forest, Jean-Claude and Paul Gillon, *Les Naufragés du temps. L'Etoile endormie* (Paris: Hachette, 1974)

Foulet, Alain, *Presque tout Tardi* (Dieppe: Sapristi, 1996)

Franc, Régis, 'Le Café de la plage 1', *Matin de Paris* [Paris], 18 February 1977, p. 21

    Le Café de la plage (Tournai: Casterman, 1989)

    Histoires immobiles et récits inachevés (Paris: Dargaud, 1977)

    Le Marchand d'opium (Paris: Dargaud, 1981)

    Nouvelles Histoires (Paris: Dargaud, 1978)

    Nuits de Chine (Paris: Dargaud, 1982)

    Souvenirs d'un menteur (Paris: Dargaud, 1979)

    Tonton Marcel. Capitaine de l'industrie (Tournai: Casterman, 1983)

Francblin, Catherine, *Les Nouveaux Réalistes* (Paris: Regard, 1997)

Franck, Frederic, *The Zen of Seeing*, 3rd edn (London: Wildwood House, 1976)

Franquin, André, *Bonjour Modeste* (Brussels: Lombard, 1959)

    L'Intégrale Franquin (Paris: Rombaldi, 1985)

    Idées noires, 2 vols (Paris: Editions Audie, 1981–1984)

    60 Aventures de Modeste et Pompon (Brussels: Lombard, 1958)

Franquin, André and Joseph Gillain, *Comment on devient Créateur de bandes dessinées* (Verviers: Marabout, 1969)

Frappat, Bruno, 'Le Gaulois universel', *Monde* [Paris], 10 July 1974, p. 8

    'René Goscinny, le Père d'Astérix', *Monde* [Paris], 8 November 1977, p. 29

Fresnault-Deruelle, Pierre, *La Bande dessinée. Essai d'analyse sémiotique* (Paris: Hachette, 1972)

Frydman, Gérard and Touis, *Sergent Laterreur* (Brussels: Distri B.D., 1976)

Fureteur, le, 'Le Fureteur vous dira', *Journal de Spirou* [Charleroi], 16 January 1947, p. 4

G.R., 'Tintin le «vertueux»', *Jeune Afrique* [Tunis], 3–9 January 1962, p. 25

Gale, Matthew, *Dada and Surrealism* (London: Phaidon, 1997)

Gaumer, Patrick and Claude Moliterni, *Dictionnaire mondial de la bande dessinée*

(Paris: Larousse, 1994)

Gaussen, Frédéric, 'La Génération du regard', *Monde Campus* [Paris], 20 November 1986, p. 8

Geluck, Philippe, *Le Chat* (Tournai: Casterman, 1986)
  Le Retour du Chat (Tournai: Casterman, 1987)
  La Vengeance du Chat (Tournai: Casterman, 1988)

Genthe, Charles, *American War Narratives 1917–1918* (New York: David Lewis, 1969)

Gifford, Denis, *The International Book of Comics* (London: Deans International, 1984)

Gillain, Joseph [Jijé], *Le Maître de la sierra* (Charleroi: Dupuis, 1960; repr. 1983)

Gillain, Joseph [Jijé] and Jean Giraud, *La Route de Coronado* (Charleroi: Dupuis, 1962)

Gineste, Thierry, *Victor de l'Aveyron* (Paris: Hachette, 1993)

Giraud, Jean [Gir], *Geronimo l'Apache* (Paris: Dargaud, 1999)
  L'Univers de Gir (Paris: Dargaud, 1986)

Giraud, Jean [Gir] and Jean-Michel Charlier, *L'Aigle solitaire* (Paris: Dargaud, 1967)
  Angel Face (Paris: Dargaud, 1975)
  Ballade pour un cercueil (Paris: Dargaud, 1974)
  Le Bout de la piste (Paris: Dargaud, 1986)
  Le Cavalier perdu (Paris: Dargaud, 1968)
  Le Cheval de fer (Paris: Dargaud, 1970)
  Chihuahua Pearl (Paris: Dargaud, 1973)
  La Dernière Carte (Paris: Dargaud, 1983)
  Fort Navajo (Paris: Dargaud, 1965)
  Général Tête Jaune (Paris: Dargaud, 1971)
  L'Homme à l'étoile d'argent (Paris: Dargaud, 1969)
  L'Homme au poing d'acier (Paris: Dargaud, 1970)
  L'Homme qui valait $500,000 (Paris: Dargaud, 1973)
  Le Hors-la-loi (Paris: Dargaud, 1974)
  La Jeunesse de Blueberry (Paris: Dargaud, 1975)
  La Longue Marche (Paris: Dargaud, 1980)
  'Lieutenant Blueberry 1', *Pilote*, 210 [Paris], 31 October 1963, pp. 16–17
  La Mine de l'Allemand perdu (Paris: Dargaud, 1972)
  Mississippi River (Paris: Dargaud, 1991)
  Nez cassé (Paris: Dargaud, 1979)
  La Piste des Navajos (Paris: Dargaud, 1969)
  La Piste des Sioux (Paris: Dargaud, 1971)
  Le Spectre aux balles d'or (Paris: Dargaud, 1972)
  Tonnerre à l'ouest (Paris: Dargaud, 1966)
  La Tribu fantôme (Paris: Dargaud, 1982)

Giraud, Jean [Gir] and William Vance, *Martial Blueberry. Sur l'Ordre de Washington* (Paris: Dargaud, 1991)

Giraud, Jean [Moebius], 'Arzach 1', *Métal hurlant* [Paris], 1 (1975), n. pag.
  'Cauchemar blanc', *Echo des savanes* [Paris], 8 (1974), pp. 39–50
  La Déesse (Tournai: Casterman, 1990)
  'Editorial', *Métal hurlant* [Paris], 4 (1975), p. 1

'Le Garage hermétique 1', *Métal hurlant* [Paris], 6 (1976), pp. 16–17

Histoire de mon double (Paris: Numéro 1, 1999)

L'Homme du Ciguri (Paris: Humanoïdes Associés, 1995)

Les Jardins d'Edena (Tournai: Casterman, 1988)

Œuvres complètes, 6 vols (Paris: Humanoïdes Associés, 1980–1986)

Quatre-Vingt-Huit (Paris: Humanoïdes Associés, 1990)

Stel (Tournai: Casterman, 1994)

Sur l'Etoile (Paris: Aedena, 1984)

Les Vacances du Major (Paris: Humanoïdes Associés, 1990)

Venise céleste (Tournai: Casterman, 1984)

Giraud, Jean [Moebius] and Jerry Bingham, *The Onyx Overlord* (New York: Epic, 1992)

Giraud, Jean [Moebius] and Alejandro Jodorowsky, *Ce qui est en bas* (Paris: Humanoïdes Associés, 1983)

Ce qui est en haut (Paris: Humanoïdes Associés, 1985)

La Cinquième Essence (Paris: Humanoïdes Associés, 1988)

La Cinquième Essence II (Paris: Humanoïdes Associés, 1989)

Griffes d'ange (Paris: Humanoïdes Associés, 1994)

'L'Incal 1', *Métal hurlant* [Paris], 58 (1980), pp. 5–14

L'Incal lumière (Paris: Humanoïdes Associés, 1981)

L'Incal noir (Paris: Humanoïdes Associés, 1980)

Giraud, Jean [Moebius], Alejandro Jodorowsky and Jean Annestay, *Les Mystères de l'Incal* (Paris: Humanoïdes Associés, 1989)

Giraud, Jean [Moebius] and Eric Shanower, *The Elsewhere Prince* (New York: Epic, 1990)

Glénat, Jacques and Numa Sadoul, 'A Bâtons rompus avec Claire Bretécher', *Cahiers de la bande dessinée* [Grenoble], 24 (1974), pp. 6–14

'Entretien avec René Goscinny', *Cahiers de la bande dessinée* [Grenoble], 22 (1973), pp. 5–18

Godard, Christian and Mittei, *Un Cabriolet pour Désiré* (Brussels: Lombard, 1969)

Goetzinger, Annie, *Aurore* (Paris: Editions des Femmes, 1978)

Golo and Frank, 'Sphinx de verre', *Charlie mensuel* [Paris], June 1980, pp. 79–93

Gonnard, René, *La Légende du bon sauvage* (Paris: Medicis, 1946)

Gordon, David, *The French Language and National Identity* (The Hague: Mouton, 1978)

Goscinny, René and Albert Uderzo, *Astérix aux Jeux Olympiques* (Paris: Dargaud, 1968)

Astérix chez les Belges (Paris: Dargaud, 1979)

Astérix chez les Bretons (Paris: Dargaud, 1966)

Astérix chez les Goths (Paris: Dargaud, 1963)

Astérix chez les Helvètes (Paris: Dargaud, 1970)

Astérix en Corse (Paris: Dargaud, 1973)

Astérix en Hispanie (Paris: Dargaud, 1969)

Astérix et le Chaudron (Paris: Dargaud, 1969)

Astérix et Cléopatre (Paris: Dargaud, 1965)

Astérix et les Normands (Paris: Dargaud, 1967)

Astérix Gladiateur (Paris: Dargaud, 1964)

'Astérix le Gaulois 1', *Pilote*, 1 [Paris], 29 October 1959, p. 20

Astérix le Gaulois (Paris: Dargaud, 1961)
Astérix Légionnaire (Paris: Dargaud, 1967)
Le Bouclier d'Arverne (Paris: Dargaud, 1968)
Le Combat des chefs (Paris: Dargaud, 1966)
'Conférence de presse', *Pilote*, 260 [Paris], 15 October 1964, p. 48
Le Devin (Paris: Dargaud, 1972)
Le Domaine des dieux (Paris: Dargaud, 1971)
La Grande Traversée (Paris: Dargaud, 1975)
Les Lauriers de César (Paris: Dargaud, 1972)
Obélix et Compagnie (Paris: Dargaud, 1976)
La Rose et le glaive (Paris: Dargaud, 1991)
La Serpe d'or (Paris: Dargaud, 1962)
Le Tour de Gaule (Paris: Dargaud, 1965)
La Zizanie (Paris: Dargaud, 1970)
Gotlib, Marcel, 'Le Clou à travers l'histoire', *Pilote*, 286 [Paris], 15 April 1965, pp.
        10–11
Gai-Luron, 2 vols (Paris: Rombaldi, 1987)
Rhââ lovely, 3 vols (Paris: Editions Audie, 1977)
'Rubrique à brac 1', *Pilote*, 447 [Paris], 16 May 1968, pp. 4–5
Rubrique à brac, 5 vols (Paris: Dargaud, 1970–1974)
Trucs en vrac, 2 vols (Paris: Dargaud, 1977 and 1985)
Gotlib, Marcel, Jacques Lob, Jean Solé and Dominique Vallet [Alexis], *Superdupont*
        (Paris: Rombaldi, 1987)
Govaert, Serge, *Mai '68: C'était au Temps où Bruxelles contestait* (Brussels: Pol-His,
        1990)
Grand Dictionnaire Hachette, 2nd edn (Paris: Hachette, 1996)
'Great Blistering Barnacles!', *Economist* [London], 31 January 1999, p. 95
Griffin, Rick, 'Oxo 69', *Zap Comics* [San Francisco], 2 (1968), p. 4
Groensteen, Thierry, 'Entretien avec François Bourgeon', *Cahiers de la bande
        dessinée* [Grenoble], 65 (1985), pp. 8–16
La Bande dessinée depuis 1975 (Paris: Albin Michel, 1985)
Système de la bande dessinée (Paris: Presses Universitaires de France, 1999)
Tardi (Paris: Magic Strip, 1980)
Groensteen, Thierry and Benoît Peeters, *Töpffer. L'Invention de la bande dessinée*
        (Paris: Hermann, 1994)
Groensteen, Thierry and Thierry Smolderen, 'Entretien avec Will Eisner', *Cahiers de
        la bande dessinée* [Grenoble], 61 (1985), pp. 86–89
Grossmann, Fritz, ed., *Pieter Bruegel. A Complete Edition of the Paintings* (London:
        Phaidon, 1973)
Guillaume, Marie-Ange and José-Louis Bocquet, *René Goscinny* (Arles: Actes Sud, 1997)
Guilmard, Pierre, *La Java des Gaspards. L'Egorgeoir* (Paris: Vents d'Ouest, 1990)
Gurgand, Jean-Noel, 'Le Phénomène Astérix', *Express* [Paris], 19–25 September
        1966, pp. 24–26
Harlé, Jean and Michel Blanc-Dumont, *Jonathan Cartland* (Paris: Dargaud, 1975)
Hayward, Susan, *French National Cinema* (London: Routledge, 1993)
Helvig, Jean-Michel, 'Tintin-Chirac et les Picaroses', *Libération* [Paris], 5–6 March
        1983, p. 6

Hemingway, Ernest, *A Farewell to Arms* (London: Penguin, 1975)

Hemmings, F.W.J., *Emile Zola*, 2nd edn (Oxford: Oxford University Press, 1966)

Hennebert, Diane, 'Bruxelles, la Ville de Tintin, n'apparaît qu'en filigraine', *Géo hors série* [Paris], November 2000, pp. 166–71

Henoument, René, *Au Bonheur des Belges. Histoire d'une identité* (Monaco: Rocher, 1992)

Hergé, see Remi, Georges

Hoare, Robert, *World War I* (London: Macdonald, 1973)

Horn, Maurice, *The World Encyclopedia of Comics* (New York: Chelsea House, 1976)

Huggett, Frank, *Modern Belgium* (London: Pall Mall, 1969)

Hugo, Victor, *Oeuvres poétiques*, ed. Pierre Albouy, 3 vols (Paris: Gallimard, 1964)

Ionesco, Eugène, *La Cantatarice chauve*, in *Théâtre*, ed. Jacques Lemarchand, 4 vols (Paris: Gallimard, 1954), I, pp. 15–54

J.L.F., 'L'Homme de l'année, Moebius et Jodorowsky', *Année de la bande dessinée* [Paris] (1981/2), pp. 197–203

Jacobs, Edgar, *Blake et Mortimer. La Marque Jaune* (Brussels: Lombard, 1956)
   SOS Météores (Brussels: Lombard, 1959)

Jigourel, Joseph and Yanna Fournier, *Costumes de Bretagne* (Brest: Télégramme, 2000)

Jodorowsky, Alejandro and Arnaud Dombre [Arno], *Alef Thau* (Paris: Humanoïdes Associés, 1982)

Jodorowsky, Alejandro and Silvio Cadelo, *Le Dieu jaloux* (Paris: Humanoïdes Associés, 1984)

Judah, Tim, 'Tintin in the Dock', *Guardian Weekend Supplement* [London], 30 January 1999, pp. 8–18

Judovitz, Dalia, 'Sex or the Misfortunes of Literature', in David Allison, Mark Roberts and Allan Weiss, eds, *Sade and the Narrative of Transgression* (Cambridge: Cambridge University Press, 1995), pp. 171–98

Klock, Geoff, *How to read Superhero Comics and why* (New York and London: Continuum, 2002)

Kubert, Joe, 'Bonhomme Richard', *Frontline Combat* [New York], September/October 1953, n. pag.

Kubert, Joe and Bob Kanigher, *Le Baron Rouge*, trans. Michèle Tingaud, 2 vols (Paris: Editions Fromage, 1978)

Kumar, Satish, *The CIA and the Third World*, 2nd edn (London: Zed Books, 1981)

Kurtzman, Harvey, 'Old Soldiers Never Die!', *Two-Fisted Tales* [New York], January 1952, pp. 1–7

Labé, Yves-Marie, 'André Franquin, le Père de Gaston s'est arrêté à 950 gags', *Monde* [Paris], 7 January 1997, p. 29

Labesse, Dominique, 'Le Comique chez Hergé', *Cahiers de la bande dessinée, spécial Hergé* [Grenoble], 14/15 (1971), pp. 52–54

Lacassin, Francis, *Tarzan ou le Chevalier crispé*, 2nd edn (Paris: Henri Veyrier, 1982)

La Fontaine, Jean de, *Fables*, ed. Antoine Adam (Paris: Garnier Flammarion, 1966)

Laity, K.A., 'Construction of a "Female Hero": Iconography in *Les Aventures extraordinaires d'Adèle Blanc-Sec*', *International Journal of Comic Art* [Philadelphia], 4.1. (2002), pp. 163–69

Lartéguy, Jean, 'Ne touchez pas à Astérix!', *Figaro littéraire* [Paris], 2 June 1966, p. 8

Laubier, Claire, ed., *The Condition of Women in France, 1945 to the Present* (London: Routledge, 1990)

Laudy, Jacques, *Hassan et Kaddour. Les Mameluks de Bonaparte* (Paris: Editions RTP, 1975)

Lauzier, Gérard and Dominique Vallet [Alexis], *Al Crane* (Paris: Dargaud, 1976)

Lavisse, Ernest, *Histoire de France: moyen âge. Cours de 1ère année* (Paris: Armand Colin, 1890)

Lebedel, Pierre, 'Astérix et Obélix Orphelins', *Figaro* [Paris], 7 November 1977, p. 32

Leblanc, Maurice, *Arsène Lupin*, ed. Francis Lacassin, 4th edn, 5 vols (Paris: Laffont, 1992)

Lecigne, Bruno and Jean-Pierre Tamine, *Fac-Similé* (Paris: Futuropolis, 1983)

Lécurieux, Roger and Norbert Morandière [Norma], *Capitaine Apache. L'Enfance d'un guerrier* (Paris: Rouge et or, 1980)

Lécurieux, Roger and Raymond Poivet, 'Les Pionniers de l'Espérance', *Vaillant* [Paris], 14 December 1945, n. pag.

Les Pionniers de l'Espérance 1945–1946, 3 vols (Paris: Futuropolis, 1989)

Leroux, Gaston, *L'Epouse du Soleil* (Paris: Lafitte, 1913)

Les Chefs d'œuvre de Gaston Leroux, ed. Gilbert Sigaux, 4 vols (Paris: Laffont, 1969)

Lewis, Leo, 'What Gaul! Asterix Plans Invasion of Europe's Theme Parks', *Independent on Sunday Business Supplement* [London], 20 April 2001, p. 1

Lindé, Pierre, 'Astérix presque Milliardaire!', *Entreprise* [Paris], 4 May 1968, pp. 61–69

Lisiecki-Bouretz, Sylvie, 'Maîtres du neuvième art', *Chroniques de la Bibliothèque nationale de France* [Paris], September 2000, p. 8

Lynton, Norbert, *The Story of Modern Art* (Oxford: Phaidon, 1980)

'Maison de la radio', *France soir* [Paris], 22 July 1969, p. 6 [journalist unknown]

Makassar, Anton, *Le Style Atome* (Brussels: Magic Strip, 1983)

Mallinson, Vernon, *Belgium* (London: Ernest Benn, 1969)

Malot, Hector, *Sans Famille*, 2 vols (Paris: Dentu, 1879)

Malraux, André, *Les Chênes qu'on abat* (Paris: Gallimard, 1971)

Margerin, Frank, *Bananes métalliques* (Paris: Humanoïdes Associés, 1982)

'Franquin' [cartoon], *Télérama* [Paris], January 1997, p. 10

Marschall, Richard, *America's Great Comic Strip Artists* (New York: Abbeville Press, 1989)

Martin, Jacques, *Alix l'intrépide* (Brussels: Lombard, 1956)

Lefranc et la Grande Menace (Brussels: Lombard, 1954)

Martin, Jacques and André Juillard, *Arno. Le Pique rouge* (Grenoble: Glénat, 1984)

Mathieu, Marc-Antoine, *L'Origine* (Paris: Delcourt, 1991)

La Qu … (Paris: Delcourt, 1991)

McCloud, Scott, *Understanding Comics* (New York: Harper Perennial, 1994)

McManus, George, *La Famille Illico* (Grenoble: Glénat, 1980) [trans. unknown]

McQuillan, Libbie, 'Between the Sheets at *Pilote*, 1968–1973', *International Journal of Comic Art* [Philadelphia], 2.1 (2000), pp. 159–77

Miller, Frank, *Batman. The Dark Knight Returns* (New York: DC Comics, 1986)

Mintz, Lawrence E., 'Fantasy, Formula, Realism and Propaganda in Milton Caniff's Comic Strips', *Journal of Popular Culture* [Bowling Green, Ohio], 12.4 (1979), pp. 653–80

Moebius, see Giraud, Jean

Mogui, Jean-Pierre, 'Tintin Orphelin', *Figaro* [Paris], 5–6 March 1983, p. 34

Molière, François, *Œuvres complètes*, ed. Georges Couton, 2 vols (Paris: Pleiade, 1971)

Moliterni, Claude, *Entretiens avec Gir, Charlier, Pratt, Gotlib, Druillet* (Paris: Serg, 1973)

Moliterni, Claude and Philippe Mellot, *Chronologie de la bande dessinée* (Paris: Flammarion, 1996)

Monnier, Henri, *Grandeur et décadence de M. Joseph Prudhomme* (Paris: Michel Lévy, 1852)

Montellier, Chantal, *La Fosse aux serpents* (Tournai: Casterman, 1990)

    'Oscar Brown n'est pas un Espion', *Métal hurlant* [Paris], 56 (1980), pp. 36–45

    'Recours en grâce', *A suivre hors série, BD polar* [Paris] (1981), pp. 82–83

    1996 (Paris: Humanoïdes Associés, 1978)

Moor, Bob de, *Cori le Moussaillon* (Brussels: Distri BD, 1976)

Moor, Johan de and Stephen Desberg, *Gaspard de la Nuit. De l'autre côté du masque* (Tournai: Casterman, 1987)

Moore, Alan and Dave Gibbons, *The Watchmen* (New York: DC Comics, 1986)

Moore, Alan and Bill Sienkiewicz, *Brought to Light* (London: Titan, 1989)

Moscosco, Victor, 'Untitled', *Zap Comics* [San Francisco], 2 (1968), pp. 6–7

Moullet, Luc, *Fritz Lang* (Paris: Seghers, 1963)

Moustaki, Georges, *Moustaki en Ballades*, 2 vols (Paris: Christian Pirot, 1996)

Murray, Doug and Michael Golden, *The Nam* (New York: Marvel, 1986)

N.S., 'Le Père de Gaston à Drouot', *Figaro* [Paris], 7 January 1997, p. 20

Oliver, Gabriel, *L'Affaire du courrier de Lyon* (Paris: Arthaud, 1966)

Orlando, Joe, 'The Ad', *Weird Fantasy* [New York], July–August 1952, n. pag

Ostrovsky, Erika, *Céline and his Vision* (London: University of London Press, 1967)

Pagnol, Marcel, *Oeuvres complètes*, 6 vols (Paris: Editions de Provence, 1967)

Peeters, Benoît, *La Bande dessinée* (Paris: Flammarion, 1993)

    Tintin and the World of Hergé, trans. Michael Farr, 2nd edn (London: Methuen Children's Books, 1995)

Pellerin, Patrice and Jean-Charles Krahn, *Aigles décapités. La Nuit des jongleurs* (Grenoble: Glénat, 1985)

Pennacchioni, Irène, *La Nostalgie en images* (Paris: Méridiens, 1982)

Perrault, Charles, *Contes de ma mère l'oie* (Paris: Gallimard, 1988)

Petitfaux, Dominique, 'La Planète ensorcelée d'Hugo Pratt', *Géo hors série. Corto Maltese* [Paris], November 2001, p. 8

Peyzaret, Richard, [F'Murr], *Génie des Alpages* (Paris: Dargaud, 1976)

Pierre, Michel, 'Franquin le Virtuose', *Magazine littéraire* [Paris], January 1980, pp. 62–63

Pirenne, Henri, *Histoire de Belgique*, 7 vols (Brussels: Lamertin, 1908–1932)

Poivet, Raymond and Bornert, 'Maquis contre SS', *Coq hardi* [Paris], 3 April 1947, p. 1

Pratt, Hugo, *Corto Maltese. Ballade de la mer salée* (Tournai: Casterman, 1975)

Propp, Vladimir, *Morphology of the Folktale*, trans. Laurence Scott, 2nd edn (Austin and London: University of Texas Press, 1968)

    Theory and History of Folklore, trans. Ariadna and Richard Martin (Manchester: Manchester University Press, 1984)

Proust, Marcel, *Du Côté de chez Swann*, ed. Jean Milly (Paris: Flammarion, 1987)
Queveau, Philippe, *Presque tout Franquin* (Paris: Comset, 1991)
Rabier, Benjamin and Fred Isly, *Tintin Lutin* (Paris: Juven, 1898)
Rabitch, Norman, *The Catholic Church and the French Nation* (London: Routledge, 1990)
Racine, Jean, *Oeuvres complètes*, ed. Georges Forestier (Paris: Gallimard, 1999)
Read, Herbert, *Art Now* (London: Faber and Faber, 1936)
Regnier, Michel [Greg], *Achille Talon. Mon Fils et moi* (Paris: Dargaud, 1970)
Regnier, Michel [Greg] and Eddy Paape, *Luc Orient. Les Dragons de feu* (Brussels: Lombard, 1969)
Remi, Georges [Hergé], *L'Affaire Tournesol* (Tournai: Casterman, 1956)
    Archives Hergé (Tournai: Casterman, 1973)
    Les Bijoux de la Castafiore (Tournai; Casterman, 1963)
    Les Cigares du Pharaon (Tournai: Casterman, 1934)
    Coke en stock (Tournai: Casterman, 1958)
    Le Crabe aux pinces d'or (Tournai: Casterman, 1941)
    L'Etoile mystérieuse (Tournai: Casterman, 1942)
    'Heure par heure', *Paris Match* [Paris], 29 November 1969, pp. 30–33
    L'Ile noire (Tournai: Casterman, 1938)
    Le Lotus bleu (Tournai: Casterman, 1936)
    Objectif Lune (Tournai: Casterman, 1953)
    On a marché sur la Lune (Tournai: Casterman, 1954)
    L'Oreille cassée (Tournai: Casterman, 1937)
    Le Sceptre d'Ottokar (Tournai: Casterman, 1939)
    Le Secret de la Licorne (Tournai: Casterman, 1943)
    Les Sept Boules de cristal (Tournai: Casterman, 1948)
    Le Temple du Soleil (Tournai: Casterman, 1949)
    Tintin au Congo (Tournai: Casterman, 1930)
    Tintin au Pays de l'or noir (Tournai: Casterman, 1950)
    Tintin au Pays des Soviets (Tournai: Casterman, 1991)
    Tintin au Tibet (Tournai: Casterman, 1960)
    Tintin en Amérique (Tournai: Casterman, 1932)
    Tintin et les Picaros (Tournai: Casterman, 1976)
    Le Trésor de Rackham le Rouge (Tournai: Casterman, 1944)
    Vol 714 pour Sydney (Tournai: Casterman, 1968)
Renan, Ernest, 'Qu'est-ce qu'une Nation?', in *Œuvres complètes d'Ernest Renan*, ed. Henriette Psichari, 10 vols (Paris: Calmann Lévy, 1947), I, pp. 887–906
Renard, Jean-Bruno, *Clefs pour la bande dessinée* (Paris: Seghers, 1978)
Restany, Pierre, *Le Nouveau Réalisme* (Paris: Union Générale des Editions, 1978)
    Trente ans de nouveau réalisme (Paris: La Différence, 1990)
Reynolds, Richard, *Superheroes. A Modern Mythology* (Jackson, MI: University of Mississippi Press, 1992)
Rivière, François and Jean-Claude Floc'h, *Le Rendez-vous de Sevenoaks* (Paris: Dargaud, 1977)
Robinson, Jerry, *Comics. An Illustrated History* (New York: G.P. Putnam and Sons, 1974)
Rodriguez Tous, J.A., 'Y ahora qué?', *Mundo* [Barcelona], 1 May 2000, p. 4
Rosenberg, Harold, *The De-definition of Art* (New York: Horizon, 1972)

Ross, Alex and Paul Dini, *Superman. Peace on Earth* (New York: DC Comics, 1999)

Rouzaud, Jean [José Perfección], 'Una Verdadera del Tío José', *Activité sexuelle normale* (Paris: Almonde Press, 1976), n. pag.

Rudorff, Raymond, *Belle Epoque* (London: Hamish Hamilton, 1972)

Sabin, Roger, *Adult Comics* (London and New York: Routledge, 1993)

   Comics, Comix and Graphic Novels (London: Phaidon, 1996)

Sade, Donatien, Marquis de, *Histoire de Juliette*, ed. Gilbert Lely, 3 vols (Paris: Union Générale des Editions, 1976–77)

Sadoul, Numa, *Entretiens avec Hergé* (Tournai: Casterman, 1989)

   Et Franquin créa Lagaffe (Brussels: Distri B.D/Schlirf Book, 1986)

   Gotlib (Paris: Albin Michel, 1974)

   Moebius: Entretiens avec Numa Sadoul (Tournai: Casterman, 1991)

Sagan, Françoise, *La Femme fardée* (Paris: J.-J. Pauvert, 1981)

Saint Exupéry, Antoine de, *Le Petit Prince* (Paris: Gallimard, 1945)

Schuiten, François and Benoît Peeters, *L'Aventure des images: de la bande dessinée au multi-média* (Paris: Autrement, 1996)

Screech, Matthew, 'André Franquin, Master of the Ninth Art', *Journal of Popular Culture* [Bowling Green, Ohio], 33.3 (1999), pp. 95–133

Seele, Herr and Kamagurka, *Maurice le Cowboy* (Paris: Albin Michel, 1986)

Segar, Elze, 'Popeye/Mathurin', *Robinson* [Paris], 30 January 1938, p. 5 [translator unknown]

Seisser, Jean, *La Gloire des Bazooka* (Paris: Laffont, 1981)

Serres, Michel, 'C'est l'Auteur qui a le plus marqué la culture contemporaine', *Libération* [Paris], 5–6 March 1983, p. 25

Severin, John and Will Elder, 'Zero Hour', *Frontline Combat* [New York], September/October 1951, n. pag

Sherzer, Dina, 'Claire Bretécher: Queen of BD', *Journal of Popular Culture* [Bowling Green, Ohio], 13.2 (1980), pp. 394–404

Sibille, Pierre, 'André Franquin, l'Invité du mois, *Libre Belgique* [Brussels], 9 April 1981, pp. 14–15

Soumois, Frédéric, *Dossier Tintin* (Brussels: Jacques Antoine, 1987)

Stang, Ragna, *Edvard Munch. The Man and the Artist* (London: Gordon Fraser, 1979)

Stein, Sally, 'Good Fences make Good Neighbors. American Resistance to Photomontage between the Wars', in *Montage and Modern Life 1919–1942*, ed. Maude Lavin (Cambridge, MA: MIT Press, 1993), pp. 128–91

Sterckx, Pierre, *Tintin et les Médias* (Brussels: Bibliothèque d'Alice, 1997)

Sterrit, David, *The Films of Jean-Luc Godard* (Cambridge: Cambridge University Press, 1999)

Stoll, André, *Astérix: L'Epopée burlesque de la France* (Brussels: Editions Complexe, 1978)

Stoltzfus, Ben, *Alain Robbe-Grillet and the New French Novel* (Carbondale, IL: Southern Illinois University Press, 1964)

Tardi, Jacques, *Adèle et la Bête* (Tournai: Casterman, 1976)

   Adieu Brindavoine suivi de la Fleur au fusil (Tournai: Casterman, 1979)

   'La Bascule à Charlot', *Charlie mensuel* [Paris], August 1976, pp. 73–96

   'C'était la Guerre des tranchées 1', *A suivre* [Paris], March 1982, pp. 9–25

   C'était la Guerre des tranchées (Tournai: Casterman, 1993)

'Un Cheval en hiver', *Pilote*, 550 [Paris], 22 May 1970, pp. 18–23
Le Démon de la Tour Eiffel (Tournai; Casterman, 1976)
Le Démon des glaces (Paris: Dargaud, 1974)
'La Fleur au fusil', *Pilote*, 743 [Paris], 1 February 1974, pp. 38–47
Griffu (Paris: Editions du Square, 1978)
'Knock Out', *Pilote annuel* [Paris], 6 bis hors série November 1974, pp. 25–30
Momies en folie (Tournai: Casterman, 1978)
Mouh Mouh (Brussels: Pepperland, 1984)
Le Mystère des profondeurs (Tournai: Casterman, 1998)
Le Noyé à deux têtes (Tournai: Casterman, 1985)
Le Savant fou (Tournai: Casterman, 1977)
Le Secret de la salamandre (Tournai: Casterman, 1981)
'La Torpédo rouge sang', *Pilote*, 567 [Paris], 11 September 1970, pp. 22–27
Tous les Monstres (Tournai: Casterman, 1994)
La Véritable Histoire du soldat inconnu (Paris: Futuropolis, 1974)
Teulé, Jean, *Copy rêves* (Grenoble: Glénat, 1984)
Thiesse, Anne-Marie, *La Création des identités nationales* (Paris: Seuil, 1999)
Thomson, Belinda, *Impressionism* (London: Thames and Hudson, 2000)
Thompson, Harry, *Tintin, Hergé and his Creation* (London: Hodder and Stoughton, 1991)
Tilleux, Maurice, *Félix* (Brussels: Heroic Albums, 1949)
Tilleux, Maurice and Francis Bertrand, *Allegro en Ford T* (Paris: Dargaud, 1968)
'Tintin au Pays du commerce', *Libération* [Paris], 5–6 March 1983, p. 26 [journalist unknown]
'Tintin est mort', *Libération* [Paris], 5–6 March 1983, p. 1 [journalist unknown]
Tisseron, Serge, *Hergé* (Paris: Seghers, 1987)
    Psychanalyse de la bande dessinée (Paris: Presses Universitaires de France, 1987)
    Tintin chez le Psychanalyste (Paris: Aubier, 1985)
    Tintin et le Secret d'Hergé (Paris: Editions Hors Collection, 1993)
Tomasi, Jean-Paul and Michel Deligne, *Tintin chez Jules Verne* (Brussels: Lefrancq, 1998)
Tomlinson, Janis, *Goya in the Twilight of the Enlightenment* (New Haven, CT: Yale University Press, 1992)
Töpffer, Rodolphe, *M. Jabot et M. Vieux Bois* (Paris: Seuil, 1996)
Trondheim, Lewis, *Les Aventures de l'Univers* (Paris: Dargaud, 1997)
    Le Dormeur (Paris: Cornélius, 1993)
    Lapinot et les Carottes de Patagonie (Paris: L'Association, 1992)
Trondheim, Lewis and Jean-Christophe Menu, *Moins d'un Quart de seconde pour vivre* (Paris: L'Association, 1991)
Tuska, Jon, *The Filming of the West* (London: Robert Hale, 1978)
Tvonvina, Led, 'Les Augures ont prononcé Franquin', *Falatoff* [Paris], November/December 1972, pp. 29–60
Uderzo, Albert, *Uderzo: de Flamberge à Astérix* (Paris: Philippsen, 1985)
Vaerenbergh, Oliver, 'Attention les Yeux, les doodles arrivent', *Soir* [Brussels] 11/12 January 1997, p. 10
Valadié, Ariane, *Ma Vie de chien. Entretiens avec Milou* (Paris: J.C. Lattès, 1993)
Van, Martine and François Mutterer, *Carpets bazaar* (Paris: Futuropolis, 1983)

Van Opstal, H., *Tracé RG* (Brussels: Lefrancq, 1998)

Van Zuylen, Carine, 'Gaston Lagaffe, Anti-héros de la bande dessinée', unpublished dissertation, Université Libre de Bruxelles, 1982

Vandersteen, Willy, *Bob et Bobette. Le Fantôme espagnol* (Brussels: Lombard, 1953)

Verne, Jules, *De la Terre à la Lune* (Paris: Hetzel, 1865)

   Michel Strogoff (Paris: Hetzel, 1876)

   Le Sphinx des glaces (Paris: Hetzel, 1897)

   Vingt mille lieues sous les mers (Paris: Hetzel, 1870)

   Voyage au centre de la Terre (Paris: Hetzel, 1864)

Vidal, Guy, Anne Goscinny and Patrick Gaumer, *René Goscinny: profession humoriste* (Paris: Dargaud, 1997)

Villon, François, *Poésies complètes*, ed. Claude Thiry (Paris: Livre de Poche, 1991)

Violeff, Jacques, *Coup sur coup* (Tournai: Casterman, 1984)

Walthéry François and Roland Goossens [Gos], *Natacha. Hôtesse de l'air* (Charleroi: Dupuis, 1970)

'War of 1812', *Frontline Combat* [New York], May/June 1953, n. pag [artist unknown]

Ware, Chris, *Acme Novelty Library 6* (Seattle, WA: Fantagraphics, 1995)

White, David Manning and Robert Abel, *The Funnies* (London: Collier Macmillan, 1963)

Wininger Pierre, *La Pyramide oubliée* (Grenoble: Glénat, 1978)

Zola, Emile, *La Faute de l'Abbé Mouret* (Paris: Charpentier, 1875)

Index